Perception:
Its Development
and Recapitulation

by
Estelle Breines

M.A., O.T.R., F.A.O.T.A.

© 1981 by Estelle Breines. All rights reserved. No part of this book may be reproduced in any form without written permission of the author.

Publisher: Geri-Rehab, Inc.
            Box 170 Hibbler Road
            Lebanon, New Jersey 08833

Library of Congress Catalog No.: 81-812-44

Appreciation is expressed to Hank Ketcham Enterprises, Inc. for permission to reproduce the *Dennis the Menace* cartoons; to Betty Edwards and J.P. Tarcher, Inc. for permission to reproduce the drawings originally printed in Drawing on The Right Side of The Brain; and to the Central Conference of American Rabbis for permission to reproduce the prayer "Birth is a beginning . . .".

Acknowledgements

Acknowledgment is gratefully accorded the many individuals who helped to make this book possible.

To my staff who listened, questioned and helped me to clarify the concepts expressed here, to Cindy Rich who took the photographs and minded the shop while my mind was elsewhere, and to Peg Felix who typed the first drafts, helping me with the language and grammar;

To Claire Daffner for repeated discussions, for serving as my mentor in matters of development, and for her friendship;

To Dr. Bonnie Kind and Dr. Dorothy Dinnerstein who advised me in the development of the experiments;

To Dr. Dorothy Strauss and Dr. Howard Gruber whose suggestions regarding the direction of my reading were invaluable;

To my family for their encouragement and tolerance, to Roxanne Breines-Sukol who typed the final manuscript, to Eric Breines whose arguments helped me to clarify my thinking, to Jacqueline Breines whose willingness and understanding helped me to write with a clear conscience, and, most of all, thank you to my husband, Ira Breines, who offered me good humor, constant support, relief from responsibility, tolerated a total change in our former lifestyle, and became an excellent cook, thereby nourishing body as well as soul.

Dedicated to
my teacher, my patient, my father

Sanford Borgman

Table of Contents

                                              Page

A. List of Figures i
I. Introduction 1
II. Preface - Occupational Therapist,
    Master of Behavioral Planning 5
III. A Framework for Human Behavior
    1. A Relational Paradigm 21
    2. Internally Expressed 45
    3. Externally Expressed 75
    4. Consentually Expressed 95
IV. A Rationale for Gerontological Practice
    5. Aging; A Definition 109
    6. Factors in Aging which Affect
       Perception and Performance 125
    7. Environmental Influences on Perception
       and Performance in Aging 143
    8. Experimental Studies Concerned with
       Environmental and Proprioceptive Memory 159
V. Gerontological Practice Applied
    9. Principles for Evaluation 177
   10. Principles for Treatment 197
   11. Selected Therapeutic Techniques 213
   12. Selected Case Studies 241
Bibliography..279

List of Figures

                                            Page

Chapter 1.
- Figure 1-1. Reversible Figures   26
- 1-2. Time/Space - Audition, Vision, Mobility Model   28
- 1-3. Right Brain/Left Brain Drawings   29-31
- 1-4. Visual Field and Optic Chiasma   37

Chapter 2.
- Figure 2-1. Dennis the Menace - "My head knows better..."   45
- 2-2. Necker Cube   46
- 2-3. Dennis the Menace - Context Dictates Perception of Events   61

Chapter 7.
- Figure 7-1. Irrigant Pole   154

Chapter 8.
- Figure 8-1. Diagram of Placement of Materials for Spatial Illusion Test for Midpoint Identification   163
- 8-2. Distribution of Ages of Subjects   164
- 8-3. Mean Scores on Ravens Coloured Progressive Matrices, Familiar and Unfamiliar Environs   164
- 8-4. Mean Scores of Spatial Illusion Test for Midpoint Identification   165
- 8-5. Raw Data, Ravens and Midpoint Identification Tests, Familiar and Unfamiliar Environs   168
- 8-6. Proprioceptive Memory Testing   171

List of Figures (continued)

Page

Chapter 9.
    Figure 9-1. Holland Tunnel Diagram -
           a) Driver's View, b) Bystander's View   181
      9-2. Side Presented Items for Stereognosis Testing 192

Chapter 10.
    Figure 10-1. Circle of Influence   203

Chapter 11.
    Figure 11-1. Sitting Position Aligned Vertically
           and Horizontally   215
      11-2. Trunk - Flexion and Extension Exercises   216
      11-3. Neck - Flexion and Extension Exercises   217
      11-4. Neck - Rotation Exercises   218
      11-5. Egocentric Orientation Exercises   219
      11-6. Arm Rests   222
      11-7. Shoulder Mobility Exercises   225
      11-8. Finger Gnosia Training   226
      11-9. Standing Balance Training   227-228
      11-10. Peripheral Stereognosis Training   233
      11-11. Exocentric Orientation Training   235
      11-12. a) Weaving Frame, Pillow, b) Wall Hanging   236
      11-13. Safe Escort Procedure   238

I. INTRODUCTION

I have recently come to reflect upon the circumstances which compelled me to write this book. What are the series of events in any one person's life that permit that person to arrive at such a strong conviction that his life is given over to the pursuit of a personal truth that demands sharing?

When Frieda Behlen interviewed me for New York University's Occupational Therapy curriculum in 1954, I can vividly recall her asking me what I expected to do as an occupational therapist. For the sake of the interview, I recall that I said something about possibly working with children or veterans, yet I somehow knew then that was not all I would do. They were merely the options I was aware of at the time. After all, what does a seventeen-year-old know of illness or aging or even the problems of living? I certainly knew very little.

Since that time my career has taken many turns. I have been fortunate enough to have practiced in a wide variety of disability areas. That circumstance, along with my opportunity as a Clinical Coordinator at Union County Technical Institute, allowed me the privilege to see occupational therapy as it is practiced by a wide variety of practioners, in all disability areas. Much of that practice was successful in helping me to develop pride in my profession. Some of that practice was abominable, making me fear for our survival.

When one has the opportunity to work with children and

adults, with psychiatric patients and physically disabled, with acutely ill persons and with chronically and terminally ill, with persons living at home and in institutions, one learns over time the nature of the persons with whom one is most successful and where one gets one's jollies. Some things are plainly more fun than others. Some problems are more interesting to solve. When people have options, they tend to be more attracted to the things they like to do and to the things they do well.

Over time I have repeatedly been exposed to jobs which have required that I rethink occupational therapy as a concept. I have set up or collaborated in setting up so many occupational therapy departments from scratch that I sometimes think that is where my true expertise lies. These departments have included those in a general hospital, a rehabilitation hospital, a drug rehabilitation program, a college curriculum, home health, private practice, myriad nursing homes, and a proprietary corporation. In each instance, it was necessary to reshuffle my thinking, throw out what experience had taught me was unworkable, and hone what I elected to retain.

At some point, it became clear to me that there were many questions to be answered that my early education had not revealed. But somehow I had been trained to observe and to ask questions. There were clearly things I needed to know.

After nineteen years away from college, I returned to formal study. I was fortunate enough to find a curriculum at Kean College in Education and Behavioral Sciences which was designed to permit its students to enhance their knowledge in their own fields of endeavor. Personal study was permitted and encouraged. I enrolled with apprehension, afraid I had forgotten how to learn. I soon discovered that I could learn better because ideas were relevant to my own experience, and made more sense to me than had my schooling the first time around.

My work had led me to questions about territoriality. I had seen similarities in behavior among my patients, the children I had raised, and the many animals I live with. I had questions about interpersonal relationships and about perception. I needed to know more about the community and agencies in the community. At the time I thought these were all divergent issues, and was pleased that I could find a curriculum which would permit me this leeway. I was also able to apply my interests toward the elderly. By now I had realized that I seemed to be most gratified with my work with this population.

Not until much later did I come to realize what there was about working with the elderly that was so stimulating. At first I thought it was that I prefer the activities and interests of the adult to the toys and games and conversation of children. I still think that is true, but I also believe that one can see far more progress in less time in the adult. Perceptual development can be recapitulated at a much faster rate than it can be acquired. Being one who prefers instant gratification, I naturally get more positive reinforcement from adults than from kids.

As a practitioner, I have developed a style of interaction with patients that seems to work well for me. As I have said, some things seem to work well and I use them. Other things I have tried and found unsuccessful, and rejected. At some point, I began to look at my practice in a critical manner, attempting to analyze what it was that made me choose one action over another. Lila Llorens has said that occupational therapists subcorticalize their own skills. They are so good at what they are doing that they do not know what it is, in fact, that they are doing. They do it automatically. With this good clue, I began to look at my practice in an attempt to determine why I chose one form of delivery over another. I was aided in my search by a very stimulating colleague, Rose Reffler. When I would say, "Don't do it that way; do it this way," I would invariably hear, "Tell me more about this." Being forced to bring to conscious attention matters that I had previously done automatically, forced me to reanalyze my choices, reexamining the reasons I had come to these choices in the first place.

Things began to fall into place. It also became clear that perceptual dysfunction could not be studied without some knowledge of normal perception. And perception in the adult was not necessarily the same as perception in the child. Up until this point, I had been exposed only to developmental theorists with a neurogenic bias. Upon becoming aware that there was a larger world out there, I opted for additional study. Two years of study at Rutgers Institute for Cognitive Studies introduced me to concepts of adult perception I could apply to what I was seeing in clinic. I was now able to generalize, where before I was only able to serve as a model.

This book is a result of a conscious search of six years duration based upon a lifetime career of questions. I am not certain that it answers too many of these questions, only that it points a direction in which to look. And, hopefully, I am not the only one who will take interest in looking in this direction.

II. PREFACE:

OCCUPATIONAL THERAPIST, MASTER OF BEHAVIORAL PLANNING

Consensus among people plays a large part in the dictates of human behavior. Performance is so often predicated upon what one is expected to do. People tend to assume the tasks assigned to roles they fill without question. For some, a time comes when questions do arise. That which has been automatically performed comes to conscious awareness and decision making becomes a part of the restructuring of behavior. Women, for example, have just recently begun to question their own roles and the task assignments inherent in those roles. Who will rear the children, wash the dishes, earn and support? A new basis for decision regarding the assignment of tasks is developing. But most people are ordinarily content to rely on customary behaviors which they perform automatically in most of their daily tasks.

That which is believed by many largely governs the beliefs of individuals. Together, mankind as a whole determines will and goals for man the individual. Expectation dictates behavior. Unity of concepts yields unity of purpose and performance among people. Standards for behavior are set by consensus, and it is expected that those standards are to be met within reasonable ranges. Custom derives from consensus between people. Agreement as to appropriateness of behavior is mutually confirmed.

Custom requires consent from those who choose to abide by custom. That choice is not always a conscious one. Automatic, habituated behaviors strongly regulate performance. Custom and consensus are difficult to regulate by formal means. Custom can be a stronger power than law. Truths of consensus can be greater than proofs of formal derivation. That Prohibition didn't work and necessitated repeal, and that there is a currently existing drug culture opposing legislation, attests to the power of consensual agreement.

Commonly understood metaphors and cliches symbolize agreements mankind expresses in communication, agreements derived over time and experience. Yet consentual acknowledgement has itself acquired a demeaned status in some quarters. Consensus has been assumed to be less than significant when compared with those scientific studies which arose from physical science and which hold that quantification provides the sole avenue to a clear and defensible study of truth. But even the mathematical science of physics has discovered that some things cannot be measured. The Heisenberg uncertainty principle demonstrates that the very act of measuring alters that which is being measured. Orne (1962)[1] indicated this to be his concern with laboratory experiments which deal with social phenomena. Laboratory research is apt to provide artifacts yielding questionable data. It is difficult to conceal from human subjects the nature of that in which they engage. In addition, an investigator often enters into research in an attempt to prove that of which the researcher is already convinced. It is recognized as a characteristic of human cognition that one tends to see an event from the perspective one has of that event. The formulation of a hypothesis for proof or disproof is evidence of such a position. When an hypothesis is formulated, a problem is expressed from a particular perspective. Being objective when one views an issue from one perspective is difficult. Perspective destroys objectivity. Bias is inherent in human cognition. An investigator must act beyond the characteristic of his species in retaining objectivity in scientific inquiry. Attitude and perspective can affect experimental design. People tend to find what they are looking for. Vested interests belie objectivity. Yet the ability to accept change is also a feature of cognition. Tolerance of shifts in attitude and their incorporation into the consensus expressed in life's tasks is a feature of human behavior. Indeed, when one is forced to change one's perspective by circumstance, one is more likely to assert one's view. Festinger (1957)[2] has entitled this inclination "reduction of cognitive dissonance." This tendency is frequently seen reflected in the behavior of religious converts who become more zealous in their religious fervor than those born to the faith. Perspective alters with time.

Many have assumed that quantification is the sole road to scientific truth. But Freud and Piaget and philosophers and scholars before and after them have added immeasurably to world knowledge without the use of statistical procedures. Observation and analysis helped them to formulate new concepts. Today again there is a swing away from quantification toward qualitative research. Rist (1979)[3] reports "that the observation of human behavior in natural settings (as opposed to measurement of human behavior) is an appropriate means by which to understand that behavior." Measure is not necessarily enlightening or growth producing. Quantification can contribute to illusion. But those professions which have developed their practice upon quantitative measure have achieved status. It may not have mattered if studies in which they have engaged might have offered humanity little toward advancing those aspects of human behavior which make us human.

Sharing and caring are distinctive human qualities. They do not carry full scientific accreditation, nor are they easily measured. The affective domain is that domain which occupational therapy educators have had most difficulty measuring when attempting to create behavioral objectives for curricula. Despite this educational deficiency in skill for measuring affect, the field of occupational therapy attracts large numbers of sensitive, caring and sharing people, but often without strong inclination toward formal research. That many occupational therapists are disinclined toward formal research seems to have biased the field in a way that directs attention toward improving practice by subjective assessment rather than measurable objectification, at least not measurable in the way that other fields have found successful for them. Occupational therapists rely upon their patients to tell them what works for them, and that has been the measure that has been used. It is the way their knowledge base has been built. Those techniques which have worked have been used and shared. Those with which patients do not mark their own successes have been rejected and forgotten. Tools of the trade are those which support successful human endeavor. Occupational therapy is a clinical practice requiring artistic skill in the performance of its craft, that of facilitating human behavior.

Just as mankind is continually developing, so too is occupational therapy. Occupational therapy is a young profession, subject to the very same growing pains that mankind has experienced. Occupational therapy began as a field which filled a need. It continues precisely because it continues to fill this same need. As Reilly (1962)[4] has stated,

> That this need will be persistent in American culture seems fairly certain. That occupational therapy will persist is not quite so certain. It is true, however, that if we fail to serve society's need for action, we will most assuredly die out as a health profession. It is also most assuredly true that if we did dissolve from the scene, in a decade or so, another group similarly organized and prepared would have to be invented. I believe, therefore, that the occupational therapy hypothesis (that man, through the use of his hands as they are energized by mind and will, can influence the state of his own health) is a natural one to be advanced in America.

Still the profession has questions. Questions occupational therapists have about themselves are the most pressing and are part of its growth. Occupational therapists have berated themselves for their lack of formal research as if this lack indicated that their profession is not valid in the absence of this research. Respected occupational therapists have publicly and repeatedly professed the view that occupational therapy is not a profession without this formal research (Fidler, 1979)[5] but in fact, occupational therapists have indeed developed a viable profession despite their lack of abundant research of a quantifiable nature. Understand that this point is made not to deny the validity of formal research, but rather to confirm the significance of that which has gone before. We have a history; a consensus.

To those who have prepared our history we are grateful for demonstrating the theoretical whole that is necessary before hypothesis can be expressed, then ratified or denied. Antje Price,[6] presenting *Laterality Revisited* at the 1979 American Occupational Therapy Association Conference in Detroit, blew holes in the concept that unilateral dominance is a sure sign of integrated neural functioning. But unless the idea that unilateral dominance as a sign of integrated function had been previously expressed, there would have been no thought to investige its worth as a concept. Concepts must be expressed before their worth can be examined, then rejected or accepted. Many valuable concepts have contributed to the development of occupational therapy. Together they have contributed to a conceptual whole, although this whole has been difficult to identify because of the diversity of its application and experience, and the broad base of education which generates from so many theoretical frames.

Not yet developed is a comprehensive means of observing and reporting its practice which succeeds for occupational therapy as well as other means have succeeded for other fields of practice, not withstanding that some attempts have been made in this direction (Llorens, 1976)[7]. The unique particulars of practice, a practice designed to resolve the unique problems which afflict individuals, need unique solution. Uniqueness is not easily measured. But uniqueness is a feature of human existence. Both Freud and Piaget, alert to this problem, resolved it by use of analysis of the clinical observations they had made. Through theories developed upon individuals studied, they contributed immeasurably to the enlightenment of mankind regarding human behavior.

Polanyi, in *Personal Knowledge* (1958)[8], has exalted the subjectivity of human awareness. He honors those special qualities inherent in cognitive performance which go beyond that which can be measured, but are nonetheless significant. The uniqueness of persons is lauded by this attitude. Uniqueness is that to which occupational therapists have specially attended in their therapeutic practice. Not only the individuality of persons, but also that of their interests, is the concern of occupational therapists. As therapists, we have within our compendia all the endeavors of humankind, defined by those people who engage in them, our clients. Tools used in treatment are those activities which mankind has designed for its own stimulation and to fulfill its own goal needs. Occupational therapy practice has been developed from empirical observations of the successful use of task-oriented treatment employed with individuals suffering mind/body impairment.

Therefore it seems necessary to look to that which distinguishes human beings as thinking, performing organisms, to define occupational therapists in their role as advocates for human performance. An attempt shall be made to see this role in light of a relational paradigm parented by gestalt principles. Gestalt psychology has offered the basis for a relational paradigm which has a theoretical base supported by quantities of research of a formal nature. Analysis of this paradigm and its application to the practice of occupational therapy may help to explain how that practice works and how more comprehensive treatment techniques may be developed.

The study of perception, cognition, learning, memory, creativity and social psychology are relevant to both cognitive psychology and occupational therapy. Cognitive psychology has studied these as theoretical constructs. Occupational therapy has concerned itself with these same constructs as health modules. Underlying occupational therapy's expertise in the use of tasks as therapeutic tools may be a conceptual model not previously identified within its own profession. These matters are complex, poorly defined and often conflicted if one views the varied speculations investigators have made regarding the nature of human thought and action. Perception, cognition and skilled performance are those features reputed to distinguish us as human beings. That so many diverse views are prevalent regarding these matters in some way frees us from the restrictions of custom and enables us to offer still another attempt at explanation. Perhaps from there we can then proceed to identify what is occupational therapy's responsibility and function.

To be able to identify what it is that occupational therapy does has long been a matter of concern and discusssion. Occupational therapists have had difficulty in identifying for themselves that their practice in a wide variety of treatment areas is indeed occupational therapy. Sometimes occupational therapists have been criticized most heartily by their own peers for wanting to be all things to all people in all areas of practice. Clarification of our role has presented questions both personally and professionally, and within the constraints of the law. Why else the recurrent dissatisfaction with a definition which changes from time to time, both nationally and as utilized in local situations? Have we not all experienced the familiar question to which we have each formulated our own reply, or not feeling capable of explanation, have committed to memory the current official definition of occupational therapy?

And yet, to whom is it least necessary to explain our practice? Clients understand succinctly what it is that their treatment is about. Involvement of clients in their own (re)habilitation clarifies for them occupational therapy's role and purpose. This is true in pediatric practice, hand rehabilitation, gerontology, psychiatry, physical disabilities and elsewhere. Clients understand their therapist's role through their own successes. Treatments are designed to provide to the client success in areas where success was not formerly available without therapeutic intervention.

What is there about this profession which makes it easier

for those who receive these services to understand it than so many of those practicing the profession? Perhaps it is that clients have only to be aware of the specifics of occupational therapy which relate directly to them or to those whose treatment they have observed. Because functional improvements are noted as a result of their effort in selected activity, clients derive their conclusions based upon evidence and faith. The evidence is the client's own success and the faith is in the expertise of the therapist. Demonstration of success has led clients to the conclusion of expertise in the facilitator of his skill development.

Too often occupational therapists themselves are not so well convinced of their own expertise. Perhaps what limits their confidence is their awareness of many other areas of practice than the one in which their own practice is bounded. Differences in the modalities which are employed in differing disability arenas has perhaps contributed toward clouding the issue. Therapists are well aware of many diverse skills and concepts necessary to successful practice in varying practice areas. But one wonders why someone else's expertise seems more impressive than one's own. What someone else knows, unknown by oneself, seems somehow more mysterious, more impressive, more important than one's own skills. Perhaps because of this, insecurity abounds. There is so much to know, but one cannot know everything there is to be known. Unfortunately, however, therapists often belittle much of what they themselves do know. In attempting to develop a conference panel in 1976, seventeen occupational therapists from all over New Jersey were approached, and asked to contribute techniques which I had observed and identified as unique and successful during the time I had been employed as a college fieldwork coordinator. All those who were approached deprecated the value of those techniques that they themselves had developed. Upon initial request, none saw that what they had designed was sufficiently significant that it could be of importance to others. Their own skill was not viewed by themselves as important. Modesty did not seem to be the issue. Therapists' own achievements and knowledge are too often seen by themselves as not significant. What is there about our profession that perpetuates this insecurity or lack of value for that at which we are indeed skilled? Is it the very uniqueness of treatment procedures that appears to negate the idea of universality? One may inappropriately conclude that even a brilliant scheme has limited applicability and therefore limited value because of the very uniqueness ascribed to human behavior. Fred Sammons has surely demonstrated the practicability of sharing demonstrated through the cost effectiveness of not requiring that we continually reinvent the wheel.

So many diverse skills and concepts are necessary for each practice area that it has been difficult for us to see the forest for the trees. Much detail often prevents one from forming a clear picture. Consolidation is difficult. One finds it difficult to attend to detail and at the same time step back in order to attain an overview. Parts and wholes are not cognitively available at the same moment. Shifting awareness is required to alert us to all that there is to know. When one is caught up in detail it takes effort to shift attention to the peripheral context of experience. One often makes that effort only if one projects a personal advantage in doing so.

The very expertise which has developed through specialization has also contributed to a further lack of positive identification for this profession. For only some treatment areas has it been commonly assumed that expertise is required. Sophisticated skills have been recognized as requisite in pediatric and physical disabilities practice. Efforts by sensory integration specialists to establish minimum competency through testing, although admirable, may have contributed to negative self images for other segments of the profession. Too many occupational therapists who accurately recognize their lack of current ability in those areas where necessary expertise has been identified, feel, because they lack current skill in those areas, they can practice in an area requiring less skill, perhaps an area such as gerontology or psychiatric practice. Presuming this to be true is faulty reasoning. These areas require as great skill in their practice as any other area. By adopting this faulty attitude, occupational therapists demean the value of the entire profession they call their own, and by doing so discourage respect for skill evidenced by master clinicians in all areas of practice. If occupational therapists do not respect their profession by practicing it well in all areas where that practice is demonstrated, who will? Some areas originating in our profession have already been lost to it through disrespect for the significance of those aspects of practice. Fidler clearly and accurately warned us of this eventuality.

Too often therapists have concentrated upon their differences rather than upon their unity. Consider then the value of occupational therapists who wave the flag of generalist, not in flight from specialization, but rather as a means of avoiding elimination from their body of knowledge a compendium of treatments which may well have application in wider areas of practice than perhaps initially conceptualized. Wide acceptance of sensory integration concepts (Gilfoyle, 1973)[9] and the utilization of those concepts in expanding areas of practice (King, 1974)[10] is a demonstration of this broad approach to treatment. Occupational therapy must be seen in its unity for each of its many practice areas to develop further. Concepts basic to all practice require expression and dissection. Proposed is a framework within which occupational therapy can be expressed, demonstrated in terms of a practice area with which this author is most familiar. Although modeled in terms of gerontological practice, I believe that this framework has applicability to all areas of occupational therapy practice.

The resolution of problems of living is the concern and province of occupational therapy. Their education and training prepare therapists with skills necessary for the resolution of these problems. Occupational therapy is a profession which has expertise in all areas of developmental performance from reflexive through conceptual and interactive behavior. Occupational therapy attends to facilitating the performance of man in his most global purview. It is the occupational therapist's role to enable healthy development by facilitating self constructed plans for behavior. Occupational therapy is a doing profession. "O.T. makes doing possible!" Occupational therapists of whatever specialization deliver their services as facilitators of behavioral plans permitting their clients to formulate behavioral plans necessary to their further development. As intervention in plans can occur at all levels of development, intervention skills at all levels become the necessary stock in trade for practice. This has been well known to be true. It is the identification of why this is true that has been of such great concern to our profession each time we have attempted to redefine ourselves (Johnson, 1973)[11].

Occupational therapy is a profession skilled in the variety of areas necessary to serve as a facilitator of behavioral plans through its global training and practice. Being a jack-of-all-trades provides a therapist with potential skill in behavioral planning. In order to plan, however, one must see the present clearly. *What is*, is a reality which may be obscured by bias. The present is seen in terms of the bias of the past. The context of the past colors the view of the present. In light of the past, the present can be seen as secondary to and dependent upon that which has gone before. Time is inherent in experience. Future is experienced in this way as well. It is seen in relationship to the present. *What was* colors our view of *what is*. *What can be* depends upon *what is*. It is necessary to resolve the clarity of *what is* in order to plan *what is to be*.

The future is alive when the reality of the present is resolved. The present may hold truths, skills and abilities which the past denies us. *What is believed to be* true clouds the reality of *what is* true. When the past dictates that things seem no longer possible, the present must be able to indicate that performance is indeed possible so that a future may live.

Developmentally, human beings are aware first of the present, then of the future, and finally of the past (Luria, 1976)[12]. Looking ahead is developmentally prior to looking back. Recall of past is dependent upon recognition and reinforcement. What has been repeated is remembered best. Time is sequential, relative, and proceeds in one direction.

The future is present for all. Living implies future. Future implies plan, but only when the future is internally constructed and directed by the one who experiences that future. Hampering performance and planning, allowing the past primacy, allowing the past to stand for the present, prevents a living future. Patients must be enabled to control their present by permitting them to learn skills they can use to plan their futures.

Needs must be identified, both those which are expressed and unexpressed. Formulation of a behavioral plan is limited by motivation and competency. Confidence and security at earliest developmental levels of performance are necessary in order to develop further in functional achievement. Lack of competency is an indication of unsuccessful attempts to resolve or integrate lower developmental units of performance. Individual component movements or behaviors may be present, yet skill may not be evidenced. Skill and competency are the baseline upon which advancing human performance is built. Where skill is not evidenced there is limitation in the ability to develop plans. This inability results from unresolved conflicts between component behaviors. Piaget's equilibration theory deals with this phenomenon. The resolution of conflict and the acquisition of constancy for the client is the goal of the occupational therapist whether attending to reflexive, motoric, conceptual or interactive levels of performance.

Throughout his lifetime, the human being is internally compelled toward planning. As Robert Browning[13] has said, "Ah, but a man's reach should exceed his grasp, or what's a heaven for?" This quotation bespeaks the essence of self directed striving. Planning exemplifies future. Future implies hope. Striving expresses within itself the concepts of future and of potential. In order to strive, one must believe that goals have the potential to be met. The occupational therapist serves to provide hope and reinforces a sense of future by enabling potential. Skill in facilitating performance by removing barriers to that performance in all activities of living permits the occupational therapist to claim the title of Master of Behavioral Planning.

REFERENCES
II. Preface - Occupational Therapist, Master of Behavioral Planning

1. Orne, M.T.: On the social psychology of the psychological experience: with particular reference to demand characteristics and their implications. *American Psychologist,* 17(11): 776-783; 1962.
2. Festinger, L.: *A Theory of Cognitive Dissonance.* Evanston, Illinois: Row, Peterson, 1957.
3. Rist, R.C.: On the Means of Knowing; Qualitative Research in Education. *New York University Education Quarterly,* New York, Summer 1979.
4. Reilly, M.: Occupational Therapy Can Be One of the Great Ideas of Twentieth Century Medicine. *American Journal of Occupational Therapy,* 31: 1-9; 1962.
5. Fidler, G.: "Professional or Nonprofessional?" In *Occupational Therapy 2001 A.D.* Rockville, Maryland: American Occupational Therapy Association, 1979.
6. Price, A.: "Laterality Revisited." Presented at the American Occupational Therapy Association Annual Conference, Detroit, Michigan, 1979.
7. Llorens, L.: *The Occupational Therapy Sequential Care Record, Revision II.* Gainesville, Florida: University of Florida, 1976.
8. Polanyi, M.: *Personal Knowledge: Towards a Post-Critical Philosophy.* Chicago: University of Chicago Press, 1958.
9. Gilfoyle, E. and Grady, A.: "A Developmental Theory of Somatosensory Perception." In *Body Senses and Perceptual Deficit,* edited by Henderson and Coryell. Boston: Boston University Press, 1973.
10. King, L.J.: A Sensory-Integrative Approach to Schizophrenia. *American Journal of Occupational Therapy,* 28: 529-535; 1974.
11. Johnson, J.: Occupational Therapy: A Model for the Future. *American Journal of Occupational Therapy,* 27: 1-7; 1973.
12. Luria, A.: *The Mind of a Mnemonist: A Little Book About a Vast Memory.* Chicago: Contemporary Books, 1976.
13. Browning, R.: *Andrea del Sarto (The Faultless Painter),* line 97.

III. A FRAMEWORK FOR HUMAN BEHAVIOR

1. A Relational Paradigm

"We owe to Gestalt psychology much of the available evidence showing that perception is a comprehension of clues in terms of a whole. But perception usually operates automatically, and gestalt psychologists have tended to collect preferentially examples of the type in which perception goes on without any deliverate effort on the part of the perceiver and is not even corrigible by his subsequent reconsideration of the result. Optical illusions are then classed with true perceptions, both being described as the equilibration or simultaneous stimuli to a comprehensive whole. Such an interpretation leaves no place for any intentional effort which prompts our perception to explore and assess in the quest of knowledge the clues offered to our senses. I believe this is a mistake, and shall say more - of the reasons for recognizing persons who use their senses as centres of intelligent judgment. At this stage it is enough to recall some features of this active personal participation. We recognize it in the signs of watchfulness which distinguish an alert animal from one rendered listless by exhaustion or neurotic disturbance. A sign-learning experiment can succeed only if we can arouse the animal's interest in his situation and make him aware of a problem which can be solved by straining his powers of observation. This may, of course, be done by offering a reward. But once he has learned a trick, the animal's inclination to repeat it without reward for the mere fun of it shows that his pleasure in solving a problem has a purely intellectual component. It has been proved also that the learning of a maze goes on even when no reward is offered. The animal's intelligence is spontaniously alive to the problem of making sense of its surrounding."

Polanyi
Personal Knowledge[1]

The self as a concept is a nebulous entity. The self is a human creation. What is defined as the self is a feeling tone, a summary of experiences, an identity. The self is a personally constructed concept which can be understood only in terms of the conceptualization of its constructor. This conceptualization does not evolve in a vacuum. The self and the world in which it develops and exists assume a pendular relationship, one to the other. While the world exists outside of the self, the world and the self are not apart. They are in constant touch. They are aspects of the same entity. The world and the self meet in the same relationship as that of body to mind. The self is a figment of mind while the body represents the world of concrete reality. Both body and mind relate to one another, exert influence upon each other, and alter in respect to one another through time. But although the world exists outside of the self, that world does not exist for any individual without having been mentally constructed by the knower of the world. Just as the world is constructed by each individual, so, too, the self is composed from experiences and encounters with that world.

The mind and the body are intrinsically unified. Modification of either aspect results in change in the other. Eastern religions, psychosomatic medicine and stress diseases attest to their unity. This inability to parse out the mind from the body is essentially that which is highlighted by the practice of occupational therapy. The use of the mind to solve problems of the body (King, 1978)[2], and the use of the body to solve problems of the mind (Ayres, 1972)[3], have been demonstrated among its treatment compendia.

The mind/body paradox has been explored since early history by scholars from Plato to Freud. How do the self and the world relate? How does the knower know? These have been problems of philosophy and psychology. This paradox is precisely the problem which is presented in attempting to define reality and in a quest to better understand what it is that our therapeutic practice attempts.

Reality is defined by the object world, but assessment of the object world is subject to the vagaries of experiences with that world. The real world is a different world for everyone. Reality differs and changes for all persons in time and in space as their perspective alters. Thus, interpretations of the mind are seen to influence percepts of the world, as bodies are seen to influence knowledge of the world within the constraints of movement and experience.

Just as the self is a nebulous concept, so, too, is reality. Reality is subject to the interpretation of the moment, the opinions of many, and the advances of world knowledge. What is true for now may be untrue within different contexts and for different individuals or groups. Consensus based upon available data dictates truth. Informed mankind shares mutual truths. For thousands of years, humanity existed without the truths of a spherical world in a universe created of particles. But once enlightened, mankind created a new consensus, never to return to its prior condition of unknowing. In normal human cognition, once knowledge is gained, one can never again 'not know.' Denial is pathology. Consolidation and retention of truth is demonstration of growth and health. Development is expansion much as a ripple grows in a pond. The world can never again be flat.

Reality is at best a shifting dimension which assumes a context/constancy relationship. Such a relationship is analogous to that which can be suggested by using as an example the origin and the insertion of a muscle. Origin as described here is not a finite point of reference, but is that point which serves as ground and to which the opposite point of insertion relates in a dependent fashion. Each point of origin or insertion of a given muscle serves relative to one another, dependent upon which point is fixed. Whichever point is fixed, the other serves as dependent and mobile in relationship to the original point. The contraction of the biceps which occurs when lifting a utensil differs from the contraction used lifting the body when chinning, in that the point which serves as origin in one instance serves as insertion in the other. That point which is stabilized serves as the foundation for a muscle contraction. Compounding this relationship are the multiple sources of stable and fluctuating muscle points evident in every task of living.

Just as the moving body demonstrates shifting points of stability, the mind, too, functions with shifting orientation. Gestalt principles alert us to shifting dimensions of cognition. Relationships dependent upon relationships highlight the transitory nature of knowledge based upon environmental encounters. These fluctuating relationships contribute to the subjectivity of that which is known, as well as the reality which is created. Relational concepts manifested in cognition have been evidenced in laboratory experiments in which variously encapsulating surrounds have been demonstrated to alter the way in which their internal components are viewed (Wallach, 1976)[4]. Space and speed relationships have been demonstrated to alter in relation to one another. The most external event dictates the context for that experienced within.

Dimensions of experience come from all sources and relate to one another as do gases in a bubble. Every component which enters the circle of inclusion provides influence upon all components and their position and influence relative to the whole and to each of the parts within the whole. Acquisition alters the character and reference of all parts and their whole whether conceptual or concrete. Thus the body and the mind can be understood to function under the same laws of relevance. They shift and flux as ground alters. Together they alter the perception of reality.

The shifting dimension of reality can be illustrated through the phenomenon of reversible figures (Figure 1-1). When reversible figures illusions are viewed, the mind outside of awareness selects to perceive that which is ambiguous first in one way, and then in the other. When no existing reference is available, either part may be viewed alternately as figure or ground. When an orienting reference exists, as it does for some individuals, there is exhibited a propensity to view reversible figures with a bias toward that inclination. Some people are more apt to view only one of a variety of possible visual conclusions. Projective techniques which utilize ambiguous material take advantage of the feature of human cognition toward biased perception in order to perform diagnostic services. The ambiguity of Rorschachs and Thematic Apperception Tests permit expressions whose characteristics are identifiable and able to be categorized. Biases can be noted. For example, testing before mealtime is quite likely to produce responses of food related content. So do compulsions and fixations bias response to testing. Bias determines the context for experience which results in orientational constancy. Orientation is a construction of cognitive derivation. Cognition functions over wide ranges. Cognition is a phenomenon which may be available to awareness or may be so well automated that conscious awareness may be absent.

Just as cognition is inclined toward bias, ambiguity is a feature of cognition which occurs at an earlier developmental level. Faced with a variety of perspectives, conflict between views may afford no resolution. Ultimately, data acquired may resolve into a perception which solves the problem implicit in the event, encompassing all perspectives. Life's encounters offer stimuli which may be resolved in one way or another. Not only in contrived illusion is ambiguity present. Normal living experiences provide ambiguity, but those same experiences permit the spontaneous resolution of ambiguous content. On one occasion as I was riding behind an automobile, the driver of the car in front appeared to be a short woman wearing a large hat. Suddenly this misperception clarified into the reality of a man whose head was shielded from view by the unusual head rest of the auto seat. The presumption that the 'hat' existed, dictated the conclusion 'woman.' It is not uncommon for such spontaneous clarifications of perception to occur. Given the same sensory information, multiple conclusions can be drawn in regard to data. Data which may be initially insufficient and ambiguous can become sufficient in time to enable drawing a more veridical conclusion. That one 'draws' a conclusion

**Figure 1-1
Reversible Figures**

Viewers presented with this configuration first see either a vase or two women's faces. Shortly thereafter, the reverse figure is perceived.

implies a creative task. Spontaneous conclusions also occur when misperceptions have been made which were based upon other than visual material alone. Accurate integration of data from multiple sensory systems is necessary for the comprehension of that data. Reliable information derives from integration of multiple sensory inputs in consistent relationship. Multiple stimuli combine to create a sudden jelling of facts into a newly created encompassing whole of reality. Such is the 'Aha!' experience. Time and perspective permit such resolutions to occur. Sometimes, of course, people 'jump to the wrong conclusions,' but time and experience, under normal circumstances, rectify such error. Unfortunately for some, errors in perceptions persist throughout life and contribute to maladaptive adjustments.

Time, or rather, awareness of time, is also determined by relational comparisons. Time is often measured by subjective means. Time passes rapidly or endlessly. A fun experience is sure to speed by. A boring lecturer sorely tries one's patience. Though the times for these two experienced may be the same, they are perceived quite differently. An hour can be a short or a long time. So can a minute. At a dog obedience trial the minute required for a dog to remain seated following the command to 'stay' feels like an eternity to the trainer and exhibitor of that dog. Time can be experienced at the same time as passing quickly or slowly. The same event can feel both fast and slow depending upon the context or the perspective of the experience. A week can drag, while the semester in which it takes place flies by.

William James (1890)[5] has suggested that time is assessed in individuals by means of comparison of the present to the past. The phenomenon in which time seems to pass more rapidly as one ages can be attributed to this relationship. Each moment in a life of time is compared to all that has gone before. As we age, that which has been experienced as previous time grows. The current moment becomes more and more brief when compared to the total experience of one human being. Einstein demonstrated that an event observed simultaneously by different observers would be interpreted differently according to the references they used. He proposed that time is not absolute, but rather occurs within a system of relativity. Time and space concepts develop from relational comparisons experienced. Those times which have occurred before our lifetimes are unfathomable. A thousand years and a hundred thousand years appear indistinguishable as they are beyond experience. Experience is necessary for assessments to be made. Internal time develops and is reinforced from expectations derived from previous experience.

Utilization of one sensory modality to circumvent the deficits of another has been voiced by Ayres. Beyond that, data offered by Hermelin (1979)[6] indicate that each modality processes according to biases referrant to the temporal or spatial dimension prevalent in that system. By comparing the performance of normal to congenitally blind or deaf children on simple tasks, she was able to show that the visual system is biased toward processing data simultaneously whereas the auditory system prefers sequential processing and that individuals are biased to perform according to the sensory processing style which they have at their disposal or are more skilled. She proposed that time offers a sequential code whereas space is of simultaneous dimension.

When one looks at motor capacity, a system exists which Hermelin proposes to be answering for the organism the question of 'Where?' 'Where' is a space coded question of dimension. Motor capacity is a space/sequential process, bridging and triangulating the dimensions of the other sensory systems. Time and space are the dimensions which audition, vision, and mobility address (Figure 1-2). Mobility

**Figure 1-2
Time/Space - Audition, Vision, Mobility Model**

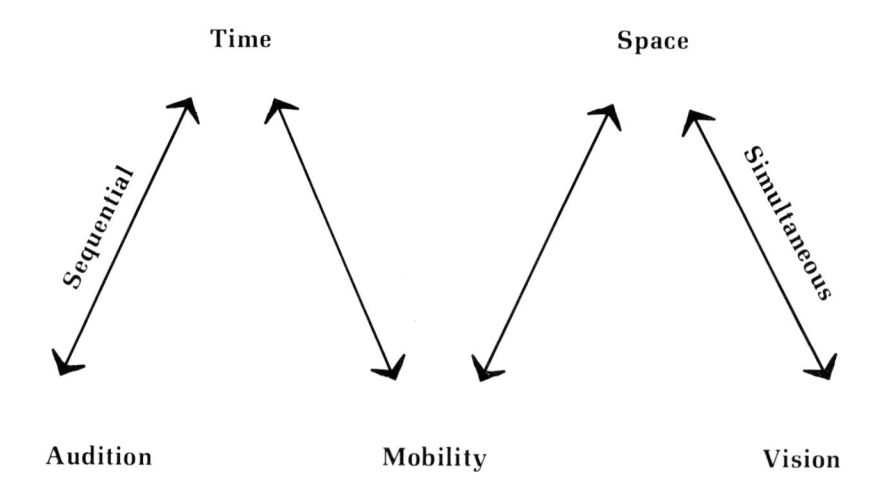

Mobility enables sequential time ordered sensory elements to integrate with the simultaneous experiencing of space.

is the common language translating the biased interpretations of vision and audition.

The issues of time and space direct us to the bicamerality of the human brain. Theorists have attributed to the bicameral brain the deciphering of these elements of time and space. Levy (1974)[7] states that "The left hemisphere analyzes over time, whereas the right hemisphere synthesizes over space." Acknowledgement of the differentiation provided by human physiology had been previously noted by Levy and Sperry (1968)[8]. "The data indicate that the mute, minor hemisphere is specialized for Gestalt perception, being primarily a synthesist in dealing with information input. The speaking, major hemisphere, in contrast, seems to operate in a more logical, analytical, computer-like fashion. Its language is inadequate of the rapid complex synthesis achieved by the minor hemisphere."In order for this division of labor to be functional requires access to each other of each element of comprehension. Edwards (1979)[9] has demonstrated through art that people are able to shift from one element or style to another. Distortions are evident in works done by untrained students. When students have been trained to shift from the analytic mode to the spatial mode with which the right brain is concerned, those distortions are eliminated (Figure 1-3). Edwards informs us that "We don't notice the distortions because we mentally adjust the image so that it fits with what we know." The consolidation of right-brained, space oriented, immediate simultaneous function with left-brained, time oriented, historically and sequentially developed material is a constantly acquiring process in normal human function. Mobility is the factor which provides continual change, enabling that consolidation or integration.

Gibson (1970)[10] states that inherent in perception is the necessity for an interactive experience with environment that requires several sensory mechanisms. Information about the world is developed through the integration of inputs and their relation to one another spatially, temporally and qualitatively. No one part is appreciated into the whole without altering the whole and at the same time each of its

Figure 1-3
Edwards (1979)[9] demonstrated alteration of perspective by shifting attention to a spatial mode.

Alice Abel
September 28, 1976

Alice Abel
November 16, 1976

Lyman Evans
April 2, 1978

Lyman Evans
May 8, 1978

A Relational Paradigm   31

Figure 1-3
Edwards (1979)[9] demonstrated alteration of perspective by shifting attention to a spatial mode.

Tom Nelson
August 8, 1978

Tom Nelson
September 3, 1978

Ken Darnell
February 5, 1974

Having completed the original course, Ken produced this drawing about a year later.

32 PERCEPTION: ITS DEVELOPMENT AND RECAPITULATION

Figure 1-3
Edwards (1979)[9] demonstrated alteration of perspective by shifting attention to a spatial mode.

John Boomer
January 3, 1978

John Boomer
March 5, 1978

Gerardo Campos
September 2, 1973

Gerardo Campos
November 10, 1973

parts. Thus the human mind expands, as the body grows and changes. Each change which occurs or is encountered must be resolved and incorporated into the whole of experience if the individual is to adapt and function. This relationship between past knowledge and new experience is inherent in development. Without the ability to synthesize experience, adaptation and skill cannot be achieved.

Spatial orientation is realized in the relational paradigm. As the world and the self are constantly moving, they are thereby in an ever shifting relationship to one another. Movement forces the use of external referents, provides the opportunity to make decisions, offers sensory feedback, and never involves a single system. Movement of self and movement of self relative to the environment provide the orientation in which the relationship between context and constancy can articulate. Our eyes move; our limbs move; and our bodies move through space. Each movement that takes place results in infinite relational changes between the parts that move and between the person and the world in which that person exists. Human physiology is designed to function most advantageously through its adaptation to movement. Visual and tactual receptors are most keenly attuned to change. We see because our eyes move, constantly offering change experiences. Saccadic eye movements are ever present and are requisites to normal vision. Otoliths and joint and muscle receptors inform people of their relationships to gravity and the space they occupy. As changes occur in visual array, in pressure, and in fluid flow, stimulation is afforded to those sensors which are designed to appreciate change.

One example in which lack of change is occasionally experienced highlights the need for movement, and therefore change, to effect retention of information necessary for function. One becomes innured to the awareness of a held object if it remains constant in pressure and position. It is commonly experienced that when one carries an object for a long period of time, one loses awareness of the object carried. Yet when two or more points of touch are experienced in changing relativity to one another, as occurs in manipulation, we are informed of position, size, shape, and concept.

Just as multiple touch points in changing relation are necessary for data assessment, so, too, the bilaterality of one's sensory systems provides a mechanism which permits one to construct orientation by comparing relations. Sound location is identified because of differences perceived through both ears. Vision uses the mechanism of comparison of data between eyes to assess distance. Two or more points in changing relativity to one another serve an orienting purpose in multisensory relativity.

Olson (1977)[11], citing O'Keefe, reports of hippocampus function

> that place units receive information from a constellation of spatial stimuli in the environment rather than from just one stimulus. Thus each place unit recognizes a particular spatial location by triangulating among stimuli in different parts of the environment much as a surveyor or a navigator determines his location in space by measuring the relative positions of fixed landmarks. Hence it appears that the hippocampus has at least two classes of cells: place units that reflect where the animal is at the present time, and displace units that reflect the distance it is about to move in the environment.

Neurological confirmation of a relational strategy is confirmation indeed.

Pick (1979)[12] reports that this process of relational comparing achieves developmentally. Single landmarks are not sufficiently powerful in contributing to the retention of orientation. A system of landmarks in which a personal triangulation judgment can be made is necessary for spatial orientation. A reference is required for spatial inference to take place. Triangulation is necessary to confirm position. Ability to perform this process outside of visual awareness requires retention of spatial coordinates. It is this retention which appears to be the factor which acquires developmentally and it is this retention which is necessary to update position as it changes from site to site. Retention necessary for updating and thus accuracy in spatial orientation has been shown by Pick to be evident in college age persons, deficient in fifth graders and absent in first graders. Updating requires a mental representation of the whole reference system of space. When an area is too large to perceive at one time through direct sensation or recollection of space, orientation is not functional. Spatial orientational updating develops through constancy within space and is acquired through movement experience within that space.

Spatial orientation is dependent upon other aspects of sensory awareness as well. Both attention information and alerting information are provided to the organism by each sensory system. The auditory system serves both an attentional purpose and alerting purpose as do the tactual system, the visual system, the gustatory/olfactory system and the kinesthetic system. These systems are alerting upon the initial change experiences of a first encounter, and can be considered attentional when ongoing multisensory experiences are being utilized in performance. Stimulated by change and movement, sound, color, touch, balance and scent serve to rapidly alert us to attend to that in the environment which is significant. A single touch serves to alert, but multiple stimuli together provide relational information upon which to attend with judgment, multiple stimuli acquired together or over time. The relationship between attention and disregard also serves an orientational function basic to goal direction. This relationship must be operational for optimal adaptive functioning. Both attention and disregard must be available to enable human task performance. Disregard enables performance. The ability to respond only to appropriate stimuli serves one's adaptive capacity. One does not ordinarily attend to or remain aware of specific performance components of living. Rather, one attends to tasks at hand. When using a hammer, the specific movements of the hand are not considered, nor is the weight of the hammer, unless that weight is unexpected, but rather one considers the progress within the task itself. How straight is the nail driven? What is the goal of the construction? Creativity and task performance require that attention be freed from diverting prerequisite component performance. It is the very subverting of attention to task that provides the relational experience necessary for orientation. Concern with cortical versus subcortical performance (Gilfoyle & Grady, 1973)[13] may well be related to this explanation of attentional performance as a relational experience.

Experience is encountered in life's tasks. As one performs, attention shifts. Attention is of short duration and variability, bringing rapidly altering data to the system for continual comparative assessment. Attention mechanisms are of cognitive derivation, based on analyzed relations between points or modes. Alerting, however, is more attuned to the periphery, preparing the organism to mobilize to central attention. Peripheral alerters have been proposed to function through a different neurological system than the attention system, probably midbrain, circuiting rapidly through primitive mechanisms that serve a protective function for the organism (Trevarthen, 1968)[14]. Goldberg (1979)[15] has shown in experiments with monkeys that stimuli in the periphery alert cells within the intermediate layer of the superior colliculus. He has been able to show that this alerting occurs prior to eye movement and is independent of eye movement, indicating the brain's role in picking out significant stimuli. Monkeys trained to perform tasks in central fields respond to peripheral alerting but retain their head positions at center unless they are unsuccessful at the tasks they have been trained to perform. Goal direction seems to direct attention. One must speculate upon the role the environment takes in directing attention as it relates to personal intention.

Trevarthen (1968)[16] has proposed that the fast old brain serving an alerting function may be attuned to peripheral information, whereas the slower attention system functions through the cortical nervous system where information is available for analysis. Eleanor Gibson (1970)[17] informs us that ambient vision processes to the superior colliculus whereas foveal vision is processed to the cortex. Review of the anatomy of the visual system reveals that upon inversion of the field as occurs when light passes through the lens, data

Figure 1-4
Visual Field and Optic Chiasma

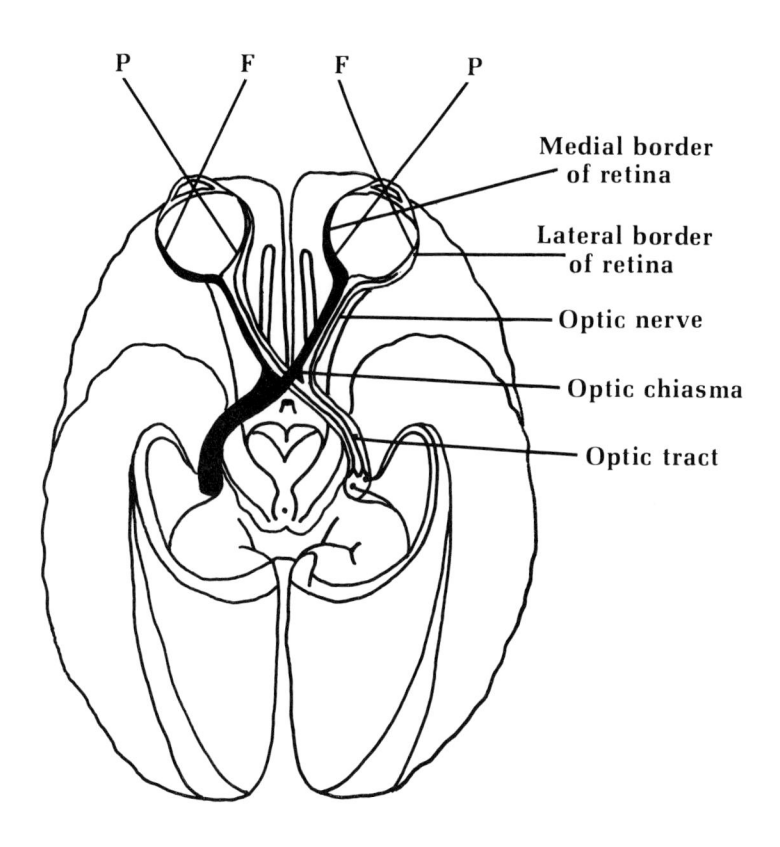

Lateral borders of the retina are stimulated by foveal visual stimuli (F). Medial borders of the retina are stimulated by the periphery (P). Medial fibers contribute to portions of the optic nerve which cross at the optic chiasma.

deriving from the periphery is received upon the nasal border of the retina and it is neural tissue in this border which crosses the optic chiasma to the opposite hemisphere (Fig. 1-4). Perhaps a temporal resolution of that which is received to different areas takes place. Varied temporal qualities may serve to confirm reality through resolved differentials in the speed of processing between the attentional and peripheral systems.

Both E. Gibson and J.J. Gibson are alert to the significance of differences between foveal and peripheral vision. J.J. Gibson (1966)[18] points out that man has developed to be an animal which has assumed greater dependence upon foveal vision. However, as humans are phylogenetically derived, sight must not be lost of the significance of peripheral vision to adaptive functioning. Trevarthen (1968)[19] has shown in his study of fish that peripheral vision is integral to functioning on an earlier developmental level.

In man, peripheral vision is not reinforced by the overlapping or duplicated visual imagery that frontal vision is afforded. Although frontal vision in both eyes does not offer identical retinal images, it is the near identity of images that offers depth information. Periphery of vision is not provided with reinforcing depth information and only retains a depth determination through constancy effects, recollection, and/or through proprioceptive reinforcement within the periphery of functional performance.

Proprioceptive memory in peripheral fields of upper extremity function in adults tends to be less accurate than frontal field function (See Chapter 8). If more numerous inputs from overlapping sensory sources reinforce the density with which things are known, it holds that the periphery is less well supplied with such reinforcing information sources, it being denied the duplicative efforts of the depth awareness mechanisms that are available to the frontal field of function. The midline has available to it all extremities and both eyes.

The periphery contributes to side/side conceptualization as well. The less well served periphery may account for the lack of side/side discrimination skill commonly found in adults. It has certainly been observed in clinical practice that left/right discrimination is a common problem even in individuals without neurological diagnosis. Several therapists I know have despaired that they are unable to administer the Southern California battery (SCSIT)[20] due to their own laterality and reversal problems.

Influence of the periphery in relationship to that to which one attends becomes critical to grounding of the self. It is the periphery which functions to provide constancy in space as it provides a context within which to relate function which takes place within foveal attention. As humans developed from lower animals, they became more skilled in manipulative tasks requiring foveal attention. Thumbs and centration united in their development. However, as changes evolved, the periphery did not become less critical to orientation. The relevance of peripheral vision to orientation is evident in the phenomenon of induced movement of the self (Rock, 1975[21]; Johannsen, 1978[22]). (See Chapter 2.) It may be relevant in the presence and absence of nystagmus. The relationships between the viewed periphery and the foveal visual field mark space and confirm self through a context/constancy relationship. Without orientation provided by peripheral experience, task performance is less possible, less proficient, less apt to provide satisfaction through demonstration of skill.

Context and constancy articulate in the myriad movements utilized in task performance. These goal directed movements serve as orienters. Movements performed while doing tasks both necessitate and establish spatial orientation. Multiple movements which occur in task performance serve as orienters through the development of spatial relationships. The consent confirmed by success in performance attests to that orientation. Successful performance serves to reinforce orientation. Success is related to skill. Skill is reinforced by appropriate or desired response from environment. Habit and skill facilitate further skill development. It is necessary to strive, to perform, to develop skill in order to achieve and to reinforce spatial constancy. Surety regarding space is both necessary and enhanced through use. Surety and skill assure that one practices that at which one expects to be successful, yielding further proficiency, further performance.

Skill is derived from drill. Repetition of task performance elicits skill. The association of movements and behaviors in conjunction with one another assures a sequential relationship with one another. The repetitive sequencing of components of behavior achieve habitual status. The retention of performance and thought enable habituation. But habit is herein described not in a behaviorist model, but within a gestalt model. It is those sequential behaviors which are in total synchrony with other previously attenuated schema of individuals that are adaptive and facilitory to higher level functioning. The concept of 'splinter skill' (Kephart, 1960)[23] can be seen to fall outside of a relational model. Splinter skills are not useful within the larger truth of integrated performance. Their recall is difficult because there is not sequential relationship defined. In order for skill to be functional it is necessary that unity exist between the part and the whole, between the task and the need to perform that task as an adaptive function. This has been confirmed in the therapeutic setting. Goldstein et al (1979)[24] reports that "It is common for a therapy to succeed in the training setting, yet fail to succeed in transferring positive outcomes to the patient's real-life environment." Optimal task performance requires integration of all relationships.

Task is that upon which skill is demonstrated. Tasks of living confirm reality. Living serves to ground the self in self constructed reality through interaction with the environment. Living, as defined here, embodies all those activities in which humans engage in the widest scope of their practical experience. People eat, they sleep, they run and jump. They work and play and love. Through all these activities of living, the world is continually re-experienced. It is repeated consolidation of relational experiences as acquired in life's tasks which enables the ascertanment of reality and thus the self. Reality is a construction of the individual confirmed by the environment and one's interaction with the world.

Reality is created from the whole cloth of experience founded in success.

An internalized awareness of constancy is necessary for the establishment of a sense of reality. Tasks provide an opportunity for the grounding reality to occur. They allow and reinforce orientation to the environment. They confirm within us feelings of self worth. When proficiency is evident, a feeling of efficacy (White, 1963)[25] results which, when projected, results in positive feedback in social encounters. Proficiency provides reinforcement in a relational model for the self/other appreciation necessary for human performance. Proficiency is measured by task performance and by positive feedback in social encounters. Human feedback confirms success experience. Consensus dictates personal image. Human interactions modify one to another. All human relationships influence one another. Change in any one yields change in the other (Asch, 1952)[26]. Self to other thus exist in a relational model. Systems theory verifies this relational phenomenon (Kielhofner, 1978)[27].

Tasks are an integral part of normal development (Ginsburg & Opper, 1969)[28] and thus must be seen as a tool necessary for developmental growth when development is impaired. Tasks have been shown to be an effective tool in health care (Reilly, 1962)[29]. As development and function can be impaired at any point in the life cycle, tasks must be considered vital to the establishment of normalcy in orientation, reality and affect. Use of tasks serves to develop relationships through experience which are necessary to achieve constancies. It may be that subverting of attention to task is the relational experience that enables development to proceed.

Through tasks, the movement of externals, of self, and of parts of self, provide orientational information. Multiple experiences of changing relativity contribute to awareness of space, the world of reality and of the self. The bilaterality of a human being's existence lends itself to a relationship between the center of that organism and the periphery of that organism's world of awareness. The concept of centration intimated or expressed by so many conceptual models is the confirmation of a center, of a self which retains its entity despite the fluctuation of all that contributes to its establishment. In tasks a treatment model has been found which confirms reality, a model skillfully performed by those who have performed their function outside of the awareness of, but within the realm of the relational paradigm.

REFERENCES
Chapter 1, A Relational Paradigm

1. Polanyi, M.: *Personal Knowledge: Towards a Post-Critical Philosophy,* Chicago: University of Chicago Press, 1958.
2. King, L.J.: Toward a Science of Adaptive Responses. *American Journal of Occupational Therapy,* 32: 429-437; 1978.
3. Ayres, A.J.: *Sensory Integration and the Treatment of Learning Disabilities.* Los Angeles: Western Psychological Services, 1972a.
4. Wallach, H.: *On Perception.* New York: Quandrangle, New York Times Book, 1976.
5. James, W.: *Principles of Psychology.* New York: Holt, 1890.
6. Hermelin, B: "Seeing and Hearing and Space and Time." Presented at the Conference on Neural and Developmental Bases of Spatial Orientation, Teachers College, Columbia University, New York, November 17, 1979.
7. Levy, J.: "Psychobiological Implications of Bilateral Asymmetry." In *Hemisphere Function in the Human Brain,* edited by S.J. Dimond and J.G. Beaumont. New York: John Wiley & Sons, 1974.
8. Levy, J., Trevarthen, C. and Sperry, R.W.: Perception of Bilateral Chimeric Figures Following Hemispheric Deconnexion. *Brain,* 95: 61-78; 1972.
9. Edwards, B.: *Drawing on the Right Side of the Brain.* Los Angeles: J.P. Tarcher, 1979.
10. Gibson, E.: The Development of Perception as an Adaptive Process. *American Scientist,* 58: 98-107; 1970.
11. Olton, D.: Spatial Memory. *Scientific American,* 236: 82-98; 1977.

12. Pick, H.: "Children's Cognitive Maps." Presented at the Conference on Neural and Developmental Bases of Spatial Orientation, Teachers College, Columbia University, New York, November 16, 1979.
13. Gilfoyle, E. and Grady, A.: "A Developmental Theory of Somatosensory Perception." In *Body Senses and Perceptual Deficit*, edited by Henderson and Coryell. Boston: Boston University Press, 1973.
14. Trevarthen, C.: "Vision in Fish: The Origins of the Visual Frame for Action Vertebrates." In *The Central Nervous System*, edited by D. Ingle. Chicago: University of Chicago Press, 1968.
15. Goldberg, M.: "Parietal Neuron Activity in Moving and Attending." Presented at the Conference on Neural and Developmental Bases of Spatial Orientation, Teachers College, Columbia University, New York, November 18, 1979.
16. Trevarthen, C.: (See above.)
17. Gibson, E.: (See above.)
18. Gibson, J.J.: *The Senses Considered As Perceptual Systems*. Boston: Houghton Mifflin, 1966.
19. Trevarthen, C.: (See above.)
20. Ayres, A.J.: *Southern California Sensory Integration Tests*. Los Angeles: Western Psychological Services, 1972b.
21. Rock, I.: *An Introduction to Perception*. New York: Macmillan, 1975.
22. Johannsen, G.: Colloquium Lecture at the Institute for Cognitive Studies, Rutgers University, Newark, New Jersey, Winter 1978-1979.
23. Kephart, N.C.: *The Slow Learner in the Classroom*. Columbus, Ohio: Charles E. Merrill, 1960.
24. Goldstein, A. et. al.: Structured Learning Therapy: Development and Evaluation. *American Journal of Occupational Therapy*, 33: 635-639; 1979.
25. White, R.: Ego and Reality in Psychoanalytic Theory. *Psychological Issues*, 3(3). New York: International Universities Press, 1963.
26. Asch, S.: *Social Psychology*. Englewood Cliffs, New Jersey: Prentice Hall, 1952.
27. Kielhofner, G.: General Systems Theory: Implications for Theory and Action in Occupational Therapy. *American Journal of Occupational Therapy*, 32: 637-645; 1978.

28. Ginsburg, H. and Opper, S.: *Piaget's Theory of Intellectual Development.* Englewood Cliffs, New Jersey: Prentice Hall, 1969.
29. Reilly, M.: Occupational Therapy Can Be One of the Great Ideas of Twentieth Century Medicine. *American Journal of Occupational Therapy,* 31: 1-9; 1962.

2. Internally Expressed

Figure 2-1

Human beings live with and interact with that with which they are surrounded. But the world in which people live and with which they interact and build experience is essentially a self constructed world. Much of that world has been created by man's hands but more so the world of experience is created by man's mind. In their minds humans conceptualize that with which they interact. In doing so they construct a conceptualization of themselves. Those concepts which are constructed dictate performance. Human behavior is controlled by what is believed as much as performance controls belief. External reality and internal construction conform to one another in a fluctuating relationship.

Much encountered in life is potentially ambiguous. Life's experiences permit the resolution of ambiguities which are faced. Multiplicative experiences tell each time anew further information regarding that which has been encountered. Knowledge of that which has been experienced contributes, fills in, permitting that which has been experienced to be known more densely and comprehensively. Time and the ability to retain experience contribute the opportunity to enhance knowledge. Some things are known very well. With some things we are very briefly acquainted. That which is known well or is more apt to occur tends to achieve greater stability. A baby recognizes first a mother's face. Recognition depends upon familiarity. A familiar set of shapes, planes, and dimensions dictate recognition. The Necker cube is such an example (Figure 2-2). People are more likely to mentally construct a three-dimensional representation of a box when the presentation is made in a plane which stimulates such interpretation (Dinnerstein, 1965).[1] Spatial relationships dictate orientation and understanding.

New knowledge is fragile. Individuals are more likely to forget that which they know briefly and that with which little is invested. A phone number can be recalled long enough for one to succeed in dialing it. That number is more apt to be recalled when dialing has been repeated or when the number is invested with critical importance. Repetition and relationship provide a sense of familiarity. The familiar provides stability. Stability and familiarity provide a

Figure 2-2
Necker Cube

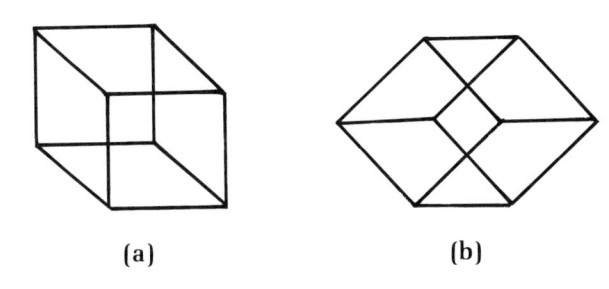

(a) (b)

When presented in the alignment on the left (a), a 3-dimensional cube is generally perceived. When presented in the alignment on the right (b), a 2-dimensional figure is generally perceived. (Dinnerstein, 1965)

context for new experience. Stability derives from constancy in orientation.

In order to learn, one must have stable and reliable systems upon which to base judgment. Constancy in awareness is critical to function. Integration of all inputs experienced enables reliance to be placed upon those inputs so that constancy can be experienced. Constancy in perception is also dependent upon subjective appreciation of the context in which that event is understood to occur. A personal frame of reference dictates whether one thinks something is heavy or light, dark or bright, or fast or slow. A prevailing set or state is an inherent characteristic of an individual at the time of a perception. Similar events are able to elicit different behavior depending upon that which has gone before. Every child knows it serves his best interests to keep away from Mommy when she has had a bad day. What would have been tolerated and even appreciated at another time, may, at some unacceptable time, be rejected with venom. The weight of prior experience shifts the dimensions with which the present world is experienced.

Some of the world of experience is of concrete structure.

Some is amorphous. People surround themselves with walls and furniture, while they also experience structure in relationships with others. Information about these structures derive through what people make of their senses. Information is afforded to the organism through its senses as that organism interacts with the environment in which it lives. Movements in space are monitored through sensors which tell us where we are as we are there. Movement and sensation are inseparable. The feedback loop unites both in an interdependent model. Sensory and motor experience are spoken of simultaneously. Integration of sensations experienced with motor functions performed is essential for adaptive behavior (Brown, 1976;[2] Ayres, 1972[3]). Perception develops from this integration of sensory motor experiences within the environmental profile of the individual. Development of reliability in perception establishes proficiency and comfort within that environment. Reliability and comfort then serve as precursors to enable learning of increasing complexity. Without efficiency in sensory motor integration, however, the effort required to effect learning is enormous. Efficient perceptual functioning underlies the development of concepts and the use of those concepts toward further cognitive functioning. When undue effort is required learning is delayed and further delays subsequent learning. Sensory input is basic to all information processing.

Miller, Galanter, and Pribram, in their book, *Plans and the Structure of Behavior* (1960)[4], propose a model for the understanding of behavior which has at origin a feedback loop system upon which all behavior is based. They envision feedback loops around larger and still larger segments of behavior. Using the analog computer model as an analogy to behavioral structure, a concept of behavior is proposed in which modular units of skill become incorporated with, or serve as bases for, the development of further skills. Each subset serves as a support entity for subsequent behaviors. Each behavioral unit, most basic to most complex, is defined as a Plan.

Some Plans are innate, deriving their programming

genetically. Others are acquired. Habits and skills are demonstrations of previously voluntary Plans that have become automatic. Once overlearned, these Plans function as do innate Plans. Progression from basic reflex behavior to advanced cognitive processing to societal role definition are proposed within this model. Plans which are no longer feasible or relevant may serve to seriously hamper function. These authors point out that "to find oneself without any Plan is a serious matter." They suggest that some forms of mental illness may be related to the inability to choose between two incompatible Plans.

All information that is received by sensory receptors comes to a total system that already has a set of experiences and references whether those experiences have been innately derived or externally generated. Each new piece of information becomes incorporated into the whole, gradually widening the scope of experience. This process is constant throughout life and occurs at all levels of experience; reflexive, sensory/motor, perceptual/cognitive, intellectual, and interactive. Basic plans depend upon information acquisition and processing. The resolution of data acquired from sensation forms the basis for acquisition and further plan development.

Sensation enters the system through receptors found within and upon the body. Information is provided to the organism through the various sensory systems which are specific in their purpose and their locations. Touch receptors are densely located in manipulative areas such as the mouth and hands, and more diffuse elsewhere on the body. The photic and tonal receptors of the eyes and ears are highly specialized to receive light and sound waves. These sensory systems in conjunction with motor performance interrelate in their role of providing information to the organism. Vocal production operates in conjunction with the auditory system to provide an auditory loop, contributing to the orientation of the individual to his place in relationship to the environment. Binaural stimulation facilitates orientation through stereophonic experience. Proprioceptive receptors in muscles, tendons and fascia are activated by stretch, compression and muscle contraction. But no sensory information acquires in isolation from any other. All information received incorporates into a whole, each part relevant to all other information and relevant to what has been previously experienced.

Not just inputs received, but processes utilized in their resolution determine percepts and thoughts. Experience is acquired whether or not attention is a component of that experience. Attention and vigilance determine which sensory experiences are alerting to the individual. The reticular activating system monitors that vigilance. Perception is selective. Perceptions may be different in the presence and absence of people. (Edney, 1972)[5] and within the different environments (See Exp. 1, Chapter 8). Age and sex differences have been reported. (Bartley, 1969;[6] Ravens, 1956, 1962[7]). Differences in perception of illusions among individuals as demonstrated in psychological testing, art and interior decoration, indicate that visual perception is not constant of itself. Allport and Pettigrew (Bartley, 1969)[8] report that urban boys are more likely to construct illusions than boys from primitive African cultures, suggesting that cultural influences are significant to perception. Luckiesh (1922, 1965)[9] offers detailed examples of illusions and the responses of individuals to those visual stimuli. He believes that judgments are based upon experiences, associations, desires and imaginings, as well as upon that which one expects to see.

Percepts are potentially ambiguous. How incoming information is treated leads one to draw conclusions about the world. The context of previous experience establishes constancies that guide people through living. Smith (1962)[10] has demonstrated that when one experiences distortion of constancy between what is viewed and what is experienced proprioceptively, the individual is capable of reconstructing new orientation constants within which to perform tasks. Stratton's (1896,[11] 1897a,[12] 1897b;[13] Rock, 1975[14]) prism adaptation experiments demonstrate that the ability to resolve conflicted visual and kinesthetic information exist for humans even when individuals have previously functioned under a different set. When Stratton strapped those inversion prisms to his eyes and lived with them for days, he demonstrated the remarkable adaptability of man. He learned to live in a reversed world and still acquired and retained skill in the performance of activities necessary for his existence. He demonstrated that humans have the ability to adapt their function, resolving conflicts they encounter, even when fully grown. A youthful nervous system is not a prerequisite for change in behavioral adaptation. The complexity of the nervous system found in adult animals of higher phylogeny does not preclude adaptation. It may indeed enable that adaptation. Lower phylogenetic animals do not have this capacity for change. Experiments in which the eyes of insects have been surgically revolved (Rock, 1975)[15] show that these creatures do not have the ability to resolve conflicts offered by the alteration of sensory experience. The bicamerality of the human brain containing a multiplicity of crossed neurological pathways arising from a variety of levels, may contribute to the ability humans have to accommodate to the changing world and person in which they find themselves. Levy (1977)[16] confirms the plasticity of the human brain.

Smith (1962)[17] devised a series of experiments in which skilled tasks were performed with vision distorted in several planes and dimensions through projections on a television screen. From observations of performance, it was determined that movement is at all times relevant to other movement. Movements provide innumerable relationships of parts to parts. Through learned experience built upon neurological feedback mechanisms, skill in tasks is built. This theory supports a view of spatial organization of motion based upon a sensory motor feedback mechanism, envisioning the internuncial neuron in the role of differential detection rather than mere connection. It was found, as had been predicted, that inversion of the visual field was more disturbing than right/left reversal and that combined inversion and right/left inversion was least disturbing to function. In this latter schematic arrangement, the relationships between sidedness and topness and bottomness

and their relationship to the self were less disjunctive. Our sides are more alike and thus less likely to resolve differences between them and the environment than are our top and bottom. Our head and feet are not as easily confused with one another as are the hands and the sides to which they belong. It was also found that there is a range of visual displacement within which normal motor activity can occur. Precision is not necessary to human function. Along with physical performance, emotional behavior was observed to be affected by the relationship of the individual to his perceptual field and to his own position within that space. It was reported that observed behavior patterns persisted and that motivated behavior increases subjects' control of their environs. Awareness of space appears to be within conscious constructive activity available to man. Smith concluded that motion is oriented to the axes of the body and that these axes serve to orient manipulative skills. Prediction of
manipulative skills were accurately fulfilled in regard to the degree of deviation from primary axial orientation cues. This concept is in concert with Ayres' view of vestibular influence upon sensory integration, and is in conformity with Knickerbocker who concludes an internalized development of spatial parameters relative to axial orientation. Knickerbocker (1976)[18] attests that functional use of perceptual skills as used in writing is based upon an awareness of self and the relation of self to the environment. Development of integrated sensory function leads to awareness of self in relation to environment. She believes that one develops concepts of self/other, top/bottom, front/back, side/side, body parts/body parts, and the ability to problem solve spatially, developing accuracy in identification of these relationships in all planes. This leads to increased skill in perception of environment, translating into the ability to write, among other skills. Orientation is shown to be necessary to functional performance. Therefore, all three, Ayres, Knickerbocker and Smith, would appear to conclude that perception and learning are space coded. Smith further proposes that concepts of self become schemata by means of the relation of motion to perception.

Despite all the change with which the body is stimulated, the impression of a solid geometrical world is created and retained, although the world is never at any one time seen or experienced in its entirety. The world is constructed in the mind, and is retained through the mind's ability to recollect space and action. I recently observed a young woman preparing to leave for college. She had to carry several cartons down a flight of stairs. They obstructed her view of the staircase. Approaching the stairs, she suddenly turned, placing her back to the staircase. Then she turned her head to look over her shoulder so she could view the stairs, took in the situation, turned again to face the stairs, the boxes again blocking her view, and she proceeded down the stairs. Her ability to retain an internal construct of space enabled her to descend safely. Proprioceptive experience confirmed the accuracy of her memory of visualized space. Human performance in space is largely enabled by skill in recognition and recollection of space.

Unique constructions of the world and relations with space exist for each individual. The uniqueness of individual orientation is vividly exemplified by students' creations in live model painting. The opportunity to view many artists' paintings of one model at the same time is evidence that each construction is so distinctive that one is often hard put to believe they represent the same subject. Perspectives differ, size and proportions differ, color differs, emphasis differs, despite similarity in talent and training. Uniqueness in orientation dictates projected content. Projective tests requiring construction, such as the Goodenough Draw-a-Person, reflect differences in spatial relationships constructed between persons. Inherent in spatial construction is the issue of memory. Internal structures must be present in memory for new data to be compared or related.

The problem of memory has been investigated but a definitive understanding of its method of function escapes our understanding as yet. Memory is the storage of information, some of which is readily available for recall, some less available for recall. That information in memory has been garnered from all the sensory systems and from the sense that is made from that content. Memory is stored perception. It is perception acquired within an earlier time frame brought forward. Memory enables creativity. What is within reception may be beyond comprehension at the time that it is received and still be retained for integration at a later date. I can recall as a child having heard a 'dirty' joke from some older children which I did not understand at the time. When I came home we had guests. I repeated the tale, asking my parents to explain what was funny. All the guests laughed, but no one cleared up matters for me. Several years later I suddenly understood the joke and became highly embarrassed at an event long since experienced. Piaget has demonstrated spontaneous resolution of problems encountered in past experience.

There is memory for all that creates perception. Memory exists for vision, audition, kinesthesia and all the senses in all the combinations or order that data has been accumulated and synthesized. Any sense or combination of same can elicit a recollection. An odor can cause one to recall an event. The scent of candy can stimulate recall. Such an experience can make one remember a happy event from childhood. A familiar melody may have associated with it a memorable incident. Manipulative skill is evidence of kinesthetic memory. The enormity of the storage capacity of the human mind is incomprehensible. Despite the remarkable mechanism which must be used for storage and recall, more remarkable is that it serves the adaptive function of human needs for the performance of its tasks of living.

Attempts to understand recollection through neurological categorization or localization have thus far failed to be significantly enlightening. Some evidence of biochemical retention has been demonstrated in lower animals. Laboratory experimentation with worms which have been maze trained, destroyed and fed to untrained worms, show that those untrained, following ingestion of trained worms, demonstrate the ability to perform the maze task. Some biochemical memory transfer seems to exist which generalizes cell to cell.

Holographic memory is another theoretical construct which is conceptualized in the same way that holograms are constructed. In this theory under investigation by Pribram (1979)[19], it is proposed that cells each retain a perspective of experience just as holograms contain perspectives of an entire picture, segments of which reiterate particulars of other segments. Much reinforcement and repetition is conceived of in this memory concept. A generalized approach to brain function is more in keeping with this theory than is a localized view. If such a concept has merit, and it seems supportive of a reverberation theory of recall, the facility of the nervous system to respond to a stimulus appears related to the number of and proficiency of response mechanisms available, as well as how often the event has been formerly experienced.

Memory may function as a reverberating response to an encountered stimulus, or can be an internally generated construct, ordinarily defined and differentiated as recognition and recall. These distinctions differ in several ways. People are able to recognize far more readily than they are able to recall. One is far more likely to recognize a stimulus than to generate a recalled response. Most students would prefer to answer a multiple choice examination than have to generate answers to fill in blanks or write essays because greater ease in recognition is expected. Recognition is stimulated by external stimuli. Recognition signifies familiarity. Ability to recognize persons, places, objects and the relationships between these serves the purpose of adaptive survival. Recall is internally generated. It is the ability to retrieve from past experience. It is not necessarily generated from an external stimulus, although offering a relevant stimulus may trigger recollection of a past experience. Recognition is a factor inherent in recall. Recognition appears to be a more primitive memory function. It serves a protective function, alerting one to the surround, facilitating fluid mobility, defining familiarity and unfamiliarity. Recall appears to be a higher level cognitive function dependent upon lower functioning recognition and is the feature of memory which permits creativity and planning. It is man's skill in reviewing data, 'seeing' this data in the mind's eye from multiple perspectives, which is enabled by recall. Just as we have near and distant sensors, in some sense we have near and distant memory. Recognition deals with the here and now. Recall deals with the past and enables the future.

Recognition is tied to the generation of perceptual constancy. Recall is less immediate, more subjective, is less readily available for confirmation. The subjectivity of recall is seen in court trials. Also, recalled events of childhood differ from confirmed reality. Freud found in a number of his cases that recalled sexual experiences identified by his clients could have not actually occurred when these events were carefully investigated. Fantasy is a feature of recall. That one is as selective about recall as people ordinarily are, is further evidence of its subjectivity. Recognition, on the other hand, is immediate and highly accurate under normal circumstances. That recognition is so reliable is what enables us to depend upon our senses. It is the basis for automative behavior. Human endeavor cannot be functional without memory in both of its aspects. Skill and facility are dependent upon recognition. Creativity is dependent upon recall. Neither function alone.

Other facts are acknowledged about memory. That which is repeated is better recalled than events of brief encounter. Repetition can be directly experienced, as in motor events, or it can be reexperienced through repeated thought processes. Studying for exams, or memorizing lines are common examples of this form of repetition designed for reinforcement. Recall is enhanced when an experience is retold. Retelling or reviewing an experience seems to reinforce its recollection. Tell a story often enough and the event will be recalled the way it was related, not necessarily the way it occurred. Remembering is our personal history. It is subject to individual construction. Two people who relate the same event will remember it differently, even with conviction. The judicial system in which evidence is heard and evaluated is in essence a social resolution of conflict in experience.

Those experiences which are not reinforced for individuals by repetition tend to be fragile in recall. Repetition appears to be particularly important to ensuring recall, especially in a system which may be experiencing diminished neurological input as a result of aging processes. Surely if cells are fewer and if synaptic connections are less efficient in aging, as has been reported by some investigators (see Chapter 6), then every source of reinforcement to provide reverberating stimuli must be utilized to retain or increase functional performance.

If related events are likely to stimulate multiple aspects of significance to function, then related events are best utilized for developing proficiency in function. Normally experienced contextual material will tend to provide more related stimuli yielding density of reinforced experience. Such multiple experiences must be in mutual contact in all four dimensions for optimal reinforcement and thus awareness. From varying perspectives, units may be seen as overlapping, providing density and comprehension, or separate, denying that comprehension of totality. A technique based upon this concept has been used to identify color blindness. Numbers can only be recognized on pseudochromatic plates if all necessary sensors are intact. So, too, multiple stimuli overlapping and synchronous for same planes and time frames provide reinforcement of memory and recognition. Asynchrony or dilution inhibits comprehension. Stimuli which enter the system but are not experienced as relevant or sufficiently powerful resist retention or recognition. Partial figures such as those designed by Leeper (Rock, 1975)[20] do not of themselves ordinarily provide sufficient data to inform subjects of the content of the figures. Gaps in the viewed field deny the formulation of a comprehensible perception.

Hypotheses have been offered which suggest that sleeping and dreaming serve somehow to 'set' information in a more permanent scheme through a computer-like sorting system. Evidence to support this view is offered by dream reports explored in psychoanalysis and which generally include in creative symbolic combination both critical material of past significance united with events which have occurred during the previous day. Time and order of acquisition are irrelevant in the construction of dream content. The process of integration of new data with past experience may explain differences in responses for short term and long term memory. It has been frequently observed as aging proceeds that recent experiences are less likely to be retained than those recalled from long ago. One wonders whether a processing resolution is inhibited by conditions which occur in later life. And does this also inhibit the resolution of recognition with recall?

All new learning of tasks and of concepts is based upon previously experienced learning. The ability to retain experiences garnered through living for use when performance demands it, enables further progressive development to occur. Reliable interaction within the world develops from encounters within that world. Confidence that consistent relationships exist between sensory experiences occurs when temporal juxtaposition occurs. That things appear to move at the same moment they feel as if they move and are viewed to move, may indicate that what is seen and what is felt is judged to be occurring. Judgment is inherent in integration. Judgment is the basis for learning.

Learning is the process of incorporation of a movement, behavior, habit, skill or concept so that it can be performed or utilized automatically. Once learned, it is available for recall. Material which can be handled automatically serves as support for the learning of new material. Learning and memory are inherent enablers for the building of complexities upon one another. We learn and develop sequentially. We learn by manipulating our environment and our information base, integrating and reintegrating our data, consolidating that data until our knowledge is secure and reliable. Learning takes place throughout life. What is learned is dictated by survival needs. That which offers no relevance is not learned well.

As development progresses, bits of information derived from sensation, recollection and consolidation build into the scheme of the verdical and are further utilized in the information base. The process by which this occurs is herein termed 'perception'. Having learned, having resolved input data with previous knowledge, is perception, and presumes integration or consolidation. Learned skills or concepts, in synchrony with all else that one learns or knows, produces efficient function. That which is learned outside of the scheme of all accumulated knowledge, as is a splinter skill, or perhaps a memorized list of nonsense syllables, does not retain or hang together, or serve to support further learning. It is difficult to recall that which provides no continuity, no relationship to its surround, a surround which may be of either concrete or conceptual derivation.

In normal growth and development the processes of integration and consolidation achieve in fits and bursts, but always in a positive progression. Perceptual development leads from innate, genetically determined components, through developed reflexes, to behaviors, concepts, and relationships. Development provides the opportunity to gradually build in necessary components for living as the need arises.

Perceptions result from constructive activity engendered by confirming experiences. It is in the adaptation of the environment to the organism that the self is grounded. Verification of the self is provided when the environment is observed to modify to confirm the existence of the organism. Individuals develop an awareness of self as they develop their relationship with the world about them. Either physical or emotional response confirms self. Action yields reaction. Action of self on space yields the manipulation of environment. The action of self causes reaction in others. Some of the time environment can be perceived to control the self. Were the self at all times to modify the environment, then confirmation is established that the self is secondary to environment and subject to its control. But the healthy self effects change within the environment. Self and environment exist in a relational mode, each effecting change upon the other, providing each other context/constancy.

In relationship reality is tested and resolved. Piaget indicates that conflict is experienced when the larger whole of truth has not yet been constucted. Analyzing characteristics of conserver behavior, Feffer (1979)[21] has proposed that vacillating non-conservation behavior is demonstrated when an attempt is made to resolve a problem beyond the available limits of the problem solver. The conserver, though, is able to see a larger truth which incorporates all apsects of truth that underlie. There is a change evidenced in the solution. Non-conservation behavior is characterized by fluctuation, limited to particulars of the components of which it has been constructed. No more comprehensive knowing occurs. As growth and change occur, more comprehensive wholes are constructed. Consolidations occur. Hierarchical development is a feature of that consolidation. Feffer has shown this to be true on all levels of human performance, sensory/motor, perceptual and intellectual. This is not essentially different from what Bronowski (1978)[22] tells us when he states:

>"The new theory—always subsumes more effects than the old. But the remarkable thing is that when it is discovered, it also wholly changes our conception of how the world works. And yet I believe that any theory that we as human beings make at any point in time is full of provisional decodings which to some extent are as fictitious as the notion of force in Newton."

Interestingly, Thomas (1979)[23] indicates that consolidation is indeed a function of all of life's existence. If one looks at the fusion which occurs in cell combination there is demonstrated contact, then combination, then unification. Such unification is reflected in the acquisition of knowledge.

One can conclude from the previous promulgations that the understanding of perception does not lie in the utilization of artificially contrived figure/ground drawings or overlapping figures as training tools, for these provide but splinter skills. These do not afford a comprehensive consolidation by integrating current information with prior knowledge, although they may demonstrate evidence of that consolidation or lack of consolidation. Rather, perception is the resolution of ambiguous, conflicted information which has been received through various sources. Perception is the integration of that which is currently experienced with that

Internally Expressed 61

which was previously known. Perception is a process. Perception is the process by which the context in which the world which has come to be known through previous experience becomes resolved into a consolidated manifestation which achieves a constant measure. Perception is an automatic demonstration of a previously resolved conflict experience leading to growth and development. Perception derives from the context of experience over time. And what is true for now is subject to reorganization at some later time.

Figure 2-3
Context dictates perception of events.

DENNIS the MENACE

"It's either buffalo comin' or a bug walkin' around in my ear."

Context phenomena show us how tenuous is the information of the world about us. We judge what we experience based upon that which we have previously experienced. We judge the weight of an object held in the hand based upon that which has been previously held. An arm which has just had a cast removed from it seems strangely light in weight. Emotions can make a task appear inordinately difficult, or delightfully engaging. Context modulates the indefinite nature of information, depending upon the situation in which those phenomena are understood to occur (Figure 2-4). Dinnerstein (1966)[24], studying context phenomena, uses the method of constant stimuli as an effective research monitor which succeeds precisely because of its attempt to approximate truth through repetitive comparisons. Constant stimuli is a research method which takes into account the approximate nature of human experience and performance through repeated measures of experienced phenomena.

Multiple experiences in relation to one another provide perceived constancy. The resolution of multiple experiences and the reliability of those experiences enable the construction of constancy. This phenomenon has been reported by Piaget to occur in the infant at approximately eight months of age. Prior to this milestone, infants do not evidence any observable recollection of the existence of objects once these objects are out of their field of vision. But constancy in performance is earlier demonstrated. Progressively developing behaviors indicate that retention of those behaviors exists, leading to more advanced behaviors. Constancy has been extensively demonstrated in the adult. The phenomenon in which a viewed object retains a perceived dimension and shape despite differences in distance from the viewer implies that somehow the viewer 'knows' the size and shape of the object of attention and retains the constancy of the object (Rock, 1975)[25]. Yet, constancy remains dependent upon confirmed experience, experience that is continually supported by concrete or consentual reality, by external influences that integrate with previous experience.

Development of perceptions results from cognitive solving mechanisms available and functional within the normally intact organism. Human beings are at the same time neurally, cognitively and functionally attuned to develop perceptions. Perception is both innate and learned at the same time in the intact system. Perception is a developmental process.

Perceptions equate with automated behaviors. In a perception, a resolution has been made of information received. A perception implies an interpretation. Ambiguous illusions such as reversible figures (see Figure 1-1), however, are evidence of unresolved conflicts. When conflict is unresolved, inability of the system to acquire a constancy in the experience is demonstrated. Previously acquired contextual experiences have not been sufficiently dense or relevant and therefore do not provide a stable base upon which to rely. Conflict may exist between that which has been formerly experienced and that which is presently evident. When such conflict occurs, either resolution of that conflict may occur, or no resolution may take place. Resolution of conflict is necessary to further development. When conflict remains, development is arrested or skewed. Information may be yielded which is experienced as in or out of synchrony, stable or unstable, reliable or unreliable. Information either makes sense or it does not. Information must make sense for it to be useful. Information must be in context in order for it to be understood. Any level of function can be demonstrated as in or out of synchrony. On a primitive level of function, failure to develop anti-gravity responses (integration of tonic labrynthine supine and prone) causes the interpretation of sensory information to be altered. This results in failure to develop awareness of upness and downness which relate to the experience of gravity. Failure in the development of rotary movement (integration of asymmetrical tonic neck reflex, neck righting and non-segmental rolling) results in the failure to determine sidedness, leading to failure to develop lateral dominance (Daffner, 1976[26], 1977[21]). Just as properly attuned reflex performance enables development of concepts of direction, so too higher levels of conceptualization are dependent upon consolidatible data. Memory has been shown to be positively enhanced when material to be recalled is relevant or comprehensible.

Development cannot proceed without the acquisition of reliable and constant contexts with which to relate. Resolution of conflict is a developmental process. Comprehension of the process of conflict resolution derives from Piagetian constructionist theory. This process follows a developmental sequence. This sequence is described by Piaget as proceeding from sensory/motor to pre-operational to operational. Each subset is prerequisite to and inherent in subsequent development. Utilization of all sensory systems, integrated in their function, provides information to the organism through sequential organization which may be experienced as veridical, stable and available for further dependable utilization.

Human maturation is prescribed. This maturation follows a sequence which enables human beings to function with increasing independence as time passes. We creep; we crawl; we sit and stand. We walk and run. We play. We acquire knowledge. We love and share. As maturation is at the same time physiologically, emotionally and cognitively experienced, both internally and externally derived, attention to the earliest developmental level of information acquisition and integration is vital even in later years. Indeed, attention to early development is inherent both in sensory integrative treatment and in proprioceptive neuromuscular facilitation techniques. Attention to reflex development is prior to more advanced function in both of these modalities. Reinforcing this view of sequential dependency, Knickerbocker (1976)[28] believes that developing self concepts related to spatial awareness is dependent upon kinesthetic, tactual awareness in conjunction with other sensory function and states that "sequential patterns in gross movements relate to the sequential fine motor patterns needed for rapid execution of script writing." Sequential resolution of information conflict both internally and externally derived is compatible for the concepts of Ayres, Miller, Galanter and Pribram, Piaget and

Freud. Sequential development is also a feature of task groups as described by Mosey (1970).[29]

In order to better understand the role of maturation and its bearing on conflict resolution, let us consider the question of sensory dominance. That some senses appear to dominate others has been claimed by researchers. Perception literature has debated the dominance of vision versus touch. Berkeley (1709)[30] attributed dominance to touch, believing that one learns what is seen through reliance upon the touch systems. Others cite evidence that there is reliance upon tactual and kinesthetic systems in early development, with increasing reliance upon auditory and visual systems as maturity approaches (Ayres, 1972)[31]. Renshaw (Bartley, 1969)[32] states that children are attributed superior tactual function, that dependence upon vision as a primary perceptor is a factor in maturity to adulthood, and that sensory dominance alters with maturation. But vision has been observed to 'capture' touch during laboratory experimentation in the adult (Rock, 1975)[33]. Rock has demonstrated that when a rod is viewed under altered vision through a prism, the rod appears bent; furthermore, it will be perceived tactually as having the same bent shape as the viewed form, although the rod is verdically straight. Vision clearly dominates the tactual experience. A cognitive judgment is made without conscious awareness, defining the shape as seen visually as correct, providing a constancy experience to the subject through denial of what is perceived tactually. Do we feel what we want to feel or presume we feel? It may be possible that visual capture results as follows.

Consider that first perceptions are made in direct relation to self, and that all subsequent discrimination is seen in light of the prior context of knowledge. Touch, proprioception and vestibular information contribute to kinesthetic awareness even before vision is available to the developing infant. Each are available in utero. These multiple sensory awarenesses contribute to the establishment of a veridical information base. Early development begins with reliance upon direct sensory systems. The direct senses from which kinesthesia is constructed offer three dimensional data to the organism. Vision and hearing are distance sensors. The gustatory/olfactory senses serve in combination providing both direct and distance functions. Taste buds are stimulated directly. Odor can derive from distance, but both smell and taste are inextricably unified in their function just as the senses of touch, proprioception and vestibular sensitivity unite to contribute to kinesthesia.

Distance sensors are more subjective. Proficiency in these senses are acquired following responses to touch and movement and gravity. Distance sensors are subject to the context of previously acquired kinesthesia. Distance sensors are seen within the context of earlier experienced, directly sensed and integrated data base. Distance sensors are dominated by direct systems unless and until learning takes place, at which time the organism substitutes reliance upon distance sensors as confidently veridical, increasing that reliance as time passes.

The essence of expansion in environmental awareness as a dimension of development is supported by the research of Pick (1979)[34] and Bremner (1978)[35]. Both report increased skill in accurately assessing spatial coordinates as age increases. A scheme achieves whereby dependency alters from egocentric to exocentric space relevant orientation as a feature of this developmental process. Bremner, deriving his approach from Piaget, reports egocentric orientation at six months. At eleven months a shift is evidenced and by eighteen months there appears to be a reliance upon external spatial coordinates. Bremner (1978)[36] has shown that "the stage IV infant's search for objects, or more generally his construction of space, need not be egocentrically defined." He considers that while the infant is relatively immobile, an egocentric strategy is adequate, and this reliance is justified until self directed mobility becomes enhanced, and that egocentric determinants for spatial orientation retain only as long as success derives from this strategy.

What is never addressed by either Pick or Bremner is the problem of egocentricity itself. When development of body schema is considered, discrimination occurs toward sharpening midline definition as well as the discrimination of body parts from each other and from the center of the self. If the body develops as object as Piaget proposes, this discrimination does not emerge whole. The cephalo/caudal, ventral/dorsal, proximal/distal progression must be taken into account as it develops in concert with external spatial awareness. Progressively developing inhibition of reflexes diminishes in the same correlation as self image acquires. Without this progression, the development of external space orientation is also restricted. Egocentricity must be seen then as a concept requiring greater definition.

Body scheme discriminates in correlation with external orientational appreciation. Although all sensory systems operate and provide influence upon the entire system, the organism begins its existence in greater touch with those systems of near appreciation. Further, these near appreciation systems achieve greater discrimination as development proceeds (still remembering that none act in exclusion from one another).

Acquisition of body scheme and self scheme acquire and modify in direct relationship to the acquisition of spatial awareness and knowledge of the world as that knowledge expands. Fraiberg (1968)[37] attributes ego development to the relationship between biological development and human environment. If one can loosely define the ego as the self it becomes possible to see that external awareness and body scheme are associated in their function and their development.

Vision permits a knowledge of environment beyond the vicinity of touch. Each eye serves as a two dimensional sensory mechanism. Each retina receives data in two dimensions only. It is in the overlay of both images in integrated experience over time, and in their interpolation, that a three dimensional analysis of the viewed field becomes possible. While the visual system acquires skill in analysis of the field through initial dependency upon the kinesthetic system in concert with the auditory system, this only happens when distance sensors are confirmed by reality to be in conformity with direct sensors by using the self and success as measure constants. As development proceeds, external space comes to be experienced as having visual primacy because vision has been determined to provide reliable information through consistent success in task performance. However, visual information does not develop significance without motion and contact. As development proceeds to adulthood, the visual system, once it becomes skilled and dependable, becomes the dominant system over the kinesthetic system. This dominance remains until or unless constancy and integration are reduced by the acquisition of unreliable or conflicting information.

When different sensory systems receive information which conflict with one another, as occurs when a prism artificially alters what is presented to the visual field, constancy is lost, or incorrectly created. But this example is a contrived laboratory experience. Such conflicts are not ordinarily experienced in normal life experience. They are experienced, however, in sudden changes experienced in acquired disability. It has already been evidenced that the human is capable of withstanding alterations in sensory input, achieving adaptation to altered experiences. But for this to occur when constancy is lost, reliance upon a veridical system is necessary for the constancy to be reinstituted. Reinstitution of constancy is necessary to resumption of function. Functional restoration can be achieved through attention to those systems which define earliest development. The kinesthetic system serves as a veridical system because of the use of self as measure constants and because kinesthesia is a composite system, deriving its data from multiple sources. However, a changing self may interfere with constancy. Reflex constants alter; relationships between body parts alter; bases upon which judgment had developed alter. Increasing reliance upon kinesthetic systems often occurs in advancing age, as the visual and auditory systems which provide distance information reduce in efficiency and reliability, particularly when environments alter and become unfamiliar. Problems arise when the function of the kinesthetic system is inhibited, a situation frequently experienced in aging, as a result of immobility, restraint, or as secondary effects of some drugs, either prescribed or illicit.

Reliance upon constants is altered as a feature of maturation and of dependability. Individuals rely upon that which functions best and that with which they can best function. Context is variable. Change is a feature of development. Development has a temporal quality in which progress and decline both demonstrate sequential change. Change must be viewed in light of the whole. The whole is altered by the alteration of the relationships between its component parts. Change occurs over time. Time is a fourth dimension within which reality is constructed.

The mind consciously or unconsciously selects from that which is experienced the data upon which it chooses to rely. That reliance has been proposed to alter as maturity proceeds. Successful behavior is dependent upon choosing correctly that to which appropriate attention should be paid and that which should be appropriately ignored. Adaptive behavior requires that these selections be made correctly and consistently. Yet even in normal function the system occasionally breaks down and incorrect judgments are created. One instance in which this occurs is during the autokinetic experience also entitled induced movement of the self. Have we not all had the experience of sitting in a vehicle, being startled by the sudden movement of ourselves, only to discover that it had not been ourselves which moved but rather the vehicle adjoining us? An incorrect judgment was made because ambiguous information had been misinterpreted. This judgment had been made instantaneously and below conscious awareness. Interestingly, this phenomenon appears to occur when unitary peripheral vision is stimulated by external movement and is facilitated by experienced proprioception such as the vibration which is experienced when a motor is running. That this sort of incorrect interpretation occurs only infrequently ordinarily permits one to confidently deal with the environment. Were all movement to be subject to unanticipated response, human confidence and performance would be seriously hampered.

Once a behavior or skill has been learned, once it has become successfully reliable, it is no longer necessary to deal with that behavior on a cortical level, but it subcortically serves as a superstructure for subsequent learned behaviors.

If, however, learned behaviors are no longer available through subcortical mechanisms, automaticity is lost, and cortical attention must be utilized in order to perform. The child who must consciously evaluate every movement equates in this regard with the neurotic depressive's avoidance mechanisms and with the elderly disabled person's inability to work through change in ability or environment. Factors which may interfere with automated behaviors include sensory deficits, motor impairment, relocation, integration and the cognitive processes of recognition, recall and consolidation.

When patients are encountered who demonstrate 'perceptual dysfunction', these may indeed be persons in whom the process whereby perception is achieved may be intact, but in whom a veridical data base is absent. The ability to resolve conflict is intact, but the information available in some way precludes integration or consolidation. It may be that underlying support data offering potential conflict have not been resolved, or old habits are serving to interfere with new learning. These interferences can be seen alike in the learning disabled child, the psychiatric patient, and the disabled aged.

Occupational therapy treatment has attended to the resolution of these conflicts. Knickerbocker (1976)[38] has demonstrated that a constancy phenomenon, although she does not term it thus, can be elicited in learning disabled children. Proprioceptive and visual inputs are combined by using a textured board upon which the child draws. Subsequently, a figure is presented for the child to trace. Ultimately the figure is rotated longitudinally reversing right and left, front and back orientations. This reversal is performed in order to develop within the child an internalized awareness of constancy of sidedness of a given figure despite the revolution of that figure. This treatment technique is founded upon proprioception and visual and spatial orientation in association with recollection and results in the ability of the child to acquire and retain a constancy effect for a spatial concept of relationships within and outside of the body of the child. Attention to multiple sensory inputs in clear conjunction with cognitive construction contributes to the success of this graded activity.

Unresolved conflict regarding information received can be at the root of psychiatric illness. We are familiar with the results of schizophrenogenic parenting (Schreiber, 1974)[39], cultural disarticulation (Krocher, 1964)[40], changing life experiences (Sheehy, 1976)[41], and crisis and stress (Selye, 1974)[42] as agents contributing to illness. Beneath all of these is conflict. The world believed or recalled is different from the world being experienced. Resolution of conflict experienced between conviction and veridicality has been unachieved. Whole truths are uncreated. To march to multiple drummers is to experience discord.

In aging and the declining functional performance frequently associated with aging, there is diminishing opportunity for the reinforcement of the orientation functions which tasks provide. Impairment of sensory systems, and the performance of these systems out of synchrony, in conjunction with decline in functional mobility impede the ongoing reinforcement necessary to ground the self. When old habits are so strong as to prevent seeing new solutions, new solutions can be facilitated in a therapeutic relationship.

The disabled, when enabled to achieve constancy in the awareness of self, have the potential to resume function. Task oriented use of gravity orienters, peripheral stimulation, and interactional relations serve the same function, that of permitting the achievement of orientation and grounding of self through the resolution of a context/ constancy relationship with the environment. Multi-sensory experiences reinforce the veridical and reduce ambiguity offered by restricted inputs. Thus it is possible to resolve conflict and facilitate self determinism in clients whether using proprioceptive neuromuscular facilitation techniques, sensory integration techniques, progressive resistive activities or task groups.

Deriving from the aforegoing are a set of principles defining perceptual development. These principles underlie human behavior. They have implication in the restoration of such development when dysfunction has occurred to the formerly well functioning adult human being as well as having implication for younger developing individuals encountering perceptual dysfunction without having ever achieved success in adaptive functioning.

Principles of Perception

1. Data derives from sensors over time.
2. Recognition through familiarity serves to permit the derivation of relational judgment.
3. Context is necessary to establish constancy.
4. The periphery of experience serves to define function.
5. The ability to recognize and associate with recollection enables performance in space.
6. Recall derives from recognition.
7. Success in tasks and expanded goals widens peripheral scope.
8. Mobility in the course of task performance yields perceptual proficiency.
9. Perception is the presumption one makes at any given time dependent upon the data one has to work with.
10. Perception is equivalent to behavior.
11. Behavior derives from that which has been concluded.
12. Behavior yields increased data acquisition.
13. Integrated experience in context yields constancy which in turn yields opportunity for development.

REFERENCES
Chapter 2. Internally Expressed

1. Dinnerstein, D.: Previous and Concurrent Visual Experience as Determinants of Phenomenal Shape. *American Journal of Psychology*, 78: 235-242; 1965.
2. Brown, H.: *Brain and Behavior.* New York: Oxford University Press, 1976.
3. Ayres, A.J.: *Sensory Integration and the Treatment of Learning Disabilities.* Los Angeles: Western Psychological Services, 1972a.

4. Miller, G.A., Galanter, E. and Pribram, K.H.: *Plans and the Structure of Behavior.* New York: Holt, 1960.
5. Edney, J.J.: Place and Space: The Effects of Experience With a Physical Locale. *Journal of Experimental Social Psychology,* 8: 124-135; 1972b.
6. Bartley, S.: *Principles of Perception.* New York: Harper and Row, 1969.
7. Ravens, J.C.: *Coloured Progressive Matrices (Sets A, Ab and B).* London: Lewis, 1956, 1962.
8. Bartley, S.: (See above.)
9. Luckiesh, M.: *Visual Illusions, Their Causes, Characteristics and Applications.* New York: Dover, 1922, 1965.
10. Smith, C.U. and Smith, W.M.: *Perception and Motion.* Philadelphia: W.B. Saunders, 1962.
11. Stratton, G.: Some Preliminary Experiments on Vision Without Inversion of the Retina. *Psychological Review,* 3: 611-617; 1896.
12. Stratton, G.: Upright Vision and the Retinal Image. *Psychological Review,* 182-187; 1897.
13. Stratton, G.: Vision Without Inversion of the Retinal Image. *Psychological Review,* 4: 341-360; 1897.
14. Rock, I.: *An Introduction to Perception.* New York: MacMillan, 1975.
15. Rock, I.: (See above.)
16. Levy, J.: "Manifestations and Implications of Shifting Hemispheric Attention in Commisurotomy Patients." In *Advances in Neurology,* edited by E.A. Weinstein and R.P. Friedland, Volume 18. New York: Raven Press, 1977.
17. Smith, C.U. and Smith, W.M.: (See above.)
18. Knickerbocker, B.: Lecture to the New Jersey Occupational Therapy Association, Princeton, New Jersey, March 1976.
19. Pribram, K.H. and Goleman, D.: Holographic Memory. *Psychology Today,* 79-84; February 1979.
20. Rock, I.: (See above.)
21. Feffer, M.: Private manuscript, 1979.
22. Bronowski, J.: *The Origins of Knowledge and Imagination.* New Haven, Connecticut: Yale University Press, 1978.
23. Thomas, L: *The Medusa and the Snail.* New York: Viking, 1979.
24. Dinnerstein, D., Cursio, F. and Chinsky, J.: Contextual Determination of Apparent Weight as Demonstrated by

the Method of Constant Stimuli. *Psychological Science,* 5: 251-252; 1966.
25. Rock, I.: (See above.)
26. Daffner, C.: Personal correspondence, 1976.
27. Daffner, C.: An Occupational Therapy Model for T of Learning Disabilities. *Journal of New Jersey Speech and Hearing Association,* 15(1): 14, 1977.
28. Knickerbocker, B.: Personal Correspondence, 1976.
29. Mosey, A.: The Concept and Use of Developmental Groups. *American Journal of Occupational Therapy,* 24: 272-275; 1970.
30. Berkeley, G.: *Toward A New Theory of Vision.* New York: Dutton, 1954. First published 1709.
31. Ayres, A.J.: (See above.)
32. Bartley, S.: (See above.)
33. Rock, I.: (See above.)
34. Pick, H.: "Children's Cognitive Maps." Presented at the Conference on Neural and Developmental Bases of Spatial Orientation, Teachers College, Columbia University, New York, November 16, 1979.
35. Bremner, V.G.: Spatial Errors Made By Infants: Inadequate Spatial Cues or Evidence of Egocentrism? *British Journal of Psychology,* 69: 77-84; 1978.
36. Bremner, V.G.: (See above.)
37. Fraiberg, S.: Parallel and Divergent Patterns in Blind and Sighted Infants. *Psychological Study of the Child,* 23: 264-300; 1968.
38. Knickerbocker, B.: *A Holistic Approach to the Treatment of Learning Disorders.* Thorofare, New Jersey: Charles B. Slack, 1980. (See Figure 40, page 215).
39. Schreiber, F.R.: *Sybil.* New York: Warner, 1974.
40. Krocher, T.: *Ishi, the Last of his Tribe.* Oakland, California: Parnassus, 1964.
41. Sheehy, G.: *Passages: Predictable Crises of Adult Life.* New York: Dutton, 1976.
42. Selye, H.: *Stress and Distress.* New York: Lippincott, 1974.

3. Externally Expressed

As we have seen, the function of man is dictated in large part by the environment in which he lives and interacts. Man's performance cannot be considered apart from the world in which he exists. Those activities of which life is constructed occur within a world which demands those activities. Structures of life prescribe behavior. Tools prescribe grasp. Shoes require feet. Mothering demands a child. It is largely the expectations of the world which dictate behavior.

Humans live in different climates, with different surrounds, well populated or isolated, in small quarters or large, in simplicity or complexity. They are desert dwellers, find purpose in jungle life, and live among concrete cliffs. The terrain of the various environs in which human beings live is widely diverse. Although life activities in which humans engage are largely predetermined by environment and cultural heritage, these same activities are created by the individual who is in synchrony with his environment. Adaptive behavior requires sensitivity and accomodation to one's specific world. Behavior acceptable in one society may be unacceptable in others. Unique cultural idiosynchrasies have been developed by man in different places. Man is an adaptive creature who has established successful life accomodations of multitudinous styles. Overall, man's function modifies to the naturally existing world in which he lives.

Humans are able to tolerate, indeed require, differences and change as part of their existence (Fiske & Maddi, 1961)[1], but this tolerance and outreach is limited by success experiences. In order to function well within a given environment, that world must meet the adaptive requirements of the individual who lives in that world. The basic needs of life must be within the reach of man. Effort requires potential reward. A person's skills must be sufficient to retrieve those needs from his world, or that person will not engage in goal directed effort. Individuals and groups select environments in which to live which are best able to provide for their needs. They select environs which offer potential reward in achievements. Given choice, they remain only if the environment successfully meets their needs.

The world in which people live today is a different structural world from the world in which the species derived. This is a world of solid walls, of corridors, of doorways, of level flooring, of ceilings and roofs, of multi-level dwellings. Man has come far from the world of sky and ground, of moving and seasonally changing surround which dictate activity. Visual distance is restricted by the carpentered environment in which man lives. One can refrain from seeing the natural light of day for weeks, and yet live in considerable comfort. People live in submarines and in total environment hotels. They transport in boxes set upon tracks, their direction determined by others. No longer is personal mobility required for survival.

Earlier was suggested the need to attend to man's origins in order to understand present function. Man's present relationship to his environment continues to dictate his development just as it molded his evolution. If man is phylogenetically derived, then it may be enlightening to reflect upon his origins in order to understand his present performance.

Much attention to the relationship of creatures to their world has been the concern of ethologists and social psychologists. Both animals and people have been observed to behave in similar ways in relation to their environments. Investigators confirm that territorial behaviors are similar between animals and people. High correlation exists between the behavior of higher animals and humans, both between neonates and adults (Held, 1968)[2]. But are we not animals before we are people? Issues of territoriality and personal space have been of interest to students of behavior. It holds that if we concur that phylogenetic development is related to ontogenetic development, it may be useful to study territorial behavioral phenomena evidenced in animals and speculate upon their significance to humans.

Territoriality is a term used by ethologists to describe behavioral phenomena noted in animals in relationship to the environments in which those animals live. Ethologists are students of animal behavior who ply their trade, not by setting up controlled experimentation, but rather by inculcating themselves within a given environment, conducting extensive observations of behaviors noted within those environs, generally specific to a particular species. One such ethologist is Jane Van Lawick-Goodall (1971)[3] who has engaged in the observation and study of chimpanzees within their natural habitat. From her work has come a model for ethological methodology along with extensive data concerned with the population she has chosen to investigate.

A significant feature of ethology is that the investigator accepts that in order to understand behavior a commitment must be made to understanding that behavior within the constraints of the natural environment of the subject to be investigated. Time, patience, and consistent, perservering observation are inherent factors in ethological study. No attempt is made on the part of the observer to alter the action. The evidence is recorded and purviewed subsequently with a hope that trends, and the perspective which time allows, will provide significant information. Accurate and consistent reporting is the token of the economy.

Observation has shown that any given territory is able to support an optimal number of residents of a given species. Human crowding has had attributed to it the maladaptive behaviors evident in center city life. Esser (1971)[4] contends that the main reason for crowding in wild species is to serve in the elimination of low ranking individuals from the population. Animal species have been observed to engage in behaviors which result in the alteration of their populations in response to environmental demands. Some species increase or decrease their sexual activity in relationship to the fruitfulness of their environment and the size of their own population. Laboratory animals become carnivorous or ill when overcrowding occurs. Lemmings destroy themselves in years when their population grows too large. Deer populations have increased in recent years in areas in which increased human population has cut down the natural vegetation available to animals. How has this population increased, if reduced forage would predict demise? Farmers have reported that greater incursions have been made by deer upon their corn crops than in former years. The result is that well nourished does are seen to produce more twinning, a curious result of depleted natural environment. But what will happen when the farms on which they presently feed turn to developments, as they are certain to do? Goodall (1971)[5] observed that species change territory in response to local conditions. Success in survival tasks must be met within the environment. The environment must have the wherewithal to meet the needs of inhabitants of that environment. Animals seek environs in which they can meet their survival needs and for which they are physiologically adapted. Tree living creatures are suited differently than are water dwelling animals. Their forage differs; their milieu differs; their structure differs, but each of these elements occurs in accord with one another. Chimps live in trees, eat vegetation, and have suitably adapted upper extremities which enable them to travel about through those trees. Fish eat small fish found in water, and breathe through gills. A fish out of water cannot survive. Environment and body integrate in their purpose, adaptive survival. Washburn (1960)[6] considers this mutuality evident in the purpose and development of the bipedal creature which became man.

In addition to Washburn's acknowledgement of erect postures associated with the use of tools, innate and unique connection between cognition and communication can also be recognized. The human ape has the unique ability to oppose the thumb, providing a remarkably dextrous tool for manipulation. In addition, man demonstrates handedness. Skillful manipulation of tools is demonstrated by the dominance of one hand. Another remarkable adaptation of man is that along with handedness, which has enabled skilled tool usage, speech has evolved. The center for speech is located in the same side of the bicameral brain which innervates the dominant hand. Clinically, one observes that loss of speech following brain damage is associated with paralysis of the right hand. The left side of the body and right side of the brain have been attributed to be associated with perceptual losses. Thus, a unique specialization of function is demonstrated in man alone. These adaptations viewed in light of one another suggest we must appreciate that all functions support one another in a creature adapted to his environment. These adaptations highlight the vastly extended periods of time necessary for this development to have occurred. And to what adapted? To the world in which the early tool handling animal had to live; a world far different in concept and horizon than that in which man must live today.

Washburn has outlined an evolutionary progression of man from prior primates. He makes the point that "each behavioral stage was both cause and effect of biological change in bones and brain." Cited is the use of tools in lower creatures which he believes is associated with the development of erect posture. The interdependence of changing features of social and physiological abilities relative to the environment in which adaptation occurs indicates how survival is effected for a species. "The reason that the human brain makes the human way of life possible is that it is the result of that way of life."

Throughout the territoriality literature by Goodall, Lorenz (1974)[7], Ardrey (1966)[8], Johnson (1972)[9], and Montegu (1973)[10], interest has been expressed in the issue of aggression. A feature noted in animals, from fish to primates, is that animals within their own familiar environment are more apt to protect that environment. Within a familiar environment, inhabitants are more apt to win when they do fight. Intruders, however, are less aggressive, less apt to win the battle, more apt to flee to their own territory when accosted by the 'owner' of that territory, when incursion has taken place.

Much aggressive behavior is noted to be ritualized. The term 'fixed-action pattern' is used to describe predetermined response behaviors noted in animals engaging in both aggressive and sexual behaviors. Many birds produce elaborate dance rituals prior to mating. Species of deer use their antlers to engage in combat, fighting not designed to injure, but instead to create display and thus dominance. Gorillas beat their chests. Much display behavior seems designed as a species protective mechanism rather than the aggressive behavior it appears to be on initial observation. These behaviors are ritualized and met by members of their species with appropriate locked in responses to signals which serve as triggers to specific behaviors. They appear to have a tight neurogenic interdetermination. When these behaviors are initiated, their full sequence must be experienced. It almost appears as if a computer has programmed their sequenced responses. Restriction in the sequence of the behavior prevents the accomplished end from occurring. It does not seem possible to circumvent the established sequences.

These automated behaviors aid in the adaptation of members of the species to the world in which they live. The fit survive (Darwin, 1962)[11]. But the higher the phylogeny of the animal, the less rigid, the more individualized and more cortically derived are behaviors noted. Ritualized or fixed-action patterns, extensively described by Lorenz, do not disappear at the mammalian level, but their relative incidence does decline, especially among higher order animals. Just as reflexes become inhibited as development proceeds (Fiorentino, 1972)[12], so too, fixed behaviors deriving from lower phylogeny become more subject to higher level control. As phyletic progression proceeds, modification through learning increases. The degree of modification from reflexive responses may be attributed to crossed sensory systems along with reduced localization of neural function in high animals. Lower animals have the inability to 'forget' old patterns of sensory motor coordination (Taub, 1968)[13]. There are circumstances whereby human beings find it difficult for themselves to forget old patterns as well. Stress may contribute to reversion to patterned responses, precluding the ability to plan beyond those automatic responses.

Human decisions about the world are made according to cognitive principles. White (1963)[14] helps us to understand that humans demonstrate a need to feel effective control. People tend to disengage themselves from that over which they feel no control. If the individual feels distanced from that over which he can effect control, he will center upon himself rather than demonstrate interaction with the periphery of attention, because he can only attend with comfort to those things about which he feels competent. That one can only perceive within a limit of focus may indeed be a primitive ontogenetic reflection of territorial behaviors evident in humans and in lower animals. Along with that which is newly acquired, primitive tendencies are retained which humans subvert as function is developed on increasingly advanced levels, and to which they revert when development is hampered.

Environment is critical to survival but environments are subject to constant change. They alter due to flood, fire and pestilence. Natural disasters and bonanzas occur. Change within a given environment predicts change in territory for inhabitants of that environment. Animals alter their environs to achieve their survival. Survival is dependent upon success in obtaining food, shelter, and comfort. The purpose of living for animals is survival. If survival is purpose, then exploration and territorial excursion are predictable behaviors. Successful territorial exchange is frequently a group effort. In chimps, territory is determined by the group, with expanded families traveling through terrain together (Goodall, 1970)[15]. Individual excursion is easily encountered by resistance. Fight or flight is the order of the day. Flight and aggression are evidence of a mechanism which serves to protect the needs for food and sex. As Freud has suggested, food is a short term survival need; sex is mankind's long term survival need. One assures the survival of the individual, the other, survival of the species. Flight and fight appears to be the monitor regulating and protecting those needs among individuals and among species. Mankind in all his activities attends to the fulfillment of these needs. Success in tasks of living is necessary for survival. Restriction of mobility in pursuit of success within environment produces stress. Human beings quickly revert to primitive functioning when stressed by isolation from personal involvement in their adaptive survival. Spatial orientation dictates perception and therefore behavior in space. Fight responses are stronger within a familiar environment while flight response is stronger within an unfamiliar environment.

Moore (1976)[16] cites ethology as the stimulus for her own interest in limbic function. She supports the importance of learning from animal behavior in order to better understand human behavior. She suggests attention to the relationship of environment to the limbic system, the seat of emotion. "Food, flight and reproduction" are concerns of the limbic system. They are also conditions of territoriality. Food and reproduction needs are served by familiarity with an environment. As a species, human beings are better adapted to deal with sudden crises of fear, flight, territorial aggression and sexual encounter than the long standing stresses with which we are confronted. Mankind's ability to remember, to plan, and to comprehend the consequences of behavior, contribute to his unrelieved stress. People often lack understanding of those factors which contribute to their own comfort. They know how they feel. Their emotions dictate their behavior. But few are able to control those emotions through behavior. People have distanced themselves from their primary needs by placing themselves in situations which continue to enhance their stress. They do not behave in ways which would result in reducing stress. The actions of human beings are often not sensitive to their physiology as it adapted for survival. The surge of adrenaline which occurs in crisis, and would have been reduced by the energy expended in fight or flight, remains undiminished.

Moore described male and female differences in response and motivation. She suggests that "the male drive is more concerned with the conquest of nature, while the female's is to nurture nature. However, both sexes have the same drive to be nurtured." Behavior, being both internally and externally directed, leads us to look briefly at differences in environmental relations exhibited by members of different sexes. Hormonal differences may direct behavior more than the women's movement would have us believe. Some evidence suggests that men may be more generalized in their adaptation to environments in that their proprioceptive memory appears to be fairly equivalent in frontal and lateral fields, whereas females tend to be more specialized in their function, showing more precision in particular fields of function (see Chapter 7).

Gender may well be a factor in spatial orientation. Learning disabled children, who evidence spatial orientation dysfunction, are more frequently boys than girls. What is presumed to be maladaptive for man's present existence may indeed be a reflection of less differentiated but more adaptive survival abilities deriving from an earlier man.

When spatial phenomena are discussed relative to animals, territoriality is often the term used. When similar environmental responses are noted in humans, the term personal space has been used. Sommer (1969)[17], discussing personal space, asserts that spatial behaviors serve to limit aggression, either by causing a person to refrain from going where he is likely to be in dispute or by engaging in ritualized behaviors akin to fixed-action patterns as a substitute for actual combat. Spatial responses are evidenced toward both people and inanimate objects. It has been observed that people tend to leave more space between themselves and another person, or a representation of a person, than they leave between themselves and inanimate objects. Testing indicates that angles increase estimates of distance; attractive surroundings decreases distance estimates (Lee, 1973)[18]. Sommer affirms that architectural demands control behavior. Square tables indicate boundaries of territory. Shoulder to shoulder placements are not conducive to conversation. Chairs against a wall seem to offer psychological security. Accustomed surroundings are a factor in comfort. Familiarity breeds increased liking for individuals' environmental preference and habituation. People like spaces they can make their own.

What is there about space that classifies it as familiar? Familiarity of space is determined from within the activities of the perceiver. Familiarity requires previously experienced interaction within that space as well as success experiences within that space. Familiarity is making space one's own.

Space is oriented by gravitational determinants. Earliest responses to space are determined by responses to gravity. Concepts of upness and downness derive from reflex responses to constant gravity. Down is that surface which is closest to gravitational pull with which there is constant contact. Up is located furthest from gravitational pull. Human beings first sense up and down as creatures who are longitudinally aligned to the earth upon which they lie. Man has only recently come to erect posture, more recently phylogenetically than ontogenetically. The derivation that mankind makes in establishing a sense of his relationship with space has been expressed variously by a wide number of theoreticians. An attempt shall be made to discuss these views regarding the development of man's relationship to his world.

Paillard and Brouchon (1968)[19] state:
> The prerequisite to the building up on motor strategies at the outside world lies in the establishment of a known system of spatial relationships among the different mobile parts of the body and a method of evaluating continually their relative position.

Thus it is believed that the body determines the spatial construction of the mind. Actions and sensory consequences produced in a stable environment provide essential sources of information. Input information is used to organize body movements in relation to each other and to targets outside the body. Action and sensory consequences result in an internalized record of space perception. The sequential ordering of these movements, their relationship with space, and their recollection, permit the development of a cognitive map.

The term cognitive map was introduced by Tolman. Cognitive mapping is a proposed process of serial transformations by which an individual acquires, codes, stores, recalls and decodes information about relative locations and phenomena in his spatial environment. The cognitive map fills in and more fully serves adaptive living as time and experience permit. Downs and Stea (1973)[20] cite, as an example of lack of familiarity related to lack of cognitive map, the disorientation experienced by Shepard and Mitchell during the 1970 Apollo moon walks. These astronauts were 75 feet from crater destination but returned without completing their mission because the lack of distinctive lunar features confused and disoriented them. Downs and Stea view the cognitive map as an analogous term indicating a convenient set of shorthand symbols varying among groups and individuals. They are based upon sensation, biases, prejudices, and personal experiences. They point out that distance can be perceived in many ways: time spent, money cost, distance in kilometers or miles, goal or direction. In this way, the individual's subjective geometry deviates from any universally ordered view of the world. Space is a personal phenomenon. The mind resolves space for each individual.

Pick (1979)[21] tells us that "localization accuracy of cognitive maps increases with age." Cognitive mapping skills and thus spatial orientation are acquired as a developmental process. Hart (1979)[22] has shown this development can be concretely demonstrated in structural form by representational means by using a map making task with youngsters. Spatial awareness as a developmental process has been described by many theorists.

Piaget and Inhelder (1973)[23] indicate that spatial concepts are based upon bicontinuous correspondences like proximity and separation, order and enclosure, and unit relationships. They believe that spatial concepts derive from personal interaction and result in macro-space concepts.

Werner (Downs & Stea, 1973)[24] describes spatial development in a sequential format. He reminds us that initially infants are unable to differentiate themselves from goal objects as they develop. Subsequently, children become active in their own actions and percepts, constructing their own universes, shifting their perspectives, enabling them to view the world from the perspective of others as well as their own. Space is thus sequentially constructed and at the same time subject to reconstruction from internal influences as well as influences external to the developing individual.

Kaplan (1973)[25] also proposes that environment is dealt with upon evolved mechanisms, but he proposes a subjective, emotional consideration of space. Anticipation and success probabilities are components of this conception of spatial concepts, suggesting that efficiency in perception is a requirement for survival, and that success is a prerequisite to spatial orientation.

Lee (1973)[26] contends that physical space and social space are inextricably linked in the mind. Schemata develop regarding surrounding physical reality. Schemata include self, familiar rooms, family, neighborhood, city and world. Each concent depends partly on the other for its development. Schema relate to one another in sequential order. But time and memory alter schema. Many have experienced return to a place known in childhood, only to discover that the place one knew is not the place that is. What was once known in terms of a child's body and seemed great in size is by the standards of an adult frame a little place indeed. People no longer fit behind the desks at which they once learned. The subjectivity of experience evidenced by the vast difference between what is and what one remembers is startling. Lee believes these schemata reside in the parietal lobes of the brain. Regardless of attempts at localization, perception of space is not necessarily relative to actual space.

Griffin (1973)[27] indicates that when extending schema to new territory, problems arise because the orientation of established schema are present and serve to confuse the new orientation. Is this a part of the disorientation experienced in relocation? One may recall having had the experience of having to sleep in a strange bed and awakening with a feeling of disorientation in the room in which one finds oneself. One is adaptively functional when this phenomenon is a transitory one, and there exists an ability to develop new schema for new territory. But intact orientational clues and memory are necessary for this to occur.

Sense of direction is the ability to retain orientation as one moves about. People vary greatly in this skill. It is a skill required for adaptive living. Lynch (1973)[28] states that way-finding is the original function of the environmental image. Adaptive way-finding requires availability and automaticity of performance in order to assure safety and thus survival. Bruner and Mandler (Downs & Stea, 1973)[29] have shown in the laboratory that once a learned maze activity has been performed and the experiment continues on, the action converts from a serial to simultaneous form, suggesting automation of activity on a brain stem level. Ability to deal with one's environment automatically, securely and safely, is a necessary survival skill.

Not only is it necessary to deal with environment securely, it is also necessary that environment be suitably attuned to the needs of the individual. In man, new and unusual stimuli from environment have been purported to produce physiological effects. Impairment of health has been attributed to excessive stress produced by change and crowding. Too, stability of social organization is important to health. To serve needs reflected by these problems, Esser[4] recommends that these principles would be served appropriately by dividing mental patients into small groups to enhance their well being. Small groups have been suggested as optimal for human function and interaction by many sources.

The relation of people with their environment has been studied by numerous investigators. Several studies warrant review for the data they provide about these relationships and the behavioral response of man to space.

Edney (1972a)[30] explored feelings about property possession as it related to permanence of residence. Posted properties were selected as target territories for study, using adjacent neighbors as a control. Substantial differences were found in residential histories related to posted signs. However, no differences were indicated by the presence of fences. Significant numbers of occupants exhibiting defense displays were found who responded to intrusion by answering the doorbell more rapidly than at unposted homes. Answering doorbeels rapidly was judged to be a measure of vigilance. It was concluded that territorial behavior increased as a person invests more time in that place, that not changing residence promotes psychological continuity, and that territoriality is a stable geographic arrangement of individuals which is practical for orientation and availability.

Edney (1972b)[31] investigated the effects of experience in a locale upon behavior. A confederate was identified to subjects as a 'telephone repairman.' Subjects were exposed to either of two conditions. In one condition, subjects were told they would be expected to return to the environment. In the other condition, subjects did not expect to return. Interpersonal distance was assessed along with environmental size perception. Subjects used a length of string to measure their estimate of personal distance from the 'telephone repairman' to themselves following the departure of the 'repairman.' The author concluded the following: that prior association with an environment, and anticipated future experience with the same environment, produced changes in feelings and behaviors; that personal territory is a place where flight behavior is absent, and that marking is not a necessary factor for space defense to arise.

Many studies of human territorial behavior have been based upon institutional life. Austin and Bates (1974)[32] studied imates in a prison bull pen, noting arrangement, dominance, and possession of valued objects. Techniques developed in ethology studies were used to guide their observations. Using video viewing, observers habituated themselves into the environment, training themselves to recognize the prisoners before they instituted recording procedures. Their hypothesis was that dominance hierarchy in humans resembles the pecking order of lower animals. They assessed personal living space, evaluating location. A single lower bunk was considered most valuable because the owner of any other bunk would have his space encroached upon by others climbing into or over it. Distance to the television set was deemed critical because this was the only source of entertainment and thus was judged sufficiently valuable to inmates to cause them to fight for its use. It was observed that mobility patterns predicted dominance, possessions, and spatial territory. Dominant inmates were observed to be more mobile.

Sundstrom and Altman (1974)[33] chose to examine spatial locations and dominance hierarchy in a residential school. Their findings confirm that dominant members use large areas of space with free access regardless of ownership, and that population changes precipitated changes in territorial habits.

DeLong (1973)[34] studied a small group of students who met for sixteen weeks during a class studying group process. Placement of these students was recorded from week to week. Notes were taken of group interactions which occurred. Placements were observed, correlating territorial stability and leadership. It was found that consistent occupation of space is evident when aggression reaches its highest level of intensity. Nearness to the leader was noted to be correlated with hierarchical placement, but only during sessions six through eleven. Spatial stability appeared to be interpreted by members as indicative of leadership capability. It was proposed that this phenomenon is a kind of vestigial ritualization of the ethological importance of staking out a territory and consistently maintaining it, thereby conveying the impression of stability which typically characterized those found high in the dominance hierarchy.

Using sociograms, Grundy and Wilson (1973)[35] applied the concept of territoriality to group orientation rather than geographic locale, suggesting that familiarity with individuals can serve to effect a territorial experience without walls. Relationships between humans dictating their influence upon one another will be explored further in the following chapter. Behavior has been observed to be influenced by the relationship of the organism with its environment. It has been demonstrated that familiarity with a place affects one's feelings of personal space (Altman, 1975)[36] and that performance is facilitated in the familiar environment (Hock, 1974)[37]. In addition, feelings and behavior within a place alter spatial perception estimates within that environment (Edney, 1972)[38]. Hart (1979)[39] has shown that children are more accurate in map production when they have had familiarity with an area. He observed as well that when mental processes were performed upon externally derived data ordinarily outside of awareness, increased skill in map making resulted when that data was brought to conscious awareness.

To adapt and survive in three dimensions the perceptual system must be capable of discriminating space and motion characteristics. The observer's familiarity with meaningful shapes is determined by prior experiences and will considerably affect what is perceived as figure or ground. Familiar objects tend to be perceived as constant under conditions of change. When one property of stimulation is ambiguous, another property which has invariable relationships may determine the perception. When I go through the Holland Tunnel I 'know' my car will never fit through that small dark hole up ahead. But then, I equally know that my car is smaller than the truck ahead and, if the truck fits through, then so shall I (see Figure 9-1). In time, I have learned that I always fit, and shall continue to do so. Much perceptually mediated behavior is a function of the individual's past experience with an environment.

Spatial behavior is in large part habitual and probably functions largely on a subcortical level. Spatial experience is accumulated, repeated, and synthesized with previous experience. Ability to recall space automatically enables safe performance within that space.

Survival is best served when information gained through constant direct sensors of the body integrates with information gained through distance sensors so that automated performance is available. The interaction of constant body with constant environment permits ease of performance within the environment. When either the body or the environment alters, difficulty ensues requiring resolution for function to be enabled. When both alter, disaster befalls. There can be no constancy within experiences encountered when there is no reliable context for those experiences.

Awareness of the importance of environment to functional performance alerts us to its critical role in the care of the disabled. Sensitivity to the influence of environment upon health, and adaptation of that environment toward improved function, are skills necessary for improvement of that function. The foveal world and peripheral world both require attention from the therapist. Attention is necessary to that which is not necessarily obvious. If the periphery serves as context for a centered constancy, then that external world and its influence deserve vital attention and manipulation as tools in structuring recapitulated development.

REFERENCES
Chapter 3: Externally Expressed

1. Fiske, D.W. and Maddi, S.R.: *Functions of Varied Experience.* Homewood, Illinois: Dorsey Press, 1961.
2. Held, R.: Plasticity in Sensorimotor Coordination. In *Neuropsychology of Spatially Oriented Behavior,* edited by S.J. Freedman, Homewood, Illinois: Dorsey Press, 1968.
3. Van Lawick-Goodall, J.: *In the Shadow of Man.* Boston: Houghton Mifflin, 1971.
4. Esser, A.: *Behavior and Environment; The Use of Space by Animals and Men.* New York: Plenum Cress, 1971.
5. Van Lawick-Goodall, J.: (See above.)
6. Washburn, S.L.: Tools and Human Evolution. *Scientific American,* 203(3); 1960.
7. Lorenz, K.: *On Aggression.* New York: Harcourt, Brace, 1974.
8. Ardrey, R.: *The Territorial Imperative.* New York: Dell, 1966.
9. Johnson, R.N.: *Aggression in Man and Animals.* Philadelphia: W.B. Saunders, 1972.
10. Montegu, A.: *Man and Aggression.* London: Oxford University Press, 1973.
11. Darwin, C.: *The Origin of Species.* New York: MacMillan, 1962.
12. Fiorentino, M.: *Normal and Abnormal Development.* Springfield, Illinois: Charles C. Thomas, 1972.

13. Taub, E.: Prism Compensation as a Learning Phenomenon. in *Neuropsychology of Spatially Oriented Behavior,* edited by S.J. Freedman. Homewood, Illinois: Dorsey Press, 1968.
14. White, R.: Ego and Reality in Psychoanalytic Theory. *Psychological Issues,* 3(3). New York: International Universities Press, 1963.
15. Van Lawick-Goodall, J.: (See above.)
16. Moore, J.: Behavior, Bias and the Limbic System. *American Journal of Occupational Therapy,* 30: 11-19; 1976.
17. Somer, R.: *Personal Space.* Englewood Cliffs, New Jersey: Prentice Hall, 1969.
18. Lee, T.: Psychology and Living Space. In *Image and Environment,* edited by R.H. Downs and D. Stea. Chicago: Aldine, 1973.
19. Paillard, J. and Brouchon, M.: Active and Passive Movements in the Calibration of Position Sense. In *Neuropsychology of Spatially Oriented Behavior,* edited by S.J. Freedman. Homewood, Illinois: Dorsey Press, 1968.
20. Downs, R.H. and Stea, D. (Editors): *Image and Environment: Cognitive Mapping and Spatial Behavior.* Chicago: Aldine, 1973.
21. Pick, H.: "Children's Cognitive Maps." Presented at the Conference on Neural and Developmental Bases of Spatial Orientation, Teachers College, Columbia University, New York, November 16, 1979.
22. Hart, R.: "Facilitating Children's Orientation Abilities." Presented at the Conference on Neural and Developmental Bases of Spatial Orientation, Teachers College, Columbia University, New York, November 16, 1979.
23. Piaget, J. and Inhelder, B.: *The Child's Conception of Space.* London: Routledge and Kegan, 1973.
24. Downs, R.H. and Stea, D. (See above.)
25. Kaplan, S.: Cognitive Maps in Perception and Thought. In *Image and Environment,* edited by R.H. Downs and D. Stea. Chicago: Aldine, 1973.
26. Lee, T.: (See above.)
27. Griffin, D.: Topographical Orientation. In *Image and Environment,* edited by R.H. Downs and D. Stea. Chicago: Aldine, 1973.
28. Lynch, K.: Some References to Orientation. In *Image and Environment,* edited by R.H. Downs and D. Stea. Chicago: Aldine, 1973.

29. Downs, R.H. and Stea, D.: (See above.)
30. Edney, J.J.: Property, Possession and Permanence; A Field Study in Human Territoriality. *Journal of Applied Social Psychology,* 275-282; July 1972a.
31. Edney, J.J.: Place and Space: The Effects of Experience With a Physical Locale. *Journal of Experimental Social Psychology,* 8: 124-135; 1972b.
32. Austin, W.T. and Bates, F.L.: Ethological Indicators of Dominance and Territoriality in a Captive Human Population. *Social Forces,* 52: 447-455; 1974.
33. Sundstrom, E. and Altman, I.: Field Study of Territorial Behavior and Dominance. *Journal of Personality and Social Psychology,* 1: 115-124; 1974.
34. DeLong, A.J.: Territorial Stability and Hierarchical Formation. *Small Group Behavior:* 55-63; February 1973.
35. Grundy, D. and Wilson, S.F.: Diagnosis and Planning of a Community Residence; A Sociometric Study. *Small Group Behavior,* 4: 206-222; 1973.
36. Altman, I.: *The Environment and Social Behavior.* Belmont, California: Wadsworth, 1975.
37. Hock, H., Gordon, G.P. and Whitehurst, R.: Contextual Relations: The Influence of Familiarity, Physical Plausibility and Belongingness. *Perception and Psychophysics,* 16: 4-8; 1974.
38. Edney, J.J.: (See above.)
39. Hart, R.: (See above.)

4. Consentually Expressed

> "—the reality of our day-to-day life consists of an endless flow of perceptual interpretations which we, the individuals who share a specific MEMBERSHIP, have learned to make in common."
>
> —Carlos Castaneda
> Journey to Ixtlan;
> The Lessons of Don Juan[1]

Human function is dependent not only upon personal efforts. It is as dependent upon the abilities and the engagements of others as personal effort, while at the same time being dependent upon the naturally existing world in which man lives. While that with which humans surround themselves is a world of personally constructed experience, man's environment is constructed from elements of experience both inanimate and animate. We live in a world of both solid and social structure. Therefore, spatial environments are not the only external influences to which human beings are subject. Human environment has long been understood to influence the behavior of others. Man's influence upon man's behavior is a critical element of human performance.

People are sensitive to the view of others. Views held by others dictate position within the social realm. Roles taken are determined by others as much as they are individually determined. Social fitness determines human status and success. Directions which are taken are determined in large part by others. People come to feel through mutual experience that they have options about only some of their world and have limited options about much else. Their options are restricted by economics, by love, by responsibility, by social custom, and by the intellectual and emotional limitations of their own minds.

In addition to being aware of man's concern for the opinions of his peers, we must be equally aware that man's interdependent action has contributed to mankind's accomplishments as a whole. Survival in our time is not directly dependent upon personal innovation and effort. Only the occasional individual is capable of providing all that he needs for survival through his own efforts. Few have the skills to survive unaided if they found themselves dependent upon their own resources. Surely few choose to do so. Man is not a creature of independent striving. Man is a social animal who elects to cooperate in interdependent effort. The symbiosis of human life is defined by mutual support systems evident within man's world. The human species exemplifies cooperative effort. Shared responsibility, with individuals assuming divergent and specialized roles, is a feature of human effort.

Because each individual lives within a personally constructed world, each world is unique for each individual. Peculiar to each person is the variety of roles he plays in that world. Demands upon each person differ. Each person's place within the scheme of things is different from that of any other person. Individuals interact with differing determinants. Placement in time differs; cultures differ; employment differs; interests and skills differ, and family size and place within that family differs. People within identical families and cultures, while similar in many respects, demonstrate great differences, individual to individual, just as peoples differ from group to group.

Within any given environment, individuals and groups survive and even gain succor from one another. A given world has ample resources to meet the needs of its multiple inhabitants. All levels of life from intracellular to social demonstrate interdependency. Living within any given environment are many, both human and animal, animal and plant, whose needs and offerings provide support to one another. Over time, man has learned to utilize this interdependency to meet his own specific needs. He farms, and in doing so, makes the product of one effort meet the needs of another. He raises corn to feed livestock and in turn uses their droppings to amplify the nutrients of the soil in which the grain is to be raised again. He spins the wool to warm his body. He drinks the milk and eats the meat. He preserves the produce for sufficient time to restart the cycle. Man, through experience and behavior, acknowledges that a well functioning ecological system survives and flourishes. Similarly, well functioning social systems offer mutual support toward survival. Families, communes, tribes and governments have developed toward communal ends. The interdependency of man is a feature of human existence evident throughout its history from earliest time to the present. Even primitive tribes which mirror our past demonstrate specialization and division of labor. The physical adaptation of man evolved to aid in their roles as hunters and gatherers and as parents of hunters and gatherers. Unity of purpose and cooperative effort developed along with physical capabilities with which to sustain those purposes (Washburn, 1960)[2].

Today, human beings live in a world quite different from that in which their species originated, although the time which has elapsed for the species is but moments within the millenia. The speed with which these changes have occurred shows signs of being potentially less than favorably adaptive for humanity. Some advances that mankind has developed in its search for new knowledge have placed all life in precarious and vulnerable conditions. Control evades the individual. There are things to fear today for which the species could not possibly have evolved coping mechanisms as yet. Too little time has elapsed. People are closer to their origins than cursory attention would presume.

Evolution occurred in such a way as to provide successfully for human needs. To this point our survival has been assured by the confirmation of success experiences in life tasks. But tasks of living show signs of alteration as history speeds by. Just as time appears to race by faster as aging progresses, a similar speed-up seems evident in the development of mankind to the present. Roles people must play today sometimes require different capabilities than those for which they were originally prepared. Success in survival tasks required in our present culture necessitates continuing adaptation to a changing world. But man has proven to be an adaptive creature, continually adapting toward his own success in survival tasks. Man's creativity and interdependency may be the features of his which will successfully solve the problems of his continued survival.

Success is a necessary feature for human development. If development is presumed to continue throughout life, continued development is predicated upon continuing success experiences. In order for success to be achieved, environments must be suitably adaptive. Not only the physical environment must support success, but the human environment also must offer consentual confirmation of success. Acknowledgment of success is a consentual experience.

But at what can one be confirmed successful? Success is measured by accomplished tasks. Tasks in which humans engage in all their varied interests are monitored and assessed by their peers. Tasks of living are limited only by human imagination, the needs demonstrated for those tasks in the world, and the confirmation by others of that suitability. Not all behavior is accorded consentual support. Bizarre behavior is defined by the lack of synchrony of tasks or behaviors to their consentual appropriateness in a given world. Genius, however, may also be defined in this way. Many ideas of the geniuses of the world were not welcomed until time confirmed the significance of their contributions. 'Before his time' is a familiar expression. Tasts appropriate in one time or culture may not be appropriately undertaken in others. Consensus determines appropriateness.

Tasks in which people engage are those which attest to accomplishment. Skill and the recognition of that skill is demonstrated in measurable production. Gross National

Product is a measure of production in the society in which we live. The contribution made by any individual is a measure of his worth to his social group. Some have been heard to say of our society that life is a game and money is the means by which the score is kept. Some would take this to be a criticism of a greed-motivated society, but all societies measure contribution in some coin. Consider, however, that the basic contribution made by any individual is his ability to care for himself. Man is the only animal who is dependent for so much of his life. Even primate infants must cling to their mothers to survive, thus contributing effort in their own behalf. Human infants, although retaining grasp reflex, do not use grasp as a functional tool for their survival until much later in their development. The human is delayed in his achievement of independence in mobility, feeding, and economics. At the other end of the life spectrum, dependence also prolongs as medical skills increase length of life, often without attention to man's need to perform creatively throughout that whole lifetime. A species dependent for so much of its lifetime is bound to develop interdependence in cultural objectives.

The expectations of society dictate a demand for independence on the part of the individual as maturity is achieved. Independence and interdependence follow a developmental path. The forms of man's pursuits change as development occurs.

Once someone becomes able to care for oneself, it then becomes further expected that that person develop mutual dependency. Sharing is a skill that parents try to inculcate in their children from the child's earliest years, but its accomplishment often takes until adulthood, if ever. Following the accomplishment of mutual dependence, tasks are directed toward responsibility for others. A measure of maturity is responsibility demonstrated. Interdependently and skillfully performed tasks of value to others are inherent in the development of human society.

Tasks in which man has engaged have brought humanity to its present state. Mankind as it exists today has developed from the experiences of all those humans who have ever lived, from the origin of mankind to the present time. Together, human beings achieved a world which could not have been achieved by individual effort. Each person incorporated his personal contribution toward mankind's total achievement through the execution of his individual efforts and strivings. One to the other, humans have contributed through time their cooperation, building achievements, achievements yielding new achievements, learning stimulating new learning, vistas ever broadening, while simultaneously focusing increasingly narrowly their individual fields of awareness. The telescope and the microscope serve as symbols which demonstrate the fluctuating direction human conceptualization and cooperation demands. Each aspect of knowledge from the most minute detail to the most comprehensive concept have resulted from mankind's compelling need for inquiry and solution-finding. Man is a curious and adventuresome animal. Seeking after knowledge and skill is ever demonstrated as a feature of human existence. What has been true of the mind of mankind as a whole is not less true for individual human beings. As people and as persons, human beings are governed by the same rules for behavior. To live as a human is to seek, to plan, to make choices and to develop throughout life. As people grow and develop, human beings encounter many experiences. They grow, they learn, they relate to others, they change, they age. They pass through various and prescribed stages throughout the course of their lifetimes. During their earliest development, they are centered upon themselves, sensitive only to their own needs, seeing themselves as the center of the world. They make the assumption that the world that they know is all there is to know. As development proceeds, humans achieve the ability to view themselves by the perspective others have of them. The views of others, for a time, control their actions. As they are reared, the behavior of young people is modified by their parents and their teachers. As growth proceeds and adolescence approaches, youngsters require the security and structure of the approval of their peers. As maturity is pursued, discord between personal needs and external pressures is resolved, whereupon personal independence and security is acquired. Individuals begin to pursue their own needs within the context of the needs of others. They become able to sublimate their short term goals toward long term ends. They understand that the wider world has reference to themselves. Their effect is seen within that world. They set themselves tasks and plan their futures. They execute their plans and modify them as necessary to the adaptation they must make to their environment. As later maturity is achieved, they reflect upon their accomplishments, reconsider their values, and reassess the directions they wish to establish for their later years. They resolve their end. They leave to those who follow a heritage upon which an expanding history may be based.

Throughout the history of mankind, civilization has been built upon person-to-person communication. As knowledge has been acquired it has been shared between persons and between generations. Gestures and body language were our earliest communication forms. Following this, language developed, permitting sharing to take an oral form. Language is a unique human achievement. The advent of the ability to utilize the mechanism of speech for communication provided a means of sharing never before available to other animals, affording to man communal memory. Parents instruct their children using oral means, sharing family lore and custom. The Bible developed from oral history. Biblical scholars delineate several styles of reporting and differing tales deriving from different ancient oral schools which combined in written form to give us The Book as known today. Oral sharing served as the basis for the written history which followed. Tribal custom and survival skills passed from generation to generation, increasing the adeptness of descendents who learned to cope with their world from the communal memory of the adventures, inventions and errors of their ancestors. *Foxfire* (1972)[3] is an attempt to retain these shared skills from the past in a modern scheme of communication.

The process of history retold was dramatically expressed in *Roots* (Haley, 1976)[4] during the recitation by the 'griot.'

How remarkable it was to see the memory of the past within the grasp of one individual. Today individuals no longer have this ability. Knowledge we have accumulated is too vast for any one individual to comprehend and recall. The Renaissance person is gone; the libraries are full; publications are vast; regulations are unending. Any one person can only know a small part of all that is known. For human beings to survive, they must continue to function as a group engaged in sharing, with roles assigned and portrayed as they have always done, but man is presently in a position which increasingly necessitates that he must trust his existence to the efforts and decisions of those whom he will never know. Man's food, shelter and intellect derive from sources beyond any one person's direct awareness.

Being a part of a society, part of a communal group, necessitates that directly or indirectly, communication facilitates concerted effort toward ends which meet the needs of the group. Group consensus within any civilization dictates the practices of that civilization. Custom results from consensus agreed upon by contributing individuals within any given civilization. Productive individuals contribute their experiences, sharing what they have learned through demonstration. That which has been seen to work well for any given culture survives in practice. Unsuccessful practices alter, or unchanging, rend that civilization unfit for survival. The people of the Bible still live. The great Roman Empire has fallen.

Group consensus presumes that those participating abide by decisions achieved by the group. For consensus to occur, individuals must modify their personal attitudes toward the development and acceptance of the group's attitudes, while at the same time individual ideas are permitted to become incorporated into the decisions of the group. People differ vastly in their influence upon group decision. Different circumstances change individual influence upon group decision. Some people lead and some are led. A process of consensus develops as time permits communication. That which the group adopts becomes truth for members of that group. Mutually confirmed truths are not less true because they have been acquired and expressed through less formal mechanisms than scientific method dictates.

While consensus is a construction of human environment, consensus derives in part from a propensity toward automated behaviors. The ability of man to recognize serves as a facilitator for follower behavior. Modeling is a primitive response endowed by recognition. Response behavior, reflecting what is observed, is a feature of early development. The infant smiles in response to a smiling face. It is a response that remains through life. A smile is always apt to generate a smile. No conscious decision is made to produce that smile. Man engages in many behaviors without conscious intent to do so. Children model their behavior after their parents and after their peers. Through the use of confederates, Asch (1955)[5] was able to demonstrate that subjects exposed to group responses will alter their own responses from that which they themselves observed and believed when their companions asserted other interpretations, even when those assertions were unfounded. Miller and Dollard (1941)[6], studying aggresson in children, found that observation of aggressive behavior elicited aggressive behavior in the observers. Experiments in which subjects were led to believe they were inflicting pain upon others demonstrate that people perform as they believe they are expected to perform, even if the tasks they are expected to do are of a nature one would expect subjects to reject (Milgram, 1963)[7]. Expectations of others apear to have profound effect upon human performance. Considerable questions have been raised as to the morality of experiments of the kind Milgram performed. Conflict experienced by subjects between their inclination and their performance has been proposed to leave subjects with severe psychic assault. The excuse presented by those who permitted Nazism to flourish: "I did as I was told." is further evidence that man has been observed to succumb to the directions of others. Man shows strong inclination to perform automatically as he perceives himself expected to, when directed to by observation, by instruction or by environmental demand. But on the other side of the coin are those abilities which man alone shows. Creativity and morality derive from the consciousness of man. Man's ability to plan, to make choices, to decide and influence his own destiny is a unique human trait. At the same time, man is able to follow while also being capable of independent judgment. But no higher functioning mental activity exists without underlying automaticity as the enabler. Discipline precedes independence and creativity. Prior to Picasso's expansions was conservative precision. Prior to the concert brilliance of Mehta were years of practice.

Man's inclination toward automatic or follower performance contributes to the function of consensus. Through familiarity and trust, the group is enabled to perform combined effort toward mutual benefit. That man has come as far as he has come in so few years is incredible evidence of the efficiency of consensus in compounding creativity. The shifting ability of man to lead and to be led, to create and respond, and to retain constancy as context shifts, serves his own survival needs as individual or as group, providing those who are led remain alert as to whom they will follow. Trust depends upon validation. Trust and security dictate the interdependent networks of social environment. Choice dictates the composition of those groups which direct society's future.

Social networks of interlacing groups afford people different positions within the various groups in which people choose to participate. Ability dictates not only position but activities in which one is apt to be engaged. Participation in family, business, golf club, school or orchestra depend upon interest and upon ability. Of all groups available to any individual living in a complex society, each person selects his own set with which to relate. Position within each group differs. A leader in one group may be a follower in another. Role is a dimension of relationship in a consentual environment. Role is given as much as it is taken. One must declare for the Presidency and be elected to the Presidency both, in order to served. Power is dictated by the role one plays against any other individual's role. Status signifies power expressed in relationship. Some of the many roles played afford greater power than others.

Time and change permit alterations in the structure of

power. A new baby born into a household shifts the relationships between the members as well as the character of the family. A mother with power over her offspring, shifts in her relations to them to a dependency role in her ultimate Dependency or low status yields automatic or follower behavior. Leadership dictates decision making and responsibility for those who consent to follow. Consent is inherent in decline. Status dictates automatic versus cognitive behavior. Responsibility dictates increased cognitive behavior. Dependency or low status yields automatic or follower behavior. Leadership dictates decision making and responsibility for those who consent to follow. Consent is inherent in consensus. Consent grants power. Roles people take in life vacillate between dependency and responsibility. Dependency has the feature of automatized follower behavior which may be seen as functioning below cortical level awareness. Responsibility places on one the burden of decision making.

The ability to make reasoned decision is a distinctly human trait, but reason relies upon automated skilled performance. Decisions cannot be made outside the scope of ability. Underlying skill enables choice. Anticipation of options becomes possible only as skill is acquired. There is no choice available if skill is not evidenced. Experience dictates options. Every activity is founded upon its component activities. The ability to perform those components outside of awareness dictates skill. Many professional golfers and bowlers will tell you that when their game is off, conscious attention to position and form does not do much to help matters. Rather, direction toward goal is useful. It is the ability to perform correctly and automatically in synchrony with the demands of the world which leads to success. One can look at someone's knitting and tell whether a beginner or an old-timer has done it. Consistent tension can be achieved only by the skilled craftsman. The brilliance of the cortex rests upon the reliability of the brain stem. Achievement is only within the range of anticipation based upon self confidence and reinforced by success. Sanity is judged by correct and reasonably accurate assessment of personal ability.

Work and play, responsibility and dependency, relate as do the concepts of Yin and Yang. This establishment of centration is related to the resolution of the extremes of experience, a centration derived from balance which can be experienced internally, externally, or consentually, throughout human experience and endeavor.

REFERENCES
Chapter 4. Consentually Expressed

1. Castenada, C: *Journey to Ixtlan; The Lessons of Don Juan.* New York: Pocket Books, 1972.
2. Washburn, S.L.: Tools and Human Evolution. *Scientific American,* 203(3); 1960.
3. Wigginton, E. (Editor): *The Foxfire Book.* Garden City, New York: Anchor, 1972.
4. Haley, A.: *Roots.* Garden City, New York: Doubleday, 1976.
5. Asch. S.: Opinions and Social Pressure. *Scientific American,* 193(5): 31-35; 1955.
6. Miller, N.E. and Dollard, J.: *Social Learning and Imitation.* New Haven, Connecticut: Yale University Press, 1941.
7. Milgram, S.: Behavioral Study of Obedience. *Journal of Abnormal & Social Psychology,* 67: 371-378; 1963.

IV. A RATIONALE FOR GERONTOLOGICAL PRACTICE

5. Aging; A Definition

AGE

Age is a quality of mind and of Life

If hope you lost and you don't look ahead

If ambition's fires are dead, "You are old."

But if of life you make the best,

And if in life you hold your zest,

If love you hold

No matter how the years go by

And how the birthdays fly,

"You are not old."

Bess Cantor
The Outlook[1]

Having defined a set of principles under which human behavior has been proposed to occur, it remains to apply these principles toward the improvement of function in those who suffer developmental arrest. We have seen that perceptual development acquires throughout life. Normal aging of itself, does not preclude that development. While perceptual development acquires throughout the life of the healthy individual, impaired development is commonly evident in disabled populations of various ages and diagnoses. When development becomes impaired at any age, impaired human endeavor is evidenced. When that development becomes impaired in later years, adaptive performance is more seriously hampered, as the potential for its recovery is too frequently denied.

Adaptive behavior is a feature for normal human endeavor. Impaired adaptive behavior is demonstrated in those suffering disability. Dysfunction in adaptive behavior is evidenced by impairment in the ability to perform familiar or skilled tasks and in the ability to acquire new skills. Tasks of mankind expressed in continued skill acquisition are vital features of life requiring adaptation for their accomplishment. Those tasks define themselves through self directed goals in concert with a properly attuned world, a world in which those tasks can appropriately be sustained.

Goal setting is evident from earliest infancy to the end of life. As life proceeds, complexity of interests and goals increase. Interests build upon each other. New goals derive from interests and capabilities. The older one gets, the more likely the complexity of one's goal interests. Interference in these naturally acquiring goal interests can occur at any age, at any level of complexity, but occurs more frequently in populations which are more likely to be disabled. When disability occurs, it is necessary to recapitulate goal achievements in order to resume functional development. When the course of development makes achievement unavailable, when adaptation is unresolved without guidance, as often occurs in disability, endeavor must be facilitated. Those goals which persons seek to acquire must be achieved in sequence, recapitulating their earliest acquisition.

Given that growth and development is a feature of living throughout life, defining that life, it is possible to see that application of that assertion to the role occupational therapy takes in facilitating that growth and development.

Yet to be described is a dimension of practice which serves to validate the verity of that application. We have chosen to specify application of principles mentioned in the previous chapters by reflecting them against a population heavily served but, as yet, poorly analyzed in practice. The adult, the aging adult, warrants more critical attention than has yet been discerned. But in order to do so, it is first necessary to define aging.

Aging has been studied under the rubric of gerontology. Gerontology is the study of old age. But what is old age? How can aging be defined? Different queries elicit different answers. Depending upon different perspectives of investigators, gerontology has been viewed in various ways. Investigators have approached the question of aging historically, politically, socially, physiologically and philosophically. In an attempt to define old age, we shall look to do so through these same avenues.

In different cultures and in different times, aged persons have been treated with varying degrees of concern and respect by members in numerous ways. Sometimes wisdom and age have been equated; sometimes frailty and uselessness have characterized age. The respect shown to elders in oriental civilizations in earlier times is well known. The shrinking of the world and the melding of cultures experienced as a result of communication between peoples, has tended to modify attitudes to some extent. Pearl Buck, in her many books about Chinese civilization, described the changes in cultural attitudes that grow from one generation to the next, and the consequences produced by those attitude changes.

In traditional Eskimo culture, religion dictated that suicide before decline or disability ensued was necessary to the reincarnation of a whole and healthy person. Only a whole person could be expected to survive in that difficult clime. This cultural inclination toward suicide in the aging had the effect of eliminating the existence of dependent elderly from the Eskimo population. This predilection has changed due to the advantages presented by present government retirement benefit programs. An elderly relative who contributes resources to the family welfare tends to be held in higher regard than is a dependent relative. This tendency has resulted in the creation of social pressures inclined towards departing from ancient customs. Encounter with other cultural groups has led to changed attitudes toward and among the elderly of the Eskimo society.

Time produces changes in all cultures and civilizations. Change is a feature of mankind's development, be it era to era or throughout an individual lifespan.

At the present time in this country, we too are in a state of flux regarding the status of our elderly. Treatment of the elderly is different today from former practices. In past years, when extended families lived in close proximity, when women were employed at home rather than outside the home, as many are today, elderly were cared for at home. Primary caretakers knew their charges well. They had lived with each other prior to the onset of illness and disability. Illness or disability was not the only experience they had together. This is decreasingly a feature of our present world. Now, those who care for the sick have never known that ill person when he was well. Being presented with a person who is met for the first time as both elderly and ill produces bias toward that individual. Disability rather than capability is perceived by those responsible for giving care. Rights and responsibilities have been transferred to others for the care of the dependent elderly. But the care provided has not necessarily improved for these elderly, despite the fact that those providing that care purport to be functioning as specialists in their field of interest.

Horror stories reach the press regularly regarding the care and welfare of the elderly ill. New York's nursing home scandal in 1976 reached national attention. One more and more frequently reads about old people who are poorly nourished and poorly clothed because their scanty funds are insufficient to provide for all of their needs. In Texas in 1979, a 91 year old woman was arrested for shop-lifting. Not having eaten in several days, and having existed prior to that time on a diet consisting only of cereal and milk, she was unable to live any longer within the law, and stole food to survive. Shades of Hugo's *Les Miserables*. As a result, she suffered arrest, necessitating subsequent court appearance. Unlike poor Jean of the French tale, long term benefits resulted from her illicit behavior. Her plight became know publicly and the community in which she lived came to her aid. This woman, however, is only one of the many, most of whom are not so fortunate as to come to the attention of those who would assist them in their survival.

Energy costs have had an impact upon the elderly as well. Automobile travel has become a luxury that many elderly cannot afford. Also, as energy costs rise, the temperature at which people on fixed incomes live reduces in winter and rises in summer. The energy that the biological system must expend to sustain homeostasis is forced to increase at the very time of life that those energy resources within the human system show tendency to diminish. Rapidly escalating economic inflation is confronted by a population whose resources are not sufficient to meet their economic need. All too often, the social and biological needs of the elderly are not being met by the culture in which they must live.

Yet one comes to realize how astute legislators are becoming in their newfound concern for the elderly. As longevity increases, as zero population growth approaches, and as the youth of this country stay away from the polls despite their earlier majority, a vast and strong political force has been emerging. Increasing legislation continues to appear which is concerned with the rights of our senior citizens. Politicians seem well aware of those factors which will invite their re-election to office. An energetic older citizenry has the potential of effecting strong political influence. But this attention to the needs of the elderly under the law is a recent occurence.

Legislative concern for the elderly began in the last century when the first retirement pension plan was established in Germany. This plan provided financial benefits to its recipients upon retirement. At that time, age 65 was set as the year of eligibility. This concept of publicly supported retirement for the elderly was originally established in an attempt to assuage disgruntled younger workers in order to provide a mechanism for the relief of the rampant unemployment being experienced at that time. It was hoped that by encouraging the elderly to retire through means of assuring them retirement income, there would be an increased opportunity for younger workers to enter the employment market when the elderly reached retirement age. This retirement plan spread to France and then to the United States, where the same age requirement was adopted in the Social Security system with no further thought as to the propriety of the selection of 65 as the critical age. Much concern has been expressed since regarding the age identified for retirement, as well as the appropriateness of retirement related to number of years of life. Issues before the legislatures and the courts have dealt with the problem of forced retirement. Recently, federal legislation raised the mandatory age for forced retirement among government employees, taking into consideration that many elderly people make suitable employees despite their age, or indeed perhaps because of it. It cannot be denied that experience is a valuable commodity.

Extensive experience has too often been met with rejection and dismissal when this experience may well have served to enhance our society. In 1977, the acting Dean of Graduate Studies at Kean College in New Jersey reached her 71st birthday. She was actively engaged in doctoral studies at the time. The Dean was a woman who had raised her family before attending college herself, and had achieved her academic position in her later years. She was retired from service to the college because of her advanced age. Having know this exciting, dynamic woman at the end of her college career, having learned a great deal from her, and having seen her value to the college, the community, and the students she served, one must wonder at a system that requires such a retirement procedure. Merit is not often related to age. Neither is reward for skilled effort.

Aging: A Definition 115

There is a law school which utilizes as professors those who have been retired from the finest of law positions due to age. This school takes advantage of a valuable resource which has been made available to them by the folly of state laws and pension regulations. Admittedly, incompetence in positions requiring brilliance and efficiency should be avoided, but establishing retirement criteria based upon age is not the only solution available, for aging does not necessarily predict cognitive dysfunction. Rather the reverse, cognitive dysfunction is often described as aging.

A gentleman with whom I am well acquainted suffers with recurrent ulcers which have necessitated hospitalization on several occasions in recent years. When he is well, which is most of the time, he is seen as a vital, dynamic individual. He is sought out for his expertise in investment matters, he goes dancing with his wife several times a week and is very active and sociable. He is, however, apprehensive of medical care. Having been admitted to the hospital one evening suffering abdominal pain, he was approached the next morning with news that a series of gastrointestinal X-rays were to be taken. He decided that he was unwilling to subject himself to this procedure and refused to comply. He dressed and discharged himself against medical advice. Subsequently a bill arrived for the X-ray procedure he had refused and for which he refused to pay. He stated that he would not pay for what he had not received. The billing department refused to comply with his position and demanded reimbursement. When the family intervened, the hospital's position was that this was an elderly, confused man who did not remember what had happened to him. The family suggested that payment would be made if the X-rays would be presented. The hospital representative agreed. Of course, no X-rays were found and an apology was forthcoming. What had doubtless occurred was that a computer charge slip went through when the order was received. Few patients ordinarily refuse treatment, making this procedure efficient on most occasions. But in this instance, a bright man with full mental capacities was immediately perceived as incompetent because he was old and he was ill. On a second hospitalization of an emergency nature, sedation was required. Again the experience resulted in the perception of him as a confused old man; medication was not presumed to be moderating his behavior. Rather, his appearance predicted to others who had not known him that his disorientation was organically determined. All too often, illness in aging is equated with cognitive dysfunction. Agism is too frequently evident toward those who are of retirement age.

While enforced retirement has shown itself to be a suspect procedure subject to discriminatory action, elective early retirement has, at the same time, been promoted by unions and legislators on behalf of their constituents. Effects of the trend toward early retirement have been largely twofold. One result which has occurred is that many people have been seeking second careers in their later years. Increased longevity has afforded this plan a good potential. We hear so often today of middle life people changing careers midstream. Shopkeepers become postal employees; housewives become office workers; executives become antique dealers. Retirement pensions have allowed people to venture into careers they could not have afforded to pursue without financial aid of some sort. Education and training remain available to persons of all ages in our present culture.

Another result of early retirement has been increased opportunity for leisure time. Excess leisure time in a society which has been built on a work ethic presents a potentially difficult conflict to resolve. Those who have never been reared to accept leisure as a viable condition of life activity will have difficulty adjusting to it as they age. For some it is necessary to retain a sense of purpose through labor, whether that labor is a source of revenue or a volunteer effort. Purpose and responsibility are features of human goal direction. It seems to be necessary for individuals to feel a need to be needed. Everyone requires a sense of purpose in his existence. Although no one is ever wholly indispensible, the illusion of such indispensibility and purpose appears to be an element of healthy human existence. Specialization and heightened expertise is driven by personal intention.

When retirement plans were originally instituted, not many individuals were expected to live to or beyond 65 years of age. Today, however, in civilized communities, life spans have increased considerably. Yet what has increased is not length of life for the species, as humans as well as other animals carry genetic programs dictating their length of life. Guinea pigs, cats, dogs, man and tortoises live for different and predictable periods of time. yet not only species dictate length of life. It is known that the best predictor for longevity in any individual is the number of years that person's ancestors lived. Some families are long-lived. Some families are composed of members who die young. The Georgians of southern Russia have become famous for their extended longevity. Much interest has been expressed regarding the factors which are at work in extending their lives beyond that which is ordinarily experienced by other peoples. In this country, centenarians are occasionally identified and interviewed by the press. They are queried as to the factors which contributed to their longevity, as if their answers would provide a solution to the quest for the fountain of youth, as if they really knew why they had lived as long as they had.

Today, more individuals than ever before are reaching their full genetic potential through improved health maintenance and treatment techniques. Antibiotics, innoculations, microsurgery, and biochemical discoveries are among the advances which have made significant contributions to longevity. There has been a distinct increase in the proportion of elderly within our society. But we have not as yet identified what old age is.

Physiologically, all animals and their components age. Aging takes place in systems, in cells and in those structures found within cells. Just as species and individuals sustain predictable lengths of lives, so too do cells. Cells are programmed genetically to a limit of cell divisions. Some cells replace throughout the life of the organism. Blood cells replace at a rapid rate. A pint of blood can be safely donated every six weeks, because these cells are replaced with sufficient rapidity to permit this procedure without endangering health. Some cells remain throughout life. Human beings are endowed at birth with all the neurons they will ever have. Cells of all lengths of life age just as does the body as a whole. Cellular components age as well. Changes occur in their physical capabilities. Collagenous fibers lose their elasticity. Chemical transfer efficiency reduces as cells age, resulting in changes of function in systems with time. Aging occurs in cells, in systems, and in individuals.

As the body ages, function alters as well. Time brings change, and with change come new problems to be encountered. Life itself offers problems to be resolved. Without problems there is no life. It is the resolution of problems which is of significance to human function. When individuals are no longer able to resolve problems, aging ensues.

What are some of the problems that befall the aged? How do these problems affect function? In the normal course of living, as one grows older, one lives to see friends and family succumb in time. A spouse dies. Friends move away, become ill or may die. Making new friends becomes more difficult. Opportunities diminish for peer encounters. Children move away from home and create their own lives. Isolation looms large for the individual who is left alone to age. Individual health problems ensue more rapidly; recovery is slower. From some disabilities there will be no recovery. Vision and hearing fade. There develops generalized weakness, paralysis, amputation, memory loss, each of which, alone or in combination, affect health. Cognition and economics often affect the administration of medication and nutrition.

"Did I take my pill today?"

"Can I afford to do what the doctor said I must do?"

"I don't have enough money for both meat and vegetables."

"Who wants to bother to cook just for one?"

Both medication and nutritious foods are necessary to the maintenance of health in the elderly.

The elderly must frequently face relocation as a consequence of social, health and financial considerations. Adjustments made to these changes are often poor. Relocation has been shown to entail high risk to many older citizens, as fifty percent of relocated elderly studied exhibited decline following the changes they encountered (Lieberman, 1974)[2]. Little is known at present regarding the critical environmental conditions which affect the well-being of the elderly. Relocation is a problem many elderly must face for one reason or another.

> "The neighborhood has changed and it's no longer safe."

> "The children want me near them but they've moved so far away."

> "These cold winters are hard on mee. I have to move south."

> "I can't take care of myself any longer."

> "Taxes keep going up but my income stays the same."

Either illness or increased costs along with decreased income may be the reason for their relocation. Financial problems for the elderly are enormous. They are our largest indigent population.

> "I'm too old and too sick to work yet my social security check is too small."

> "My home is paid for but I can't meet the taxes."

> "The price of food keeps going up."

> "The stairs need repair but I can't afford to fix them, and I don't have the strength to do it myself. My husband used to take of those things."

Ability to get about is reduced. When that hip won't let someone make it onto the bus, it doesn't warrant going out as frequently anymore. Independence is lost. Self care becomes a problem in the selection and maintenance of clothing, in personal hygiene, in food preparation, in communication and in dealing with the breaking of old habits, because it can't be done that way anymore.

Sexual outlets become more limited. One's partner is aged or absent. Courting is something new to have to deal with after all those years. And,

"I have no privacy any longer."

Then,

"I have to get ready to die myself."

"Is life worth living?"

The suicide rate is largest among our older population (Rennick, 1978)[3]. Human beings are the only animals who have the ability to anticipate their own deaths. That humans are capable of reporting their understanding of cause and effect from generation to generation has provided this ability. Much of religion has been designed to attend to the insurance of a future beyond physical demise. As aging proceeds, it seems that people expend greater time in pursuit of their religious interests.

Who ages well? Not necessarily the person who retains his health, but the person who can make the necessary adjustments that the social, physical and emotional pressures of living and dying require. Death has been viewed as a friend of the aged. If one can begin to view death too as a part of a normal progression of experiences, then one has made a large step toward completion of the task of living (Kubler-Ross, 1975)[4].

Despite the myriad problems which may be encountered in aging, many elderly are gainfully employed, involved in their communities and in advocacy, interested in teaching and learning, broadening their intellectual horizons, and are seeking and gaining leisure skills. Visit any retirement community or speak to a Grey Panther if you want to see vitality in the aged.

So what is it that defines aging? Not number of years, for that has been shown to be a poor reflection of criteria. Rather it appears that decline in function is equated with aging. But a critical look at decline will reveal that decline begins with the cessation of growth. Twenty year old gymnasts are over the hill. The old man of sports is well known. Thirty-five year old ball players are beyond the pale. When people stop growing, they begin to age. Predictable functional decline sets in at programmed times; for example, presbyopia occurs in close association with the fortieth birthday, a milestone no longer equated with old age. Human beings are all aging as they are engaged in living. As aging proceeds, the body is assaulted from within and without. In each individual's lifetime, breakdowns in functional ability occur due to trauma. Emotional stress, fractures, infectious disease, surgical repairs of failing systems or merely failures of those systems themselves occur. Illness and disease ensue as a course of life. Aches and pains increase as time passes. As aging proceeds, and as illness is more frequently encountered, changes occur. Critical illness results in devastating feelings of reduced self worth. Illness creates feelings of deprecation and dependency. Depression often ensues. Along with depression comes reduced strength as a result of the immobilization which ordinarily occurs in association with illness, as well as being a result of illness itself. Illnesses which assault the elderly are apt to affect their ability to get about, preventing them from performing in the same way they performed prior to the onset of disease.

It is when diseases serve as barriers to function, and when these barriers are perceived by oneself and by others as signs of aging, that aging occurs. The question "Who is old?" is answered by mutual consent. One is old when one believes one is old, and when the reality of this conclusion is confirmed by the world in which one lives. Grey hair is not a definition of old age. Individuals who are fully functional are often not perceived of as old, despite their length of years. We are all acquainted with vital individuals of advanced age. Disabled people, on the other hand, may be considered elderly before the time ordinarily assigned to healthy members of their community. A rehabilitation project for the elderly blind who live in their own homes exists in Newark, New Jersey. These people are transported daily to a center in downtown Newark. This project has been federally funded and included as eligible were persons who are 55 years of age and older. Although most projects for the elderly are defined by the Office on Aging as available to those 60 years of age and older, disability was determined to reduce the criteria by which individuals were classified as aged within this program. Disability increases the perception of one as an elderly person. Fifty-five and sixty appear younger to this author every year.

Disability equates with aging. Disability in the elderly is somewhat different from disability in younger persons. The multiple problems encountered by the elderly are unique, perhaps more so than in many other patient categories. Disability is rarely experienced in one system or area alone. Frequently, sudden disability occurs to an individual who is at the same time coping with bodily changes associated with progressive dysfunction. Long term disabilities associated with cataracts, arthritis, diabetes and circulatory diseases are all to be dealt with along with the suddenness of strokes and hip fractures. The multiplicities of decline of function associated with disease processes, traumatic injury, psychosocial needs and relationships present unique problems to patients and therapists for resolution. No patient presents the same combination of abilities or disabilities. And number of years has no correlation with expected performance. It is a poor correlant in the 'normal'. It makes as poor a correlant in the disabled population. The only expectation is that increased age will yield expected increases in physical limitation for each individual over time, but not for all the population in any given number of years. Elderly run the marathon. I have never been able to comfortably walk up a flight of stairs. I do it to reduce decline, but I don't like it. So too, patients will do what they feel is important, even if it isn't pleasant. Adults are experienced in sublimating present desires for long term goals.

Aging is a process in which all persons are engaged. That we identify this process in ourselves is a prerequisite toward development of the respect for aging required if we are to achieve competence as gerontological specialists, or indeed if we are to age well ourselves. Therapists must not look upon their clients as 'they' and upon themselves as 'we'. All of us are engaged in the same excursion. We are all on a trip through life, with some of us closer to the beginning and some of us closer to the end with no sure way to know which of us is at which point along the way. Our role as therapists is to make the trip easier.

REFERENCES
Chapter 5. Aging; A Definition

1. Cantor, B.: "Age." In *The Outlook*. Green Brook, New Jersey: Greenbrook Manor Nursing Home, October 1979.
2. Lieberman, M.: Relocation Search and Social Policy. *Gerontologist*, 14: 494-501; 1974.
3. Rennick, H.L.P. and Cantor, J.M.: Suicide and Aging. In *Readings in Gerontology*, edited by H. Brown. St. Louis, Missouri: C.V. Masky, 1978.
4. Kubler-Ross, E.: *The Final Stages of Growth*. Englewood Cliffs, New Jersey: Prentice Hall, 1975.

6. Factors in Aging Which Affect Perception and Performance

Various changes occur to the human body as time proceeds. From the tiniest embryo through to the end of life, the human is involved in change. These changes which occur have been entitled development. Development has traditionally been equated with growth and progress. Decline may also be perceived as developmental as it acquires sequentially and progressively, though less predictably. As changes are evidenced in growth, then in decline, change is at all times also evident in behavior. Together, the mind and the body change and adapt with one another as time passes.

With the onset of aging, many changes become increasingly evident in the physiology of the body. Varied sites and sequences of reduced function affect individuals, yet reduced function occurs in aging as surely as walking follows crawling. Reducing sensory-motor function is expected following a peak attained in young adulthood. At different levels of human development, there are varying levels of function of various sensory end organs. Predominance of systems change with development. The human fetus responds tactually on a different level than the newborn infant. Prior to birth there is limited cutaneous pain response. This factor aids in the birth process. Sensory and perceptual change is an aspect of all development. Adaptation to change enables function throughout life.

Change intimates a before and an after. In human performance, the after is dependent upon the recollection of the before. Prior context sets the tone for subsequent change.

Some age related changes commonly occur which contribute to disability and have been shown to be accompanied by changes in cognition. The mind and the body often show reciprocal decline. Functional performance of both mind and body depend upon the chemistry and physics of the energy plant that is the body in which the mind resides. A look at physical changes which underly performance may help the better understanding of that performance.

Collagen is a critical element of living tissue, found within interstitial tissues located between cells, and serves as a bond between those cells. As tissues age, physical properties of the collagenous components of those tissues reduce in the elasticity of their fibers. Time, for some undetermined reason, produces this diminished capacity for elasticity in live tissue. Wherever tissue requires flexibility for function, reduction of that flexibility hampers the performance of that tissue. As muscles and fascia reduce in flexibility, mobility is reduced.

Neural tissue also alters in aging. Neural endplates change their structure. Synapse metabolism becomes affected. Chemical transfer speed declines. Neuro-chemistry alters. Thatcher and John (1977)[1] report that aging is accompanied by a flattening of dendritic neurotubules through which neurotransmitters are transported. This alteration of neural structure, they feel, appears to be partially responsible for diminished function of brain cells in the very old.

As aging proceeds, these two major changes, loss of flexibility of tissue and loss of neurotransmission capability, represent the major components of the deficiency which results to the feedback loop system. Loss of tissue flexibility demonstrates both reduction in motor capacity and secondary sensory losses which result as a feature of this lack of mobility. Losses in neural capacity of afferent and efferent pathways also provide both losses in sensory input and in motor production. Both deficiencies are the major manifestations which occur in aging physiology which contribute to sensory motor malfunctions and thus to functional decline.

Responsiveness to sensory stimuli has been shown to diminish after 60 years of age and to increasingly diminish in later years (Bender, 1975)[2]. Experimental studies reviewed by Corso (1971)[3] reveal that studies of pain sensitivity indicate a significant decline past 60 years of age with responses varying among different areas of the body. Degenerative changes in receptors and in the peripheral nervous system, as well as decreased skin elasticity, were reported. No recent data regarding tactual sensitivity was available. Vibratory sensitivity was shown to be intact below 80 years of age, with some indication that lower extremities were affected more than upper extremities when these losses were evident. Lewis (1979)[4] reports to the contrary that vibratory sensibility diminishes in aging. Certainly it would be useful to determine more accurately the proficiency of vibratory sensation related to aging. Despite this disparity regarding vibration, greater functional disorders in touch, vision, audition and mobility have universally been observed to develop as aging ensues and as tissue changes occur.

Other physiological changes occur in aging as well. Cell and organ metabolism slows. Facilitory and inhibitory enzyme production alters. Joint capsules alter. Hormone production reduces or ceases. Myriad age-related changes have been identified. In those studies reviewed by Corso, much physiological and functional decline was evident in normal adults as they age. Crystalline lenses accumulate inert tissue at the center and become less transparent. Pupil size diminishes, resulting in decreased acuity and accommodation. Blue-green discrimination has been shown to be poorer than red-yellow discrimination. Loss of proficiency in color viewing has been attributed to the yellowing of lenses, which appears to produce a filter effect. Changes were noted in fluid loss, in reduced accommodation and in reduced dark-adaptation. Elderly, when tested with visual overlay colored cube projections, were observed to be slow to shift retinal rivalry. Color accuracy increases up to the twenties and then demonstrates decreased proficiency. This early loss of sensory capacity is an indication that aging and decline begin earlier in life than most people are accustomed to thinking of it occurring.

Auditory losses related to aging were reported in four areas. These were defined as sensory presbycusis, neural presbycusis, metabolic presbycusis and mechanical presbycusis. In addition, Corso reported a reduction in afferent nerve cells in the cerebral cortex after age 75. This cell loss was reported to contribute to impaired hearing and secondarily to the inability to communicate effectively. Speech discrimination problems were described in which environmental noises were attributed to mask consonant speech sounds, a figure-ground problem here expressed in audition. Healthy aged were reputed to hear better than less healthy aged. But one wonders what criteria were established to identify good health. It is questionable in such a report, which is cause and which is effect. Could it be that retention of functional hearing might be a factor in the retention of health rather than a sign of its decline?

Corso concluded that, although age decrements were clearly evidenced, onset of decline occurred at different ages and rates and that a broad explanation across modalities was necessary, suggesting further research. In concurrence with this view, an attempt shall be made to present a position which will summarize conditions which appear to contribute to losses evidenced in aging.

While sensory motor deficits have been shown to increase as aging proceeds, and because motor losses demonstrate inherent sensory loss, it appears necessary to consider the significance of these sensory deficits to the performance of the aging adult. These acute or prolonged sensory deficits which the elderly person experiences cause that individual to experience a condition of sensory deprivation. Sensory deprivation is a term referring to the removal of stimulation to sensory end organs at all possible sites of origin, resulting in the inability to discriminate inputs. Some sensory deprivation can be produced through bombardment stimuli as well. White noise or ganzvelt are examples of such over-stimulation. Too much stimulation prevents discrimination and thus denies data accumulation, just as does restriction of stimulation. Since sensations are received to the eyes, ears, nose, mouth, skin, muscles and joints, restricted stimulation or sensory deprivation to sensors in these areas may be induced through contrived means, or they may occur as a natural course of events, such as occurs in aging. It is commonly acknowledged that sensory deprivation has profound effects upon young children and animals as well, resulting in disorientation, bizarre behavior, as well as failure to thrive. The rearing of young requires stimulation offered by changes which result from movement and interaction. This does not appear to be less so in the aged.

Effects of sensory deprivation upon behavior have been studied by many investigators. In order to study the problem of sensory deprivation, researchers have induced sensory deprivation through various methods, all designed to isolate the subject from the world he would ordinarily experience. In some instances, underwater experiments were devised in an attempt to equalize pressure surrounding the body and neutralize gravitational effects prior to testing.

Some concern has been expressed regarding the methodology of sensory deprivation experiments. Rossi (1969)[5] points out that because subjects are exposed to testing following isolation, it is not possible to differentiate sensory deprivation effects from abrupt change effects. Nevertheless, something very unique occurs to individuals who have experienced altered states of sensory stimulation. Many experiments have been executed in which normal young adults were studied in their responses following sensory deprivation. A look at some effects to the young adult who has been exposed to sensory deprivation may help us to understand the effects that similar deprivation can provide when it occurs in the aged body.

Gross disturbances of perceptual responses have been noted as a result of sensory deprivation experiments. Deprivation to one sensory system has been observed to produce facilitory or inhibitory effects in other systems. When visual deprivation alone has been afforded the subject,

130 PERCEPTION: ITS DEVELOPMENT AND RECAPITULATION

it has been seen to produce distortion and changes in perception. Kinesthetic deprivation, too, can produce behavioral changes. In the normal adult, a two day period of such deprivation has been shown to produce greater effects than periods of shorter or longer duration. Positioning in prone or supine for prolonged periods of time, as frequently occurs during hospitalization or illness, will affect perception of spatial environment. This apparently occurs because the restriction of movement and the changed relationship of the head and body to gravity cause insufficient stimulation to sustain orientation. Depressed scores on tests of spatial relationships have been recorded in children who have been restricted to horizontal positioning, as is often required post surgery or orthopedic repair (Daffner, 1976)[6]. Zuckerman (1969)[7] reports that lying on one's back appears to be more conducive to reported visual hallucination than other positions. You will recall that prolonged supine posturing is the most commonly observed position noted in patients in the hospital setting.

Data regarding the cognitive effects of sensory deprivation indicate that memory is undamaged by this procedure, and even may be facilitated, but deficits in problem solving abilities have been evidenced. Considerable impairment has been noted in projective test performance (Suedfeld, 1969)[8]. Increased susceptibility to suggestion appears to originate with lack of informational anchors. As has been previously suggested, context serves to orient one to the surround, permitting constancy to be effected. Loss of input from the surround enhances disorientation. An organism which has no orientational constants deriving from personal experience is likely to latch on to the experience of others in a consentual model. Destruction of self through the deprivation of dependable orientational anchors is a mechanism that has been used in the brainwashing of prisoners of war.

Though cognitive deficits have been demonstrated to have resulted from sensory deprivation, Suedfeld further reports that exercise has been shown to decrease those deficits. That exercise has been shown to reduce sensory deficits should be no surprise. Body movement provides the system with greater sensory information through stimulation of all sensors in concert. Kinesthesia is vital to performance. Movement in space is critical to auditory and visual perception. Eye movement is necessary to sight. Movement reduction serves to reduce stimulation of the central nervous system. Movement provides orientation. If movement provides stimulation and orientation, then deprivation of movement can be demonstrated to reduce constancy, particularly when experienced in an unfamiliar environment.

As a person ages and as sensory deficits occur, the amount of information available to the individual reduces or alters in the same way that similar deficiencies have been induced in sensory deprivation experiments. Many diseases of aging yield decreased neural functioning, either as primary or secondary effects. Diseases and disabilities which produce decline of movement of the body and of movement of the body through space, reduce sensory inputs, and serve to alter perceptual function. Hip fractures, strokes, arthritis, cataracts and cardiac conditions are not uncommon among the elderly and are conditions likely to reduce mobility. Medication administered for the treatment of some conditions have been shown to contribute to decreased function (Foley, 1975)[9]. Decreased sensory inputs directly related to disease, or indirectly a result of immobilization, are features of disability in aging.

O'Neill and Calhoun (1975)[10] surveyed a nursing home population of 42 residents over 70 years of age. They administered tests of auditory function, visual function, two point tactile sensitivity and assessed mental status. A nurse's rating was included in their assessment battery. Sensory deficits and cognitive and behavioral deterioration were noted. Senile manifestations were defined as deficits of memory, comprehension, orientation and organization occurring in later life. It was noted that patients with or without arteriosclerosis did not differ as to mental ability. These authors concluded that senile manifestations are related to overall sensory losses. This is a departure from the commonly held attitude attributing 'senile' behavior to a form of brain tissue disease. Rather, these investigators attributed these behaviors to the inability to make sense of their senses. Sensory deficits reduce the amount of available information to the individual. Sensory input has been determined to be crucial to the maintenance of cortical arousal through the reticular activating system. Sensory input was expressed to be essential for adaptive behavior.

Research studies of performance ability in comparative age groups were consistent with the evidence that sensory ability reduces as aging proceeds. Denny (1974)[11] studied 214 individuals from 35 to 95 years of age, of which 49 were male and 165 were female. A mixed population of subjects were selected for study, some of whom were nursing home residents and some of whom were obtained for the study by canvassing the community. Stimuli of varying sizes, colors and shapes were presented to subjects. Subjects were told "to put the ones that were alike or the same together". Three groups of different ages were compared. Subjects over 60 ordinarily performed in more primitive grouping patterns. However, they were able to utilize more sophisticated grouping if requested to do so. Further testing was administered to determine if modeling would elicit more sophisticated patterns of grouping. For this study 24 of the subjects were utilized from the first experiment. Subjects consisted of those who did not group the stimuli according to complete similarity on their own. These subjects were 65-91 years of age. All resided in nursing homes. Twenty-two were female and two were male. Both a modeling and a control condition of experimentation were used. In the modeling condition, subjects watched the experimenter go through obvious search and trial and error machinations before being required to perform on their own. Subjects then performed the task with the same set of stimuli. This was followed by a post test in which a second set of stimuli were used. More improvement was noted in the modeling group than in the control group. The author concluded that reversion to primitive grouping patterns was probably not due to neural degeneration. Once again, we see that behavior altered due to other than neural dysfunction. This author suggested that isolation from occupational and educational demands to perform activities of this nature may have been responsible for the grouping patterns utilized.

Patterns of problem solving have been observed to alter in children as they develop, but Riegal (1973)[12] claims that it has never been demonstrated that formal operational intelligence characterizes mature adult thinking. He poses questions about adult cognition which suggest that individuals have the ability to switch back and forth from sensory motor to operational mechanisms of thinking, and that several different levels of cognitive functions may be simultaneously utilized. When Papulia and Riely (1974)[13] reviewed research based upon Piaget's theories, they suggested that young children and elderly performed similarly. It was claimed that both responded to the perceptual appearance of transformed stimuli rather than logic. No significant sex difference existed, but educational levels had a significant effect on task performance. Considerable variability in cognitive function was found among subjects. Isolation from occupation, education and social experience, as well as place of residence, appeared to contribute to lowered performance levels. It was their feeling that cognitive ability appears to disintegrate in reverse of acquisition. However, cessation of developmental progression may manifest itself in apparent decline. If re-establishment of constancy is requisite for function in the changing organism, then cognitive styles may indeed be uniform for both children and adults encountering change. Continual re-establishment of constancy is here proposed to be a feature of all human development. In the normal healthy adult, constancy remains because fewer changes are experienced. When change occurs, re-establishment of constancy is necessary to maintained or improved function.

In evaluating Rorschachs, Klopfer (1974)[14], concludes that difficulty in seeing, which frequently befalls the elderly, results in vague perceptions. Inferiority is manifested. Klopfer described restricted thought contact and emotional instability, both of an inhibited or egocentric and impulsive nature. He stated that old people respond to kind attention, and that they are intellectually slower, more inefficient, more unproductive. Yet he found the elderly more efficient in dealing with practical matters than theoretical problems. One wonders on what bases these generalizations are made, particularly when he ultimately concludes that the elderly cannot be distinguished by age alone.

Reduced speed of processing and performance appears to be a characteristic of aging repeatedly cited in the literature. Gaylord and Marsh (1975)[15] studied the influence of age on the speed of a spatial cognitive process. They tested ten right handed males ages 18-24 and ten right handed males ages 65-72 using depth rotation figures. Subjects were asked to respond to presentation of figures with a response of 'same' or 'different'. Reaction latencies were timed. A significant difference between the responses of the younger and older group existed, with longer reaction times and more errors evidenced in the elder. The authors attributed this to a slowing of cognitive processing as well as a slowing of motor response and sensory encoding. They also suggested this reflected similar losses found in memory scanning speed and felt that these results may indicate a similar decline for serial processing which rely upon recent memory processes.

Waugh et al (1973)[16] investigated the effects of age on choice reaction time. They tested 203 males in four groups with median ages of 33, 45, 55, and 68 years. Forty responses were required of each subject. Subjects were average in health with educational backgrounds ranging from some high school education to those with graduate school education, although older subjects generally had less edication than younger subjects. Subjects were required to release a key with their right hand when a red light was illuminated on the right of the subject. A key was to be released with the left hand when a green light on the left was illuminated. A brief auditory signal was presented two seconds before each trial. Ten to fifteen seconds between trials was permitted. Both repeated and alternated stimuli were presented with a total of forty correct trials for each subject. The study indicated a significant difference in response time beween the oldest and the youngest age groups, while demonstration of performance efficiency were equivalent. Response latencies increased with age. The authors concluded that the older individual's longer choice reaction time reflected impaired psychomotor performance rather than decision making efficiency. Botwinick and Storandt (1973)[17] in their study of verbal abilities which did not show decline in aging, took the position that speed of response should not be considered a measure of cognitive function. Despite their position, speed does often stand as such a measure. Reduced speed of neurological processes which is evidenced in aging by many sources, appears to be a major contributor to impaired cognitive functioning observed. As speed is an indicator of skilled performance, reduced speed is significant to skill loss. Lost skill reflects upon the subject adversely by those he encounters and with whom he must deal.

Memory was explored by Corso, who reported that forward memory span for digits in the aged was reported to be six digits, whereas younger subjects demonstrated the ability to remember seven digits. However, when different digits were presented to each ear, young subjects recited only one or two digits. Short term memory was shown less efficient in aging. Smith (1974)[18] reminds us that historical evidence holds that memory declines with age and that short term memory is that which is more involved; yet, he was able to show that old and young alike were not differentially affected by response interference.

We have seen that tissue changes, reduced feedback proficiency, reduced speed of performance and reduced cognitive proficiency are repeatedly reported in studies of aged. The results of these changes may be explained in the following way.

Decreasing proficiency of the sensory mechanisms upon which adults ordinarily rely (see Chapter 2), produced inhibited functional ability in the elderly. Reduction in dependable visual performance results either in a return to reliance upon the tactual/kinesthetic sensory mechanisms upon which earlier development had been based, or may result in confusion when reliance remains unchanged. Constancy is dependent upon integrated sensory performance. Early reliance upon kinesthesia was based upon a physical being which had different qualities as a measure of constancy, a person who in terms of physical identity no longer exists. Re-establishment of constants by which to assess present performance is prerequisite to that performance. Reliable constants are necessary to comfort and security.

Comfort and security are revealed by Corso as motivators in seeing and hearing events as previously accustomed. Older people tend to adhere more rigidly to the expected perception and resist or are incapable of reorganizing a perception. But this may be a means that people construct to retain a measure of reality which was based upon previously constructed and intact schemata.

When there are faulty or faltering systems, data may be provided which may be in conflict with one another. Temporal alteration may contribute to this conflict experience. Conflict in data received does not occur in the elderly alone. It is a reflection of change in body scheme. There is a phenomenon evidenced in young people who are experiencing growth spurts, whereby feedback systems based upon previously acquired information about space have not kept up with the evidence provided the central nervous system. Experience determines that coordinated muscle contractions will propel the body a given distance in space. The growth process of lengthening of limbs and increased muscle volume which occur in the absence of processed integration of input, causes increase of force in movement beyond the expectation of the mover. Vision says it is necessary to move a given distance, yet movement is not equivalent to expectation, causing the clumsiness often observed in adolescence. A similar phenomenon manifests itself in the elderly, especially in acute disability. Sensory motor performance and cognitive assessment are not synchronous. As has been seen in Chapter 2, conflict in experiences serves to delay or hamper further development.

Sensory deprivation alters the interpretation of one's relationship with the environment. Since sensory deficits occur as a facet of aging, the deprivation experienced has the same effect as that experienced in induced deprivation. Decreasing proficiency of the sensory mechanisms upon which adults rely appears to inhibit cognitive function. When this occurs, it seems to be useful to return to reliance upon the sensory mechanisms which children utilize for learning. This means of encountering the world aids in permitting the aging individual to maintain a hold on reality thereby avoiding the necessity for a critical analysis of every novel situation. When cognitive processing must be utilized for performance which has been formerly accomplished automatically, reduction in self image results. Speed in processing is also diminished. If sense of space is in part determined by temporal assessments and if speed is altered along with differences in relationships between sensory system processing, affect is vulnerable.

Foley (1975)[19] has reported that with aging is found decline in capacity for adaptation. It appears that the more sudden the loss of neural function, the more difficult is one's adaptation to disability. Denial to the individual of sensory experience or inability on the part of the individual to make sense of sensory experiences profoundly affects function. When functional loss is gradually acquired, gradual accommodation to the loss is more easily accomplished. Adaptation to a sensory loss in one system may be accomplished by transferred reliance to the use of other systems. Hermelin (1979)[20] has shown that children rely upon preferred systems, yet individuals have the capacity to shift reliance among systems, altering their dependency. The human organism is well equipped to tolerate change. This tolerance of change is what is experienced in the therapeutic situation. Gradual change can heighten performance.

We have seen much evidence of decline of function in aging, but by no means is aging exclusively categorized in terms of decline. Corso informs us that many functions remain unchanged in aging. Food complaints among the elderly were determined not to be based upon sensory impairment. Critical flicker frequency is not an indicator of age. Figural after effects is not an index of the functional level of the central nervous system as it ages. No age related errors were identified in graphesthesia (palmar cutaneous perception of number writing). There is no correlation of age to error in large/small figures testing reported in the absence of organic mental syndrome. However, defining perception in this manner should be criticized, because diagnosis of organic mental syndrome is based upon responses to functional testing. In this report, the cart has been put before the horse. The very absence of perceptual dysfunction cannot be seen to be an indication of absence of organic mental syndrome if its presence defines it.

Investigators have shown us that there is clearly not total predictability of decline associated with aging. Possible explanation for this lack of clarity regarding cause and effect may come to us from additional resources. Evidence cited by Buell and Coleman (1979)[21] indicates that although brain cells die as one ages, it has also been found that dendrites of living neurons continue to grow throughout life, enabling the neural system to maintain and expand its function. Eccles (1972)[22] indicates that it is neurological disuse which results in deterioration of dendritic fibers. However, these very same fibers can be restimulated to growth by use. Thatcher and John confirm that usage has been seen to produce changes in brain cells. Use implies growth and development. Disuse implies atrophy. Although the number of neurons in any individual reduces as time proceeds, dendritic fibers of remaining cells are able to grow and construct new synaptic connections providing increased opportunity for the transmission of enzyme produced energy across those synapses. Loss of brain cells is apparently not as significant to function as it would appear. All persons lose cells in huge quantities, yet great numbers of elderly citizens remain alert and functional despite those cell losses.

Although much evidence has shown, as we have seen, that aging brings decline in function, this is by no means a one way street. Facilitated performance can act to increase and further new performance. That the elderly can benefit from exercise and skill learning has been evident for quite some time. Gains made as a result of treatment attest to the benefits of goal-directed activity toward increasing functional performance despite aging. Purposeful movement in the elderly can serve to retard and diminish perceptual disorientation.

Most studies concerned with development of perception have attended to what has been observed in children; perception has been less well documented in advancing maturity (Piaget, 1972)[23]. Sequential acquisition of skill has been noted in children. Spatial orientation which has developed from kinesthesia contributes to this progression. Despite insufficient analysis of developmental changes in normal aging, sequential recapitulation of spatial/cognitive orientation has been demonstrated in the recovery of patients (Chapter 12). Restoration of perception and performance in the aged appears to recapitulate early perceptual development. Gerontogeny recapitulates ontogeny.

Defining problems encountered by the aged as learning disabilities, perceptual deficits, or cognitive processing deficits, may clarify mechanisms which occur when individuals fail to perform functionally. In children, learning disabilities which are encountered may be the result of innate malfunctioning processing systems. Inadequate inputs or depressed or hypersensitive synaptic mechanisms, or inadequate feedback systems may be at fault in preventing the child from learning. In the adult, these same factors interfere with learning. However, the term innate cannot be used to describe the problems encountered. Rather, these problems are acquired. Learning disabilities of adults are not those which confront a clean slate. They occur to an organism which has previously acquired a large body of knowledge on sensory-motor, perceptual and conceptual levels acquired through past integration of sensory inputs. So the disabled adult is both served by his previous experience and may be hampered by that same experience. Therapeutic intervention requires the inhibition of habits that hamper in order to utilize the skills that will facilitate further adaptive survival.

REFERENCES
Chapter 6. Factors in Aging

1. Thatcher, R.W. and John, E.R.: *Functional Neuroscience, Volume I: Foundations of Cognitive Processes.* Hillsdale, New York: Lawrence Erlbaum, 1977.
2. Bender, M.: The Incidence and Type of Perceptual Deficiencies in the Aged. In *Neurological and Sensory Disorder in the Elderly,* edited by W.S. Fields. New York: Stratton Intercontinental Medical Book, 1975.
3. Corso, J.: Sensory Processes and Age Effects in Normal Adults. *Journal of Gerontology,* 26: 9-105; 1971.
4. Lewis, S.: *The Mature Years: A Geriatric Occupational Therapy Text.* Thorofare, New Jersey: Charles B. Slack, 1979.
5. Rossi, .A.M.: General Methodological Considerations. In *Sensory Deprivation: Fifteen Years of Research,* edited by J.P. Zubek. New York: Appleton-Century Crofts, 1969.
6. Daffner, C.: Personal correspondence, 1976.
7. Zuckerman, M.: Hallucinations: Reported Sensations and Images. In *Sensory Deprivation: Fifteen Years of Research,* edited by J.P. Zubek. New York: Appleton-Century Crofts, 1969.
8. Suedfeld, P.: Changes in Intellectual performance and in Susceptibility to Influence. In *Sensory Deprivation: Fifteen Years of Research,* edited by J.P. Zubek, New York: Appleton-Century Crofts, 1969.
9. Foley, J.M.: Sensations and Behavior. In *Neurological and Sensory Disorders in the Elderly,* edited by W.S. Fields. New York: Stratton Intercontinental Medical Book, 1975.
10. O'Neill, P.M. and Calhoun, K.S.: Sensory Deficits and Behavioral Deterioration in Senescence. *Journal of Abnormal Psychology,* 84: 579-582; 1975.
11. Denny, N.: Classification Abilities in the Elderly. *Journal of Gerontology,* 29: 309-314; 1974.
12. Riegal, K.: Dialectic Operation, The Final Period of Cognitive Development. *Human Development,* 16: 346-370; 1973.
13. Pauplia, D.E. and Reily, D.D.: Cognitive Function in Middle and Old Age Adults; A Review of Research Based on Piaget's Theory. *Human Development,* 17: 424-443; 1974.
14. Klopfer, W.G.: The Rorschach and Old Age. *Journal of Personality Assessment,* 38: 420-422; 1974.

15. Gaylord, S.A. and Marsh, G.R.: Age Differences in the Speed of a Cognitive Process. *Journal of Gerontology*, 30: 674-678; 1975.
16. Waugh, N.C., Fozard, J.L., Tolland, G.A. and Erwin, D.E.: Effects of Age and Stimulus Repetition on a Two Choice Reaction Time. *Journal of Gerontology*, 28: 466-470; 1973.
17. Botwinick, J. and Storandt, M.: Speed Functions, Vocabulary, Ability and Age. *Perception and Motor Skills*, 36(3), Part 2; June 1973.
18. Smith, A.D.: Response Interference with Organized Recall in the Aged. *Developmental Psychology*, 10: 867-870; 1974.
19. Foley, J.: (See above.)
20. Hermelin, B.: "Seeing and Hearing and Space and Time." Presented at the Conference on Neural and Developmental Bases of Spatial Orientation, Teachers College, Columbia University, New York, November 17, 1979.
21. Buell, S.J. and Coleman, P.D.: Dendritic Growth in the Aged Human Brain and Failure of Growth in Senile Dementia. *Science*, 206: 854-856; November 1979.
22. Eccles, J.C.: *The Understanding of the Brain.* New York: McGraw Hill, 1972.
23. Piaget, J.: Intellectual Evaluation From Adolescence to Adulthood. *Human Development*, 151: 1-12; 1972.

7. Environmental Influences on Perception and Performance in Aging

Environment and the relationship that a person establishes with his living environment is important to individual performance within that environment. The living environment in which one finds oneself dictates human performance. This relationship of functional ability to environment has profound implication for the elderly. Some environments in which the elderly live are conducive to health. Some residential choices may profess to be intended for health care, but indeed may ill serve their stated intention. Care of the elderly ill in this country takes place in several environments. Elderly are served medically in their homes, in hospitals and in nursing homes. Each of these may be familiar or unfamiliar environments, depending upon a variety of factors including length of residency and the degree of interaction they have experienced therein. Each of these environments can facilitate or inhibit function and mobility.

The home has been shown to be an effective treatment environment for the aged ill all over the world. In our own country, that home may be the home in which the resident has raised a family and has had a variety of experiences freely directed. One's own home, however, familiar and loved, at the end of life may restrict liberties. A residence of 70 years may become a prison when the bedroom and bathroom are up a flight of unmanageable stairs, making it inaccessible to both resident and friends. Or the home in which the older person lives may be the home of his son or daughter, in which no personal rights are perceived by the client. The tendency today is for people to live in nuclear family units in which rights are determined by ownership, not age. The elderly relative often is seen as an extra person not quite fitting into the core family without considerable adjustment. Roles and responsibilities are unclear or a source of conflict. For example, the kitchen may be off limits.

"It's not safe."

"It's not Mother's place."

"I don't want her to have to work so hard."

"Having Mother help out takes too long."

"Two women in the kitchen is one too many."

The elderly relative may look upon matters from another perspective.

"They're so short with me."

"The living room has toys strewn about and I'm afraid of falling."

"They like to entertain there and don't want an old lady's company."

"I can't hear the conversation anyway."

"It's so far to the bathroom and I can't get there in time."

> "I'm so ashamed when I'm wet, but I can't tell when I have to go."

> "I'm better off in my room."

Too often, the result is reduced mobility and greater isolation.

In a health care facility, things may not be better. There are routines to be followed. The sick patient often must stay in bed, or may be transferred for his outing to his bedside chair. Mobility is not simplified. Biased attitudes along with pressuring responsibilities color behavior.

> "Wheelchairs clutter the corridors, and besides, we need them to transport patients to therapy."

> "Old people need lots of help."

> "Here Mother, let me feed you. It's faster."

> "It's faster to bed pan a patient than take the time to transfer her to the toilet."

The patient is complaining of pain.

> "Let's not hurt her by moving her. Dr. Crotchet will have our heads if we get any more complaints from the family."

> "The patient was up all night, agitated."

> "Let's order some Haldol and see if everyone can get some sleep tonight."

> "Patient's disoriented. Diagnosis, organic brain syndrome."

The kiss of death. No one recovers from that. Or if he does, it must have been an acute variety. Not acute blood loss following surgery, depriving the system of vital oxygen to the brain; not reaction to anesthesia or mood altering drugs; not relocation; not stress or fear.

"Mother's not the same anymore."

"We can't take care of that Foley catheter. We work all day. Who will feed her, keep her clean? Let's find a nursing home."

"You go there to die."

"I promised Mother I'd never put her into one of those places. And now I have to break my promise. Daddy asked me always to take care of her. But we don't have room. The bedroom is upstairs. The children need their lives too. And how can I quit work? There's Betty's college tuition. And Joe's business is doing worse. Expenses are going up."

Dilemma and guilt. Families frequently cannot allow themselves to believe that Mother can do things for herself while still justifying her nursing home residency. For, indeed, if she is able to care for herself, her need for nursing home residency may be suspect. Families often seek out nursing homes which will treat their parent exactly the way they fantasize that that person should be treated, 'better' than they would. Rest and total bed care is too often their ideal.

LET ALL THOSE WHO ENTER HERE BE FEEBLE!

In order to withstand the traumatic experience implicit in relocation to a nursing home, in order to prevail against heightened anxiety, in order to elect to advance in living, the patient must be able to muster the wherewithal to meet the unknown with courage. The patient must also be able to view himself as having potential, a difficult image to muster when he recognizes the attitudes of others toward himself. Patients can elect either to control their change-stimulated anxiety by remaining within the familiarity of their rooms, or learn to live with, relate to, and participate in the unfamiliar. Schactel (1959)[1] has stated that remaining with the familiar has the "character of a flight activity", and has said of human performance in states of anxiety:

> "The determination to go forward to such encounters keeps the doors open to an expanding life while the seeking of protection in the embeddedness of the familiar makes for stagnation and constriction of life."

It is precisely the ability to encounter which can be facilitated and tolerated through graded approaches to living. If one does not, then,

> "the disruptive, paralyzing function leaves no such choice; its function is to make man avoid the separation from embeddedness by paralyzing him and taking away from him the power of decision and action."

The understanding of the difference between fear and anxiety has also been well expressed by Schactel.

> "It has often been remarked that the difference between anxiety and fear is that while both are related to expectation, while both are about something, in anxiety the object of the expectation is unknown, while in fear it is known."

Perhaps this is so, but the difference may also lie in the issue of control. That which one can potentially control, that which one can understand and can deal with, does not lie within the realm of anxiety. Once a situation is known, it can be dealt with. When it is so overwhelming that control cannot be potentiated, anxiety results. The unfamiliar yields anxiety. The residence the elderly person encounters when disability occurs is often unfamiliar and stress provoking. This residence is often a nursing home.

A nursing home is an institution. The best of nursing homes is still an institution. The word institution causes one to conceptualize an ill-suited environment. Yet a nursing home can and should be a suitable alternative where restorative care can be provided for the elderly disabled. Good nursing homes exist, and can permit independence and control to their residents. Nursing homes should be thought of as minimal care facilities, with the goal being the attainment of minimal care and maximum independence for each resident. Unfortunately, too many nursing homes are organized to provide maximum efficiency in the care of patients who reside therein, to the exclusion of personalized attention to individual patient needs. Maximum efficiency means that each patient must be fed, cleaned, medicated and entertained with effectiveness and concern for the needs of all. Too often this care is provided in a fashion which denies the needs of individuals, while paper proposals relating to total care and discharge planning are studiously prepared. It is, however, possible to provide cost-effective treatment which does attend to individual patient needs. A conscious concern for their life space, with attention placed on familiarizing patients with their total environment and its relationship to themselves through interaction with its space, is appropriate and necessary for those residents of nursing homes.

In order to move about, perform and relate with ease, individuals must be facile in their interactions with space, objects and persons within their environment. This facility is aided by familiarity and certainty about that environment. Predictable response dictates people's inclination to perform. Certain awareness of distance and of the energy requirements necessary for performance permit individuals to make judgments about their interactions with their environment. Predictable human response from others also dictates inclinations to act and interact. People tend to attempt that at which they are assured potential success, and that which will provide them consentual affirmation. Risk is taken only when probability of success is felt, or when the rewards are potentially sufficient to warrant the risk. Some risks are of a short term nature, some long term. Some actions entail great willingness to risk self. There are some things people accept the risks of easily. But small risks to some are great risks to others. To lose at a game can be insignificant or defeating depending upon one's orientation. Priorities people establish determine the value or worth they attribute to activities. As development proceeds, people ordinarily become increasingly willing to take larger risks. The taking of larger risks, however, is dependent upon success experiences in earlier behaviors. Inherent in the taking of risks is that invested effort is a feature of success. One must feel that it is worthwhile to expend effort. Anticipation of positive responses is a prerequisite for risk experience. Normal human beings do not expose themselves to risk unless reward is anticipated by that exposure.

A familiar environment is devoid of many features of risk. If one has had previous experience with a given environment, one has already had to deal with the newness of experience which that environment offers. It is commonly accepted that new experiences are fraught with anxiety. First experiences entail risk and stress. Anxieties associated with the new job, the first day of school and the traditional wedding night are related to unfamiliarity expressed in terms of territory, space, relationships and altered self.

Familiarity with environment and anticipation of reencountering that environment has been shown to be a factor of perception created within that environment (Edney, 1972b)[2]. Environmental experiential factors determined by testing and clinical evidence have been cited as pertinent to the acquisition and maintenance of cognitive abilities in old age (Schultz, 1976)[3].

In order to perform efficiently in an unfamiliar environment, there must be awareness of surroundings through integration of all sensory inputs. Confusion results when different sensory mechanisms report divergent information. Inability to rely on formerly dependable information systems is extremely threatening. This may account for the inferiority which has been reported manifest among the aged (Klopfer, 1974)[4].

The ability to remember how to move through space is vital to function. This ability is automatically available throughout life. When disability occurs, movement becomes limited, whereupon recollection of movement patterns diminishes with disuse. Difficulty in locomotion, which accompanies disability, interferes with adaptation to environment. Performance in the lateral fields seems more likely to diminish than performance in the frontal fields. The periphery is not as well served by the normal physiology and function of man. Lateral arm movements are not ordinarily necessary in order to function in the stable milieu of the disabled. Most necessary bed performance occurs in frontal position. Performance of tasks is generally restricted to the frontal field. Foveal vision is necessary to performance of frontal tasks. When one is still and attendant to the front alone, peripheral vision is not utilized or stimulated. But both movement of objects and movement of self through space causes stimulation of the peripheral retinal field. Peripheral vision receives diminished stimulation when movement is reduced. Peripheral vision is a supportive visual system providing orienting and alerting, permitting and enhancing functional performance. Conscious awareness of information available in the periphery is not ordinarily present either to the patient or to the therapist. But when the periphery serves to alert, response to the periphery occurs even without conscious attention. Thus reflexive responses to alerting cause movement which result in enhanced orientation when the focus of attention becomes the frontal field. Repeated movements convert to a subcortical storage model where these patterns remain available in order to release the orientation function from attention as occurs in habit or skill development. Familiarity of environment reduces the necessity for this process to take place.

Environments which patients are exposed to are not only unfamiliar to them, but are too often restrictive of their movement. Health care environments tend to restrict patient movement. Bed railings, close quarters, medical equipment, bed heights and the absence of clothing and/or mobilization aids all serve to retain patients in or around their assigned beds. Medical or nursing restriction frequently and inadvertently contribute to effect immobilization upon the patient. All too often, patients become increasingly debilitated physically and emotionally from the circumstances of their environment to a greater degree than their admitting illness. Medical or nursing procedures are often devised for staff efficiency, enhancing decline in sensory input and mobility beyond the awareness of the practitioner. Adaptation to the needs of hospital and staff causes an inherent denial of concern for patient needs, even if lip service to patients' needs is professed. Attention to the effect of procedures and regulations upon the patient is advisable in order to reduce the devastating isolation and immobility which occur with disability.

The health care environment constantly gives clues to the patient which indicate to him that moving out of personal territory is contraindicated. Elsewhere is others' territory. Going elsewhere is an act of invasion. But invasion requires aggression (Lorenz, 1974)[5]. The aggression required to enhance territorial outreach is absent in the ill. A dynamically active limbic system is necessary for active incursion into foreign territory. Reduced movement both results from and results in retreat to the only territory perceived by the patient as his own.

Superficially, it is obvious that lack of movement of self enhances weakness and debilitation. Yet it is absence of movement within space causing perceptual dysfunction which is a further concern. The difficulty in mobility which is encountered in 'health care' environments reduces the very orientation necessary to efficient perceptual functioning. In order to maintain or enhance functional perception and interaction with the environment, it is necessary to stimulate those systems which offer derived spatial orientation. Propulsion, particularly self induced, yields increased orientation within space. Vestibular stimulation has been shown to be of necessity in neonates, learning disabled children and psychiatric patients (Wilbarger, 1978[6], Ayres, 1972[7]; King, 1974[8]). It is not less so in the elderly who are suffering sensory decline and induced sensory conflict, along with sensory deprivation and relocation. The kinesthetic systems of tactile, proprioceptive and vestibular derivation appear to be particularly critical in response to reduced stimulation. The reticular formation has been cited for its response to movement (Moore, 1978)[9] as well as the thalamic region associated with affect. Experimentation with normal subjects has demonstrated aberrant psychological reactions, including hallucination and confusion, when sensory deprivation has been provided (Zuckerman, 1969)[10]. Movement appears to be critical to the normalization of neurological and psychological tone.

Movement is not a conscious element of health care. It is foreign to the orientation of most health professionals. In the eyes of most nursing staffs and of patients themselves, patients are there to be assisted. So often, when patients have demonstrated their independent capabilities, they have requested that this information remain unshared with anyone who will expect them to perform, even when this self imvolvement would produce a tone of self competence. Even the patient who is capable of mobility is restrained in his mobility because his actions are perceived to interfere with 'routine'. Patients do not wish to be veiwed as 'uncooperative' lest they be denied services they deem necessary at the time that they wish them.

Each factor preventing mobilization must be attended to, and eliminated or modified, to maximize the patients' mobility, in order to instill orientation in the patient along with feelings of self responsibility and worth. Rehabilitation is designed to maximize the functional performance of the individual. Without maximal movement experiences within the environment, functional performance is seriously inhibited. An honest look at the real reasons for patient immobility must be taken and effort made to reduce the influence of artificial or arbitrary hindrances to patient mobility. Sometimes it is necessary to alter the environment. Floors, doorways, corridors, location of furniture and furniture itself should be designed or modified for the maximum locomotion and performance of patients. All too often, furniture is placed for the convenience of housekeeping or other staff or to please aesthetic sensibilities of the administrator. Bed locks should be secure. Often they are not, for the convenience of the staff in cleaning or transport. Patients who are insecure about moving will not and should not jeopardize their precarious vestibular systems by using unstable equipment. It is security in movement which should be established so that patients can automatize their movements rather than deal with movement on a cortical level. Moving, utilizing cortical systems, enhances insecurity (Moore, 1978)[11], and results in decreased willingness to move. Decreased mobility, in turn, provides sensory deprivation, and thus depressed reticular activation.

In order to facilitate patient mobility, each patient who is not fully independent in ambulation must have a wheelchair, walker or other appropriate aid available to him at all times and must be well trained in the use of these aids. Patients may require special adaptations made for their wheelchair so that it best serves their particular needs. Adapting wheelchairs for individual use can decrease immobility. In too many hospitals and nursing homes, wheelchairs are for universal usage, rather than specifically assigned and adapted to the use of particular patients. It is not necessary that the patient only be provided an appropriate wheelchair if at a rehabilitation center. Early application of rehabilitation principles can be provided in all health care environments. One way in which wheelchairs can be adapted to individual needs is by suspending urinary irrigants from them. Wheelchairs adapted in this fashion are less restricting than pole plus chair. (Figure 7-1) Staff are less likely to move cumbersome equipment. Patients requiring urinary irrigation are ordinarily incapable of moving a wheelchair without such rigging. Patients must be instructed in transfer techniques, and encouraged to practice these skills until supervision is no longer necessary, as measured by patient performance. Easily available clothing, along with skill in self dressing techniques, enhances mobility. Patients should have clothing accessible to them, within their easy reach, permitting their self care. The use of diapers can serve to reinforce incontinency. Closures on diapers are difficult to manage without assistance,

Figure 7-1

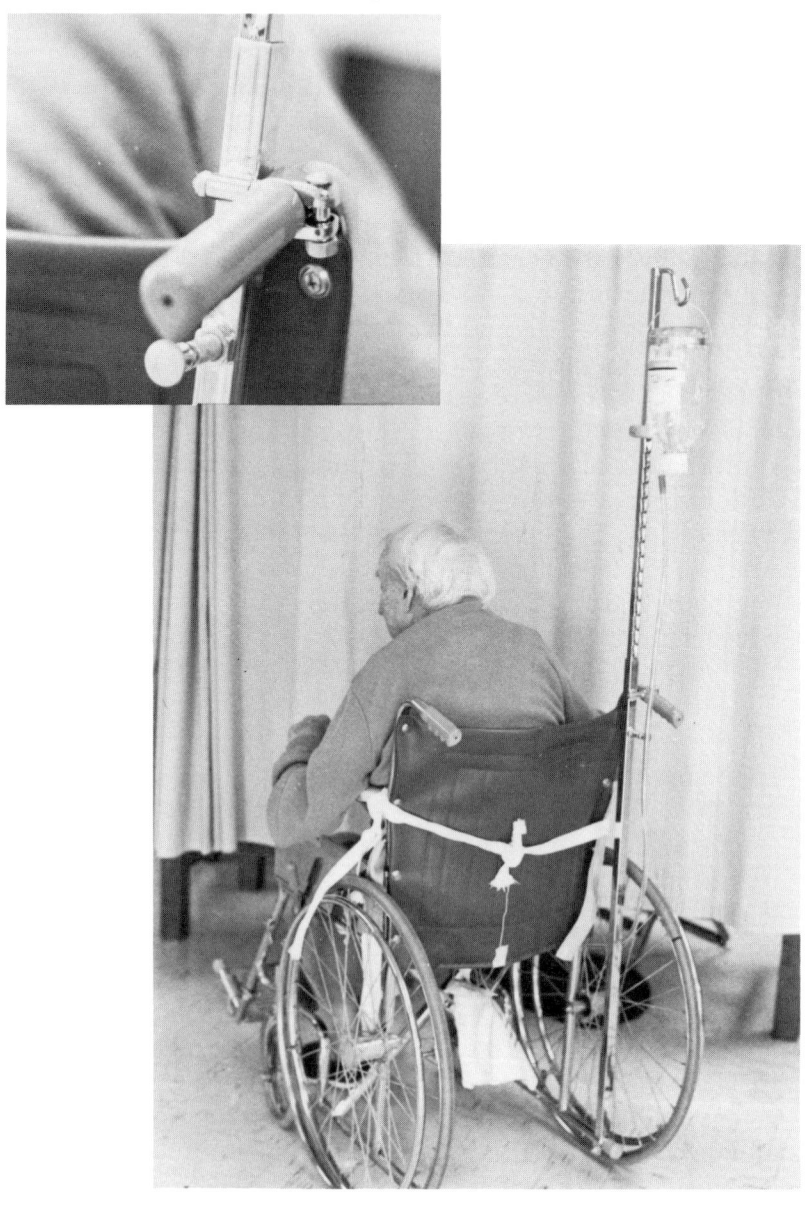

A wheelchair adapted with an irrigant pole permits mobility to the patient, whereas freestanding equipment is impossible for the patient and difficult for the staff to maneuver.

particularly when balance is insecure. A patient who can transfer and manage underpants is more likely to achieve continency, confidence and respect, in self and from others.

Destinations to which patients are expected to go should be incorporated into patients' programs. Mobility should be expected as part of the patient's plan for self. Staff and families should be instructed not to aid patients in movement if the patient is at all able to proceed independently. Graded partial independence in mobility is invaluable, as well as graded utilization of learned skills, as a requisite and effective treatment measure.

The best treatment for the reduction of fear of movement is movement itself. Habituation enhances skill. Use of skills within the living environment provides a means for the development of perceptual constancy through the resolution of sensory conflicts by experience within the environment (Breines, 1978)[12].

The comfort in familiar surroundings which the elderly express and the desire of many to remain in their own homes, may be attributed to the discomfort they feel in unfamiliar environs. Pastalan (1974)[13] proposed that housing environments for the aged be designed with awareness of the psychosocial and physiological changes which occur in the life cycle. He reported that the organization of space should be such that compensation be permitted for sensory deterioration and the reduction of life space that occurs in aging. The elderly should be able to maintain use of their environment for stimulation and prevention of further functional decline. Skill in evaluating function and environment clearly defines the therapist's role here.

As function decreases, perceptual function decreases, resulting in reduction of the human organism's ability to adapt to a changing environment. Those disorders which restrict locomotion interfere with adaptation to environment. Living schemes of the elderly which cut down on activity reduce function. The aged, in effect, become subject to sensory deprivation as a facet of living. Sensory deprivation experiments give evidence of the need for environmental stimulation as an alerting and orienting condition.

Yet individuals adapt throughout their lifetimes. Adaptation, however, is easier and quicker within a familiar environment as people age. Learning which has taken place in younger years serves one well in aging. Perceptual constancy orients one in a familiar locale. The overstuffed chair remains the same conceptual size, despite the changing feedback information as receptors conflict in information processed. Perceptual constancy is a requisite to function. When perceptions are not reliable, as occurs in children with learning disabilities, there is interference in the ability to build upon experience (Bartley, 1969)[14]. Unintegrated reflexes and/or interference in sensory input and/or the integration of inputs are factors which interfere with accurate perceptual functioning. Losses in sensory proficiency functioning in combination with relocation, are proposed as possible contributors to disabilities often seen in the aged. To counteract deficits experienced through dysfunction, relocation and disorientation, familiarization with environment through self directed mobility is recommended.

REFERENCES
Chapter 7. Environmental Influences on Perception and Performance in Aging

1. Schactel, E.G.: *Metamorphosis; On the Development of Affect, Perception, Attention and Memory.* New York: Basic Books, 1959.
2. Edney, J.J.: Place and Space: The Effects of Experience With A Physical Locale. *Journal of Experimental Social Psychology, 8: 124-135; 1972b.*
3. Schultz, N.R. and Mayer, W.J.: Feedback Effects on Spatial Egocentrism In Old Age. *Journal of Gerontology,* 31(1): 72-75; 1976.
4. Klopfer, W.G.: The Rorschach and Old Age. *Journal of Personality Assessment,* 38: 420-422; 1974.
5. Lorenz, K.: *On Aggression.* New York: Harcourt, Brace, 1974.
6. Wilbarger, P.: "Clinical Aspects of Vestibular Stimulation." Presented at the Conference on the Vestibular System, Washington University, St. Louis, Missouri, June 1978.

7. Ayres, A.J.: *Sensory Integration and the Treatment of Learning Disabilities.* Los Angeles: Western Psychological Services, 1972a.
8. King, L.J.: A Sensory Integrative Approach to Schizophrenia. *American Journal of Occupational Therapy,* 28: 529-536; 1974.
9. Moore, J.: "Neuroanatomical Aspects of the Vestibular System." Presented at the Conference on the Vestibular System, Washington University, St. Louis, Missouri, June 1978.
10. Zuckerman, M.: Hallucinations; Reported Sensations and Images. In *Sensory Deprivation: Fifteen Years of Research,* edited by J.P. Zubek, New York: Appleton-Century Crofts, 1969.
11. Moore, J.: (See above.)
12. Breines, E.: *Perceptual Changes in Aging.* Lebanon, New Jersey: Geri-Rehab, 1980.
13. Pastalan, L.: The Stimulation of Age-Related Losses: A New Approach to the Study of Environmental Barriers. *New Outlook for the Blind,* 68: 356-362; 1974.
14. Bartley, S.: *Principles of Perception.* New York: Harper and Row, 1969.

8. Experimental Studies Concerned With Environment and Proprioceptive Memory

Conditions which have demonstrated themselves to be critical to performance in the elderly have shown themselves to be environment, recall of space, and loss of sensory inputs and relationships. Mobility and peripheral stimulation have also been seen to modify performance. Each of these factors are inextricably united within functional performance; but in order to analyze their contribution toward function, it is necessary to measure their role and contribution. Proprioceptive memory and perceptual performance in different environments are two aspects of function which have not as yet been well studied. Each influence function in space. An attempt has been made to gather some data to help enlighten us in the direction further study should take.

Accurate proprioceptive functioning tells the body's parts where they are, as movement shifts the relationships of body parts to one another. That movement occurs within an external world. Some of that world is familiar, some unfamiliar. In order to evaluate evidence of environmental perception and performance differences in aging, it seemed necessary to assess a population of elderly citizens in their response to perceptual testing, comparing their responses on perceptual tests within both familiar and unfamiliar environments. In an effort to reduce the artifacts inherent in illness and in change of life style, a population of well elderly people were sought who resided in their own homes, conducting their normal lives. It was hypothesized that proficiency on perceptual testing would diminish in an unfamiliar environment and that this could be demonstrated in an elderly population. It had been indicated in the literature (Corso, 1971)[1], that visual perception is considerably affected by age, that perceptions persevere, and that there are significant differences in perception between older and younger subjects, with older subjects less flexible in judgment and demonstrating poorer performance in extracting information from complex figure configurations. This evidence, combined with personal clinical experience with patients treated in hospitals, in their own homes and in nursing homes, led to the hypothesis that familiarity of environment would provide better perceptual skills. As a result, an experiment was devised to test the hypothesis that people over 60 years of age would demonstrate better visual perception in a familiar environment than in an unfamiliar environment (Breines, 1977)[2].

Experiment A

The subjects were twenty healthy volunteers over 60 years of age. Seven subjects were male; thirteen subjects were female. All were residents of Hunterdon County, a rural, white community in western New Jersey. Contact with subjects was made through the assistance of the Hunterdon County Office on Aging, through personal contact and by word of mouth.

Subjects were tested with both the Ravens Coloured Progressive Matrices[3] and a Spatial Illusion Test for Midpoint Identification devised for this experiment. (Figure 8-1) Subjects were tested both at their own homes, which served as the familiar environment, and at the researcher's home, which served as the unfamiliar environment. The researcher's home was selected because it would serve as a

Studies Concerned with Environmental and Proprioceptive Memory

constant source of unfamiliarity to each of the subjects, and was a local residence similar in many respects to their own homes. All the subjects lived within thirty minutes driving time from the researcher's home, and no subject had ever before visited this house. They were driven to and from their homes for testing by the researcher. Each was alone in the car with the researcher, except for two married couples, who travelled together with the researcher.

Subjects served as their own controls as each was tested two times, one time in the familiar home, one time in the unfamiliar home. Alternating random selection determined which site was used for the initial test in an effort to control for test familiarity. Subjects were telephoned in advance to set up appointments. It was explained to the subjects that the study required normal adults over the age of sixty, and was designed to learn how people over sixty see. It was also presented to those who were approached, that many studies of the elderly are done with populations of sick people in nursing homes and that it was necessary to achieve the cooperation of well people who are able to function in their own homes. Subjects were informed that a letter was filed with the Hunterdon County Office on Aging stating that the project was being performed as part of graduate studies. Subjects were assured that names and addresses were needed only to enable the researcher to find their homes, and that they were not to be graded as individuals. Only their age and scores would be of interest to the researcher. Subjects were told they would not receive individual scores following testing, but overall results of the study would be shared with them when the study was concluded. At the conclusion of the study, a copy of the thesis was filed with the Office on Aging and subjects were advised of its availability.

Ravens Coloured Progressive Matrices were selected because they had been designed for use with young children and old people, for anthropological studies and for clinical work. It is a test which can be used with people who have communication problems associated with both physical dysfunction and unfamiliarity with a language. It was not designed to be a test of intelligence in its sole use. The thirty-six problems in the three sets of twelve were designed to assess mental development up to the stage of ability to reason by analogy. This ability to reason by analogy had been reported to be the earliest to decline in later life.

Success on the Ravens is not restricted by slowed motor or analytical capacity, as the test is untimed. Little verbal explanation is necessary. Selection of one of six figures is required to accurately complete a form which is located directly above the choice figures. The figures are brightly colored. The complexity of choice increases within each set of twelve figures. The book form of the test was administered and a separate answer sheet was provided to each subject. The answer sheets consisted of three numbered columns within which the subject wrote the correctly numbered answer. This test was selected because it has been validated on a population of normal older persons as well as on elderly depressives and on those with senile dementia.

The Spatial Illusion Test for Midpoint Identification was devised and included because the experimenter felt that a gross task could possibly test different capabilities. It was quick and easy to perform. There were no right or wrong answers, thereby presenting no risk to the subject. It assessed the subjects' evaluation of space. In this test, subjects were asked to estimate the midpoint of a paperboard strip, 3½"x49", placed on the floor. A black plastic sheet, 3½"x6', made from a garbage disposal bag, was placed under the strip to eliminate the possibility of estimating size by cues on the floor. The paperboard strip was placed on the black plastic sheet with the narrow border of the paperboard placed against an adhesive tape mark. Subjects stood on the plastic sheet facing the paperboard so that it was perpendicular to the subjects' feet which were touching another adhesive tape mark located 12" before the paperboard. The pointer, a short pool cue, was marked with chalk by the researcher and was handed to the subjects. Subjects were asked to draw a line with the pointer, as nearly as possible dividing the paperboard in half across the width. Subjects were praised for their performance each time.

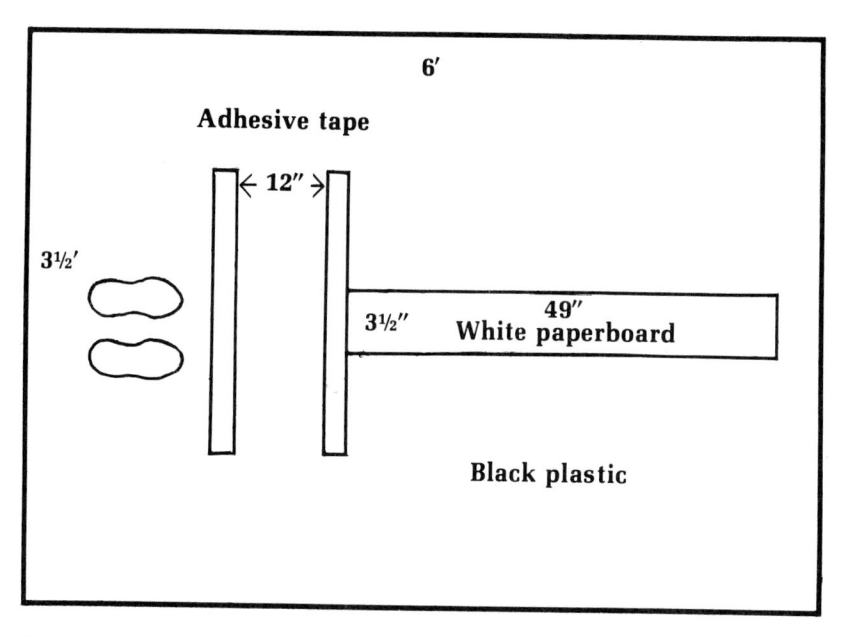

Studies Concerned with Environmental and Proprioceptive Memory 163

Figure 8-1.

Diagram of placement of materials for Spatial Illusion Test for Midpoint Identification.

The data were analyzed for all subjects without regard to sex. As can be seen in Figure 8-3, there was a tendency for subjects to perform better in the familiar environment than in the unfamiliar environment on the Ravens. A t-test on this data showed the trend was not significant. (T=1.03, P=.16). As can be seen in Figure 8-4, there was a tendency for subjects to perform better in the unfamiliar environment than in the familiar environment on the Midpoint Identification Test. A t-test on this data showed the trend was not significant (T=.94, P=.18).

Only for the Ravens did the data show a tendency to support the hypothesis that elderly people would perform better on perceptual tasks in a familiar environment. Data from the Spatial Illusion Test for Midpoint Identification showed an opposite trend in that subjects performed better in the

164 PERCEPTION: ITS DEVELOPMENT AND RECAPITULATION

Figure 8-2.

RESULTS

Table 1 shows the distribution of ages of the subjects. The median age was 71.

Table 1
Distribution of Ages of Subjects

Ages of Subjects	
	60
	65
	66
	66
	67
	67
	68
	70
	71
	71
	71
	72
	75
	80
	82
	83
	84
	86
	87
	90

Figure 8-3

Mean Scores on Ravens Coloured Progressive Matrices, Familiar and Unfamiliar Environments

	Mean Errors
Ravens, familiar environment	5.9
Ravens, unfamiliar environment	7.2

Figure 8-4

Mean Scores of Spatial Illusion Test for Midpoint Identification, Familiar and Unfamiliar Environments

	Millimeters from midpoint
Midpoint, familiar environment	27.9 mm.
Midpoint, unfamiliar environment	23.9 mm.

unfamiliar environment. The difference between trends was unexpected. Attention was directed to possible explanations for the results obtained. In comparing these two tests, it can be noted that each measures different skills. The degree of cortical versus subcortical functional primacy differs between tests. The Ravens is a visual perception test requiring conscious decision making. Inherent in the Ravens is no gross physical performance skill. In order to perform accurately, it is necessary to select from among specific finite responses in which a right or wrong answer exists. Subjects probably assume that there is only one correct response and that correctness is in some way a measure of their intelligence and thereby worth. On the other hand, Midpoint Identification was probably not viewed as a measure of self worth or intelligence by the subjects. There are gross motor skill components in this test. Subjects perceived themselves as accurate when they approximated the midline within several inches. This difference in the way subjects perceived the two tests may account in part for the different results. Perhaps subjects perform better in a familiar environment only when they perceive a task to be related to their intellectual functioning or worth.

Subjects seemed more cautious in assessing the paperboard before marking it in the unfamiliar environment, whereas they appeared to perform more confidently at home, though less accurately. This subjective appraisal could have been monitored by timing performance, if this response had been anticipated. Possibly subjects could do better if they tried harder in the familiar environment, which they did not appear to do. Perhaps their comfort within the familiar environment interfered in some way with the ability to perform newly learned gross motor tasks.

The position of the subjects during testing differed in both tests. The Ravens was administered while the subject was seated. Attention was restricted to that which is ordinarily experienced in a table task. The person and the environment was still. The Midpoint Identification was performed while the subject was standing and had been recently mobile. Central nervous system alerting mechanisms may have served to enhance sensory motor function within the unfamiliar environment, or positioning or mobility may alter effects in some way. Differences between systems utilized to perform these different tasks may be facilitated or inhibited in the same way that has been shown in sensory deprivation experiments. (Zubek, 1969)[4].

The effect of constancy in perceiving things as previously accustomed may account for the greater inaccuracy in subjects' homes where familiarity may actually alter the perception of items newly introduced to the environment. In the completely new environment, each thing is assessed in relation to each other new thing and thereby viewed in relation to one another. A well adult population, although aged, surely does not show decline in spatial awareness regarding newly encountered surrounds.

Studying the normal aged in the manner of this experiment was fraught with difficulty. A brief test normally administered in less than ten minutes became an enormously time consuming project. Elderly people in their own setting have control over their own time frame. It was necessary for the researcher to sublimate her needs to those of the subjects in order to effect maximum cooperation. In much laboratory experimentation, this is not the case.

Subjects were difficult to obtain. Resistance was encountered on several scores. Among them were, not wanting to be a 'guinea pig', fear in regard to the motives of the examiner, insecurity about being able to perform adequately, aprehension about being compared to others, concern about traveling in hazardous weather, and being too busy. Several confirmed appointments resulted in no data, because the subjects changed their minds for one reason or another after the arrival of the examiner. On the other hand, several subjects made obtaining additional subjects their personal project.

Those subjects who cooperated with the examiner and participated in the experiment may have reflected a unique segment of the population and were not necessarily representative of the aged population they purport to represent. The data thereby obtained from these cooperative older citizens might be biased because data from those individuals who refused might yield a different picture of perceptual ability. It is conceivable that refusal to participate reflects insecurity which may be related to perceptual decline. Ability or willingness to cope with risk may be associated with function within a given environment.

Exposure to all the normal aged encountered during examination, even those who were not able to or did not wish to participate in the experiment, was a valuable learning experience regarding attitudes, life styles and philosophy of the aged. No difficulty encountered obscured this at any time. In order to understand the aged, it is necessary to encounter them on their own ground and on their own terms. Those individuals of 87 and 93 years of age who were genuinely too busy with their own lives to participate in an experiment, although gracious in their refusal, may tell us more about the criteria for health and function in aging than anything experimental studies have thus far revealed.

Experiment B

Having found evidence that perceptual testing often measures different aspects of function than those functions which the investigator intended to explore, invited inquiry regarding which factors in perception and performance seemed to differ between elderly and younger adult populations. In the aged ill, a tendency had been observed toward differences between ranges of upper extremity performance. Ranges of performance means those areas of function directly before the subject, compared to those

Figure 8-5
Raw Data, Ravens and Midpoint Identification, Familiar and Unfamiliar Environs

Subjects	Sex	Age	Ravens, fam.	Ravens, unfam.	Midpoint, fam.	Midpoint, unfam.
1	F	80	18	24	26	28
2	M	87	12	8	41	31
3	F	67	3	5	22	16
4	F	83	10	13	25	24
5	M	66	4	9	15	11
6	F	84	8	3	5	4
7	M	86	4	3	46	60
8	F	68	9	4	6	8
9	F	70	1	9	18	8
10	M	71	4	5	34	29
11	F	66	0	1	7	1
12	M	75	0	1	64	0
13	F	60	2	2	33	47
14	F	82	4	3	15	45
15	F	72	1	1	35	3
16	F	71	1	0	20	9
17	M	67	2	4	28	35
18	M	71	19	12	32	31
19	F	65	2	4	45	18
20	F	90	15	33	41	64

Odd # Ss were tested first in unfamiliar environment.
Even # Ss were tested first in familiar environment.
Ravens scores are expressed in terms of errors.
Midpoint scores are expressed in terms of mm. deviated from center.

lateral to the subject. Nursing home residents with whom this investigator was most familiar, are generally seen seated, usually in wheelchairs. When seated, these persons frequently had been noted to have adequate performance and manipulative skill when they performed in front of themselves. Often, despite the absence of diagnosed neurological disease, these same individuals exhibited difficulty in the performance of unilateral manipulative skills, when the upper extremities are lateral to the body, a skill necessary to wheelchair travel. Proprioceptive memory appeared to be impaired in lateral ranges. Some degree of astereognosis had frequently been demonstrated to be associated with this loss. This deficit seriously hampers the ability to operate a wheelchair. Recognition and recollection of hand position appeared absent or seriously impaired. Attempts to grasp wheelchair arms rather than wheels had been noted repeatedly, indicating inability to differentiate wheelchair armrests from the wheels, even in patients who were cognitively aware and had received instruction in wheelchair use. These patients need to turn and look at their hands to cause correct placement of their hands and thus use of the wheelchair. It is only following hours or days of practice that this visual ascertainment is no longer required. It was also noted that as wheelchair proficiency and usage increased, affect normalized and skill in other areas increased as well. Conjecturing about what might be occurring in wheelchair travel led to several observations. Stimulation of the periphery of vision and of upper extremity function seemed somehow to be associated. It was observed that when the arms are efficiently used in wheelchair travel, the eyes are focused ahead. As travel proceeds, the periphery of vision becomes stimulated by the change experience offered by movement of space into and past the periphery. In propulsion, change is greater to the retinal fields of the periphery than foveal ranges of vision. Observing patients in whom wheelchair skill grew, it appeared that a reestablishment of utilization of peripheral field function may have wider effects than initially suspected. However, it is uncertain whether peripheral upper extremity function or peripheral vision is generating the effect. Reduced peripheral vision has been attributed to occur in the elderly, both as a condition of aging or as a function of lenses to correct vision following cataract surgery, a common occurrence in the elderly. Data on proprioceptive memory comparing various fields of function in either young or old did not appear to be available. It seemed necessary to determine measurements of normal proprioceptive memory in lateral function in order to speculate upon the importance of lateral function to perceptual development and thus to the regeneration of that development in the aged.

Keeping these considerations in mind, an experiment was devised to obtain base line data from a well population, comparing memory for arm placement in several areas of space with which one could ultimately compare the effects of aging and illness on this aspect of proprioceptive memory. Those areas delineated for study were described as the far frontal field, the near frontal field, the near lateral field and the far lateral field (Figure 8-6). The frontal field (1) was defined as those four positions directly before the foveal visual field of the subject, had vision not been occluded. Lateral field (2) was defined as those four positions lateral to the side to the body for which peripheral vision would be necessary, had vision not been occluded. Both the dominant and the non-dominant sides were tested.

It was hypothesized that memory would be more accurate for movement of the dominant than of the non-dominant upper extremity; that age might be a factor in frontal and lateral function differences; and that frontal field function would be more accurate than lateral field function. Twenty adult subjects, ages 17-48 years volunteered, ten of which were male, ten of which were female. Eighteen subjects were right dominant, two left dominant, one of whom is ambidextrous and is left dominant for gross motor activities only. This subject was treated as left dominant for statistical purposes. Data was calculated as dominant and non-dominant. The subjects fell into two age groups.

    1. 17-22 years - called young
    2. 36-48 years - called middle aged

No elderly subjects were used in this experiment anticipating further testing with an aged population at a future date.

Materials used included a premarked horseshoe shaped paperboard form which was presented resting upon a

Figure 8-6

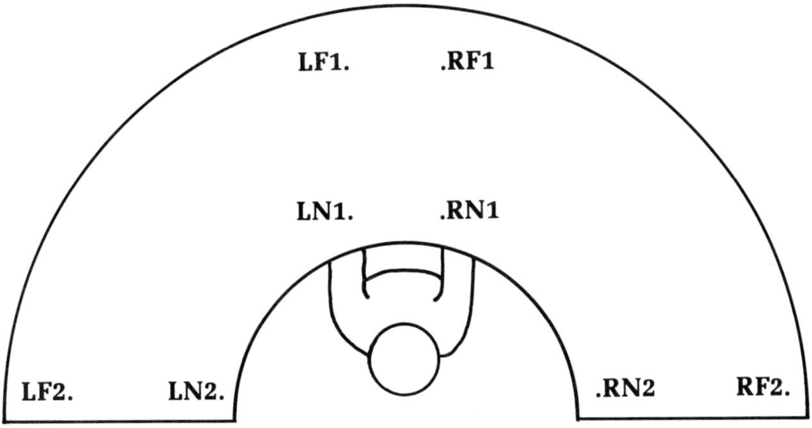

Proprioceptive memory testing

1. Foveal field
2. Lateral field
L. Left
R. Right
F. Far
N. Near

wooden table of the same dimensions. The table was hinged to enable portability. Five colored marker pens were adapted to attach to the subjects' forefingers in an attempt to reduce the variability of grasp position upon the accuracy of measurement.

Subjects were seated within the horseshoe and were requested to close their eyes. A mask was offered to subjects if they desired to use it. Few elected to use the mask preferring to close their eyes. Subjects were alternately begun at testing on the right or left side. Sequence of target points was ramdomized across subjects but held constant for each subject's right and left hands. All subjects were tested in eight positions five times. The examiner placed the tip of a colored marker attached to the subject's forefinger on the target point. Subjects were asked to bring their hand to their chest and then to return to the same target point. In subjects tested on the right first, subjects targeted four right positions, then four left positions, changed colored markers and repeated the procedure four more times. The purpose of the test was explained to the subjects after testing. Testing each subject took approximately 15 minutes.

Non-parametric statistics for small groups (Mann Whitney U) revealed that, for men, there was no significant difference between performance among the eight sectors of space. A .05 difference in function was noted between middle aged and young subjects in the non-dominant far lateral field where older subjects performed better. For women, differences were found between field functions and between ages. The non-dominant near front field was most accurate, a highly unexpected result. It was significantly better in skill than both the non-dominant far front and dominant far front fields at .01. No significant difference was noted between dominant and non-dominant front fields, however, the non-dominant front field was more accurate than the dominant, contrary to expectation. When both dominant and non-dominant far front fields were compared to both dominant and non-dominant near front fields, near fronts were more accurate to the .05. When both near front fields were compared to both near lateral fields, front fields were more accurate than lateral fields to .01. No significant differences were noted between far front and far lateral positions. Decline at .05 was noted in the dominant front field.

These results do not reveal answers, as much as they stimulate questions.

> Do men and women begin life and continue to experience life with equal functional ability in proprioceptive memory?

> Do women excel in orientation and decline in function of alerting, peripheral responses?

> Is decline in the peripheral skills a demonstration of 'forgetting' resulting from disuse, or is it an innate difference between men and women?

What is there about female performance or development which enhances non-dominant proprioceptive memory (orientation to space) in the frontal range?

Are there aspects of child rearing (carrying) potentiality present?

Shoulder girdle and elbow structure differs between men and women. Are there differences, too, in the joint and muscle receptors stimulated?

As the non-dominant upper extremity is used for carrying, while the dominant upper extremity is used for skilled motor function, is it that females receive less joint compression over greater periods of time with the exception of more specialized use for carrying, providing increased joint and muscle compression only in the non-dominant frontal plane?

Men are generally stronger and less skilled in fine motor skills than women, and may tend to be less specialized in their upper extremity function. Upper extremity function is developmentally prior to other movement. Is continuance of upper extremity facility a factor in the retention of perceptual facility? If so, this would support the view that disuse would further highlight losses in proprioceptive memory, perhaps through reductions in synaptic interconnections over time, resulting in reduced perceptual orientation, particularly in unfamiliar environs.

People tend to do what they do well and avoid that which they do poorly. As skill reduces, they avoid that at which they have become unskilled. Further, people tend to gain skill in what they succeed at, or what their life requires them to do. The dominant hand may well increase in skill with use at the expense of the loss in skill demonstrated in the non-dominant hand.

Few tasks in life require skilled use in near lateral fields. People tend to turn and attend with frontal orientation when a task is within reach and they tend to use the skilled upper extremity for tasks requiring skilled movement. This may explain the decline women experience in the right near lateral field as they grow older, particularly if trunk rotation is more facile in women than men, an area uninvestigated here.

These questions and speculations suggest that greater attention should be paid to adaptation of performance in relationship to the environment. Environment which one has had the opportunity to know through interaction permitted by movement, enables and sustains the development of relationships. But familiarity alone does not guarantee orientation. Neither is it motility or recall of motility, but rather it appears to be that disorientation occurs when motility, and thus sensory stimulation, is restricted within an environment in which there has been insufficient opportunity for new experience to gel and incorporate with former experience. If reduced interaction with environment reduces ongoing relational experience and thus orientation, then attention to the causes of reduced interactions will provide the means for intervening in that anticipated progressive decline.

REFERENCES
Chapter 8. Experimental Studies Concerned with Environmental and Proprioceptive Memory

1. Corso, J.: Sensory Processes and Age Effects in Normal Adults. *Journal of Gerontology,* 26: 9-105; 1971.
2. Breines, E.: *The Effects of Familiarity of Environment on Perception in an Aged Population.* Bound Brook, New Jersey: New Jersey Occupational Therapy Association, 1977.
3. Ravens, J.C.: *Coloured Progressive Matrices (Sets A, Ab and B).* London: Lewis, 1956, 1962.
4. Zubek, J.P. (Editor): *Sensory Deprivation: Fifteen Years of Research.* New York: Appleton-Century Crofts, 1969.
5. Breines, E.: *Proprioceptive Memory; The Recall of Frontal and Lateral Space in Upper Extremity Function.* Previously unpublished, 1979.

V. GERONTOLOGICAL PRACTICE APPLIED

9. Principles for Evaluation

As one ages, it is to be expected that, with time, there will be increased encounters with disability. Time brings more opportunities for all experiences. Multiple existing disabilities are likely to ensue and accrue as time proceeds. Various illnesses and dysfunctions in varying combinations acquire in the older population. Each individual is likely to have a unique combination of these disabilities.

Disability may be experienced sequentially or simultaneously. Illnesses or disabilities may acquire gradually or may occur suddenly and unexpectedly. When these disabilities occur, they often result in changes in life styles. These changes may be either of a temporary or permanent nature. When sudden change occurs to persons who are apt to be experiencing decline in the function of many systems, the ability to overcome these problems is often overwhelming. Visual and auditory systems are diminishing in proficiency. Some diseases that are likely to occur in later years affect the tactual system. Olfaction and gustatory discrimination diminish. When comfort within environment declines or when disabilities cause the reduction of movement within space, kinesthetic input thereby becomes reduced. Upon what systems can the mind rely for accurate and consistent information regarding the world, as aging occurs?

When multiple systems become assaulted, and when increasing alteration is encountered in what is being experienced, input received from multiple sensory systems may be perceived as garbled. If integration of sensory experience is a necessity for functional performance throughout life, when integrational dysfunctions become increasingly apparent as when crisis occurs in aging, confusion is likely to result from the lack of certainty regarding self awareness and orientation which results. Relocation necessitated by loss of independent ability to care for oneself, encountered in association with uncertainty regarding self and one's place, often results in problems of overwhelming proportion.

Problems inherent in new living experiences, met in new environs, with new bodily constraints, must be met with new and creative problem solving mechanisms. Independent solving mechanisms are within the capacity of some individuals, but for many individuals these abilities are absent. Assault upon the body and upon the mind can leave the formerly competent individual in a role of dependency and a state of disorganization which seriously impairs that person's ability to problem solve. The devastation of sudden illness can be paralyzing.

Strong habit formation may also contribute to the interference in a person's problem solving ability. Habit may be defined as automated sequenced performance. Habit and habit formation are ordinarily adaptive, enabling development. But subcortical, automated performances which have served one well prior to disability and displacement may serve to interfere with new skill learning. Disabled systems have been observed to circuit through habitual behavior which is unable to lead to a successful end goal any longer. Perseveration is one example of habitual performance which is not directed toward goal accomplishment. Ordinarily, automation of performance is facilitory to further performance. But habit may in some instances be maladaptive, such as when a habit no longer facilitates, but inhibits performance. A predilection to perform in a habitual pattern may prevent adaptive performance when the successful conclusion of the sequence of the habit is not feasible. The therapist must be alert to this possibility and must acquire the ability to observe and understand fluid movement patterns in applied activity, and the purpose of those movements toward adaptive living. The ability to observe movement and its application is critical to the accomplishment of a skilled evaluation. Skilled observaton is a prerequisite to the development of new sequential patterns designed to replace unsuccessful habits.

Loss of necessity to attend is provided by habit. The facetious expression regarding former President Gerald Ford—"He can't walk and chew gum at the same time."—is an example of the fact that certain tasks are automatically expected to be performed in conjunction with one another. It is ordinarily impossible to attend simultaneously to multiple new issues or tasks. Recall of lists of items has been demonstrated to interfere with the recollection of subsequently learned items. Proactive inhibition is a feature of human cognition. In much the same way, it is difficult to rub one's belly and pat one's head simultaneously. Attention to one event interferes with attention to the other. In this sense, attention may then be viewed as inhibitory to automated performance. Habitual performance serves to free up attention so that new learning or skill building can take place.

When former habits are not relevant, they cannot serve this aforestated function. Automatic performance which does not bring the individual to the point at which cognitive attention can assume its role in goal performance is then inhibitory. Because habit occurs on a non-conscious level, its involvement is outside of awareness. The direction habit takes in the disabled adult when it is askew from his present needs for adaptation, therefore, dead ends within itself. The system short circuits relative to goal direction. No goal, no motive can be considered when goals are not seen as possible. When habitual performances are not adaptive, conclusions drawn by patients and their caretakers alike is that successful goal performance is not possible. Goals can only be set when goals are believed to be possible.

Motivation posits within itself consciousness, whereas habit predicts unawareness. But habit and motivation are inextricably integrated. Habit can only be viable when it serves as a facilitator to motivation. Only then is motivation able to serve as the foundation for new habit formation.

When a crisis occurs in aging, the individual must now restart life as if a new entity beginning to learn and experience. Having to deal with life tasks in a new way is much like starting at the beginning. Matters which were once handled automatically must now be dealt with cortically and repeatedly explored, as do Piaget's children repeatedly handle their environment while they go about their sensory motor period of learning. This sensory motor period does not cease in childhood. It is carried through life and is reencountered as new matters are experienced, matters that must be dealt with cortically and resolved. That most of that which one is ordinarily capable of doing can be performed automatically, enables the performance of new behaviors. When previously automatic behavior must now be performed on a cortical level, subsequent behaviors are hampered. In dealing with the limitations of movement and the fear associated with a fractured hip, for example, the ability to perform simple tasks of living is formidable within the constraints of the new person.

It is to be expected that patients will demonstrate loss of abilities directly associated with the diagnoses which required their institutionalization. However, older patients are often far more disabled by dysfunctions not directly associated with the diagnosis for which they were admitted to a care facility. Certain whole movement or behavioral patterns have been observed as lost with no diagnosed neurological disease to account for those losses.

It is not unusual for patients to demonstrate loss of proprioceptive memory for actions required in lateral areas of space. But recall of movement or proprioceptive memory can be stimulated when new patterns can be triggered by other automatic actions which still retain. Reflexive or habitual patterns of movement can be used to elicit performance wholes. It is as if a gap has to be bridged to fire the engine in a new way, like hot wiring a car if the key is unavailable. That does not mean the key cannot be found, but it may be the solution of the moment which can enable

Figure 9-1

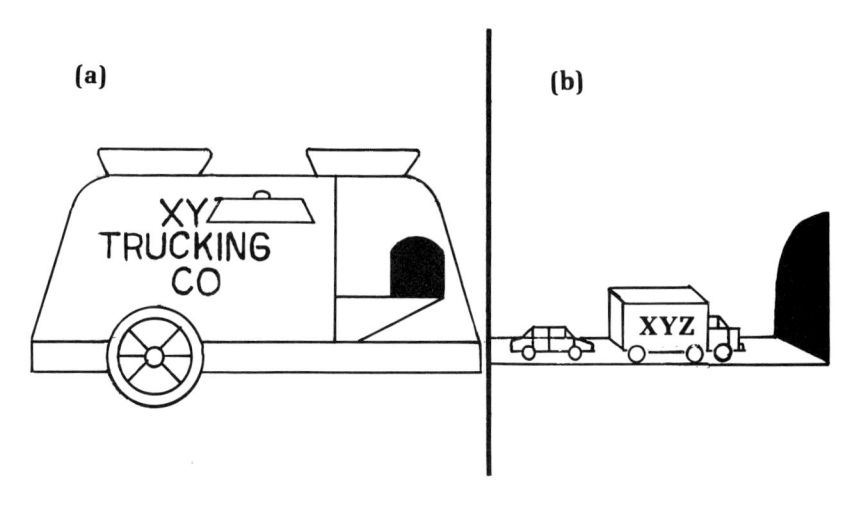

Holland Tunnel Diagram

(a) Relationship viewed from automobile interior

(b) Relationship viewed by bystander

performance and reduce the tendency toward further decline.

This Hot Wire Principle is one of the Breines Automotive Principles which undoubtedly originated from the time spent in the Breines automobile. After all, an itinerant therapist encounters inordinate quantities of mobility in her practice. The other principles are described as follows:

- The Holland Tunnel Principle - (Figure 9-1)

> My car can't fit into the Holland Tunnel. It's too big to fit into that small hole in the world. But the trailer truck ahead of me fits in and I am smaller than that trailer truck, so I must be able to fit, and I do.

- The Automatic Pilot Principle -

> When you drive to your home, you put the key into the ignition, depress the accelerator, and go. When you drive to my home, no more automatic pilot. Cortical pilot. The trip is longer, harder, and requires more decision making.

- New Car, Old Car Principle -

When you are in a new car, that car feels foreign and 'other.' There comes a time when a car at whose use you have become skilled and with which you have become familiar becomes an extension of self. You and your personal world are a whole hurtling through space, acting as a complete unit effecting change upon the universe. Familiarity and habit permit the extended self to function automatically.

The Hot Wire Principle equates with facilitation, a facilitation which serves to circumvent barriers provided by formerly developed habits which are inhibiting present performance. The goal of this facilitation is to utilize intact engrams by circuitous route.

The Holland Tunnel Principle equates with the cognitive, albeit below conscious, development of perceptual constancy.

The Automatic Pilot Principle equates with subcortical versus cortical performance.

The New Car, Old Car Principle expresses the relationship of self to other. The self/other dichotomy shifts with familiarity, skill and comfort. The self grows and encompasses increasing bits of world, space and objects, almost introjectively as Freud has postulated.

Thus, information proceeds from sensory input to subcortical integration of inputs to cortical manipulation and awareness to subcortical availability, and translates into relationships with the world around us. Learning proceeds throughout life as each new experience is incorporated into the whole.

However, learning ceases when insurmountable barriers to learning occur. No one knows better those functional impairments which befall the aged than the occupational therapist. Slowed motor responses with resultant decreased generalized strength, in combination with particular disabilities associated with diseases found more frequently in aging, are noted. CVA, arthritis, Parkinson's disease, hip fracture, cardiac and respiratory insufficiency as well as visual and auditory deficits all result in direct or indirect reduction in interaction with environment, leading to reduced sensory motor capacity. Combinations of disabilities compound the problems of recovery of the elderly ill.

Barriers to performance must be identified in order to delete those barriers by remediation or circumvention. If the progressively encapsulating feedback model of Miller, Galanter and Pribram (1960)[1] is recalled and envisioned as an onion, evaluation can be conceived of as a tool for peeling that onion.

In order to achieve effective treatment, ideal assessment should be made within the living environment of the individual to be evaluated. Environment should include location and significant persons within all time schemes. Early assessment is the wisest course (Breines, 1979)[2]. If habits are permitted to develop toward maladaptive ends, then recovery of function becomes all the more difficult.

Evaluation of the patient should follow a mode designed to elicit recognition of everything which interferes with that individual's ability to function within his environment and goals. Remediation which will be of no functional use to the patient is generally invalid. This does not mean that only patient stated goals are attended to. Sometimes it is necessary to aid the patient by expressing for him his unstated feelings as the patient is guided through the assessment of his abilities and disabilities. It is necessary to aid patients to set goals which are realistic in order to work out problems of new life styles, either permanent or temporary. Planning for a change in life style is an extension of the behavioral plan.

When entering into a relationship with an elderly client, as with all clients, a relationship of trust must be established with all due speed. A sequence of assaulting circumstances have brought the patient to this therapeutic encounter. These circumstances are such that they are very likely to have led the elderly patient to believe in his imminent demise. And the longer the disablement, isolation, and depression have been experienced, the more inclined that self expressed prophecy is apt to be believed. It is the rare individual who can withstand multiple devastating experiences with courage and hope, and without assistance. Only the rare individual can withstand further and further ego assault and still survive. Progressive decline predicts further decline. What becomes lost as one ages is difficult to retrieve. Skilled assessment and planning are designed to counteract that decline.

The presence of the occupational therapist at the earliest moment in the recovery process says to the patient - someone thinks I may be able to recover my skills. The attitude of the therapist further confirms this supposition when emphasis is placed upon functional performance rather than diagnosis. Diagnosis and medication are foreign and unfamiliar and anxiety provoking to the patient. Functional performance is familiar and easy to understand. The patient's ability to understand and relate to the concerns of the occupational therapist serves as a comfort to that patient. The concerns of the patient are the basic concerns of the therapist. Areas to be evaluated in the assessment of the patient are those with which the patient is familiar and primarily concerned. What parts of me work and what can I do with them? Patients often have fantasies about their limitations. Due to fear and ignorance on their part and on the part of their families, patients have not ordinarily had the opportunity to openly analyze their abilities and disabilities. For them to make realistic plans with a respected expert serves to reduce their anxiety and build confidence. Without this opportunity for exploration and ventilation, patients often magnify their disablement and draw unjustified conclusions about their potential recovery which can be a hindrance to their recovery.

People are apt to perform as they are expected to, and as they expect themselves to perform. If people believe themselves incompetent, they surely will be. Early recognition of potential serves as a modifier of behavior. Discussion is not sufficient to allay fears. Patients will be more inclined to believe in themselves when techniques are learned which make a difference in their ability to perform. Therefore it is necessary to determine that which is most critical to the patient in order to teach those skills which the patient feels makes the greatest difference to himself.

It is through goal directed activities that the occupational therapist performs, but who dictates the goals? The adult patient must collaborate in the design of his own treatment plan with a clear understanding of what is intervening with his ability to perform skillfully. After all, this patient has had a lifetime of experience and responsibility for self as well as for others. To exclude the patient from the development of his own treatment plan is to treat that elder with less than the respect which he deserves. Patients' needs must be assessed from the vantage of the patient's own view of what is critical in his own life. The therapist must be able to ascertain what the patient desires for himself, and work through decisions integral to these plans. Recall that motivation is both basic to, and derives from, habit formation. If an individual is attuned to his world, his motives will direct his attention. As skill and proficiency increase, habituation develops, enabling the setting of new goals. Attention to intention will serve to effect the most efficient application of treatment.

It has often been heard that a given patient is difficult to motivate. This perspective is a reversal of what should be understood as the concept of motivation. It is not the therapist's job to motivate the patient. Instead, the therapist's task is to identify the motivation of the patient, and facilitate the development of behavioral plans, to enable the patient to reach goals the patient has for himself. Evaluation of the patient should include a determination of where function is impaired and where motivation lies, for it is only through patient motivation that goal direction is an effective treatment tool.

The evaluation is an experience for the patient which can serve as a balm or as another onslaught. Highlighting dysfunction, exposing the patient to increased attention to that dysfunction, does not generally serve the therapeutic purpose. It is far better to highlight potential. The evaluation period can be used to indicate to the patient that remediation is a possibility. If the patient wishes something from his drawer, the patient can be positioned so that the patient can perform the task for himself. The evaluation period should be used to indicate to the patient that you will not be doing tasks for the patient, but are skilled at enabling the patient to perform necessary tasks for himself. The patient should be afforded the opportunity to express his feelings and hopes with the affirmation that these dreams remain a possibility. The evaluation can be used to stimulate attitudes while investigation proceeds. The spoken and silent language of the evaluation says more than is obvious.

"MAY I COME IN AND TALK WITH YOU? MAY I SIT HERE?

This request says to the patient, "This is your place where you have rights. I defer to you. You are respected by me and you control this encounter." Once invited, sit face to face with the client with no barriers between you. Place yourself where the patient can see your face and lips and slowly and clearly state:

"HELLO. MY NAME IS   (full name)   . I AM AN OCCUPATIONAL THERAPIST. MY JOB IS TO FIND OUT WHAT YOU CAN DO—"

The first thing that the patient hears is a concern on the part of someone to know his capabilities. Someone believes he is capable of something. It is likely that no one else has delivered this message before. Previously the hidden messages have been expressions of perceived incompetence. ("It must be that I cannot help myself. Why else is everything being done for me? There is no hope for someone like me. I'm finished. My life is ending.")

"WHAT YOU ARE HAVING DIFFICULTY DOING—"

Not "What *can't* you do?" The implication is of mere difficulty, not impossibility. A subtle but important suggestion has been made leading to:

"AND TO HELP YOU DO THE THINGS YOU WANT TO BE DOING FOR YOURSELF."

Why would someone want to help another person with such matters unless potential exists for those gains to be made?

Smile, pause as if you expect a response; listen; communicate. Responses which come from the patient are genreally those which are of most immediate concern to him. He has found a person who is expressing his faith in him, a person who is taking time to listen, a precious commodity in a health care facility. Here is a person who intends to help him with those things which are of his greatest concern. The patient constructs his own idea of what occupational therapy is and how it can help him. Occupational therapy is to the patient a means for solving problems. Whatever expressions the patient makes leads to a potential solution in which the patient can be involved. The therapist can help the patient seek the solutions for himself.

As the patient reveals himself, take the patient's hand as if to say, "I care. I understand your needs. They can be met." Act on the patient's expressed concern. If the patient says, "My back hurts," show him how to turn in bed. If he says he fears for his family, assist him in the use of his wheelchair to get to the phone or to the nurse to inquire. If he needs to use the toilet, instruct him in a toilet transfer. If he is cold, show him how to put on his sweater or to pull up the covers. Thereupon becomes established a relationship of faith. One who can facilitate the solution of a major problem can be relied upon to lead one to further solutions, solutions which are relevant and enabling. Once this relationship begins to be established, then further exploration can be made.

"I HAVE SOME FUNNY OR PECULIAR THINGS I'D LIKE TO ASK YOU TO HELP ME TO KNOW YOU BETTER."

What are the things you need to know to assess patient performance? Now is the time to find these things out. But they are best discovered in as natural a fashion as possible. Range of motion, strength, sensory and perceptual performance, praxis, synergies, ability to follow directions, fine and gross motor skills, ADL skills, cognitive ability are all among those abilities the therapist will wish to investigate.

You should already know the condition of your patient's memory from listening to the patient and from having prepared yourself with a review of the patient's chart, comparing data from both. Do not overlook the fact, however, that the chart is not always accurate. Ask simply, "When did you get here?" "From where?" or "What brought you here?" The patient's perspective will often reveal a substantially different answer to this question than the family or the physician would give. Often the answer is more genuine and revealing of the problems to be solved.

Questions of this sort appear to express interest, not to put someone on the spot. Affect and appropriateness are easily observed. If the patient shows any dysfunction in his ability to respond or appears stressed by difficulty with these questions, it is best to make light of things and cease this course of questioning. Using your own frailties may help to reduce the stress to which the patient has been exposed. "I always forget names," or "I have trouble with telephone numbers," or "Sometimes people have trouble remembering things after surgery (or a move when they've been sick) but that usually clears up." Hope instilled. It is not necessary to belabor these losses. The patient is frightened by their presence. It is important that the patient not be stressed by his own inability to perform adequately.

A few well selected performances, skillfully observed, will tell a great deal with little stress produced in the patient.

"HOW HIGH CAN YOU RAISE YOUR ARMS?"

This sort of question is usually received by the patient with surprise. After all, the patient didn't receive medical care for any problem he was experiencing with his arms. At that point, you might say:

"SEE, I TOLD YOU I WOULD BE ASKING SOME FUNNY QUESTIONS."

Any humor which can be elicited will serve to reduce stress and develop the relationship you are trying to build. Too, there are no right or wrong answers to raising one's arms. Active shoulder range of motion will tell a great deal about the patient. Range below 100° shoulder flexion limits ease in dressing and grooming. It may be an indication of scapular weakness, which strength is necessary to perform transfers, wheelchair travel and ambulation using a walker. If active range is limited, you will want to know the patient's passive range.

"SHOULDERS STIFF? LET ME SEE."

Full passive range of motion tells us that there is muscle weakness. If the shoulders are tight, painful, there has probably been a long-standing condition, and arthritic joints. If only one hand is raised by the patient determine why. Were the instructions understood? Is the patient compensating for muscle weakness in shoulders, neck or back using one extremity to provide stabilization in order to raise the other? Does the patient understand the concept up? And, if understood, is 'up' accurately reproduced? If one hand is up, ask the patient which hand is up. If the answer is correct, praise is in order, but indicate you expected an accurate answer. Adults are normally expected to know their right from their left hand. If incorrect, note by observation if the patient is aware of his error or not. Determine whether the decision was automatic or consciously arrived at. At the same time, observe neck range of motion, trunk shifting and fluid or restricted movements. Fluidity in neck and trunk mobility will tell you something about the patient's relationship with his periphery of awareness, as will observation of the patient's position. Extensor thrust or asymmetrical trunk posture should be noted. Observe tasks the patient performs while in conversation with you. Can the patient rise from lying or sitting?

"CAN YOU PUT YOUR RIGHT HAND ON YOUR LEFT EAR?"

Speed of processing, accuracy of laterality, identification of body parts, ability to cross the midline are revealed. Allow the answers to lead you in your investigation. If the wrong response is given to a directive, what is at the base of the error in performance? Were you heard? Is vision hampering responses?

Vision can be functional at different levels. Can the patient recognize people and objects? Peripheral vision may be a factor in orientation proficiency. Does the patient have sufficient vision with which to perform activities in which he wishes to be engaged? Frequently patients have corrective lenses at home which may be obtained. Or they may have glasses which are not current in their correction, or may be scratched, or may not fit.

Dentures, too, may be ill fitting. If the patient has been ill for some time it is not uncommon for his mouth to have changed in shape while the dentures were unused. Ability to eat may be affected by disuse or weight change as much as it is dependent upon vision, hand usage and the ability to swallow. It is vital to determine exactly what is at the core of feeding dysfunction.

Observe if the patient is able to hear normal speech. Hearing losses are common in older persons. Some patients have had prior conditions of hearing loss and have hearing aids. If patients do not have hearing aids, or if the hearing of patients with hearing aids does not appear to be improved through the use of the hearing aid, these patients may be good candidates for an audiology consultation. Patients with hearing aids must have functional batteries. Does the patient know how to insert the batteries himself? Are there batteries available to him? Can the patient converse on the telephone? Would special adaptations be recommended for his use?

Observe and note what other adaptations would facilitate function in the patient. Adapted arm rests, removed or raised leg rests, bed height and positions, reaching equipment, padding, splinting, feeding or other adaptive aids each may be recommended.

Determine the discharge plan for the patient. This plan will make considerable difference in the goals set for living adaptation. The needs of a patient who is to live at home alone are rather different from those of a patient who is to remain a nursing home resident. Each must acquire different skills. Ambulation tolerance needs may be greater in the nursing home than within a small apartment. Shopping for groceries and preparing meals is not a skill commonly required by the nursing home resident.

Test all patients for stereognosis. Simply request of the patient if you may place something in his hand to identify without him looking at it. Use familiar objects. Request if you can take an item from his drawer for this purpose. Personal items are less apt to evoke stress. Use a different item for each hand. Shield the item from view and present it to the patient at the side of him and request him to avert his eyes (Figure 9-2). If the patient has difficulty in closing or averting his eyes, use a towel or the bedcovers over his hand to keep the item from view. Again, tell the patient that some people cannot help looking. It is not necessary to use any contrived equipment. Stereognosis is the ability to mentally construct what one is feeling when vision is absent. For our patients, we wish to know whether familiar objects are unfamiliar to them unless viewed. If the patient is correct in his assessment, then one can assume tactual sensitivity is intact. Ability to perform well in some areas would indicate no necessity to assess underlying capabilities. If there is stereognostic dysfunction, one must determine if the error or absence of response is due to losses in tactual functioning, processing, or if it is a demonstration of anomia. If the error occurs in the first hand tested, use the same object in the second hand. If the patient identifies the object correctly with the second hand, then a naming problem does not exist. Further assessment will reveal the presence of sensory losses or finger agnosia.

Some patients state that they are not crazy or simple-minded, and that they resent being tested for this apparently simple skill. I have found that patients are satisfied and cooperative if I explain that I test everyone this way because some people come out of the hospital with problems in touch

192 PERCEPTION: ITS DEVELOPMENT AND RECAPITULATION

Figure 9-2

Side Presented Items for Stereognosis Testing

Object is presented at the patient's side for stereognosis testing. Note therapist shielding object from view of patient without use of elaborate equipment.

that have not been noticed before. I state that we just want to be certain that touch is not a problem for them. This is usually sufficient to allay their defensiveness. Patients are cooperative when they are not forced by the situation to be defensive.

Sometimes astereognosis has been identified for the first time in the patient. Oddly enough, it is usually a comfort to the patients to understand that this is precisely the reason for much of their demonstrated dependency and/or confusion. Being able to isolate the dysfunction to a touch deficiency helps the patient to achieve an improved self image. Prior to this point they have not understood their own behavior. They fear approaching senility. Why else can they no longer perform simple tasks which they have been capable of accomplishing for as long as they can remember?

Once a disability has been identified it is possible to tell the patient that this is something that can be worked on. No promises, but it is easier to correct or work around something when you know what is wrong. Each dysfunction will determine the focus of treatment. Some will respond to remediation, others will require circumvention.

And so the evaluation proceeeds. Balance, reach, plans. The order of assessment is not critical. The situation often dictates the sequence. While the sequence of assessment is not critical, it is necessary to retain a mental list of areas to be assessed. Diagnosis will often alert you to areas of potential dysfunction, but do not limit your investigation to those areas alone. It is important to allow the patient plenty of space and time to express himself at his own pace, for problems will then be more likely to surface.

It is not necessary or desirable to proceed through a contrived and lengthy ADL evaluation at the primary meeting. Initially, it is sufficient to determine that the patient is dependent or independent. It is the unusual patient who is independent in all ADLs upon admission to a nursing home. If the patient had been independent in self care, it is unlikely that he would have been admitted. Schedule ADL training to occur at the normal time for ADLs to be performed and there determine the degree of dependency. Can the patient roll in bed, reach necessary items? Dress? Difficulty with what items? Feed self? Stand, transfer to chair, toilet, cleanse self? Wheel chair, proceed through space, direction find, socialize? Manage time, develop leisure skills, assume responsibility, endure both sitting and ambulating through life skills?

Initial observations must be carefully recorded. Notations should be expressed in measurable coefficients. The patient's progress or lack of progress must be assessable. If the patient demonstrates gains, then further treatment is warranted. One must be able to note any gains made in measurable quantities. Baseline evaluation data are critical to this approach.

A patient's capabilities must be based upon sophisticated judgments, not from prejudices deriving from those untrained in functional performance. *What is* is not *what may be* and assessment alone cannot predict prognosis. Only performance can accurately predict prognosis. Sophisticated identification of barriers to patient performance is requisite to the construction of treatment plans. Once barriers have been identified, then those barriers can be eliminated or compensated for to enhance performance and mobility.

Treatment derives from evaluation. Once assessment has been made of patient ability and disability within the world in which the patient must function, a plan for treatment can be established. Each deficit noted should be expressed in terms of treatment. Recommendations should be stated. If strength or range of motion are diminished, then recommendations would include a goal to increase strength and range of motion. If a deficit is determined to be of a permanent nature, then it is necessary to express a means of circumventing the problem. If the patient is blind or partially sighted, then an appropriate treatment would be visual compensation training. All deficits noted can be expressed in terms of treatment.

It is appropriate and desirable to refer to other specialists when those specialties would appear to be of benefit to the patient. Referrals may be made to physical therapy, speech and audiology, dentist, psychiatric services, or dietary.

Consultation with ophthalmologists and orthopedists, cardiologists and social service will frequently help in providing information to enable the most comprehensive care of the patient. Other occupational therapists may have particular expertise for which referral or consultation would be useful. A practice which attracts a variety of experience may not offer the opportunity to develop sufficient expertise in certain disability areas, whereas other occupational therapists may have that expertise. Consultation is available from those working in specialty programs in dialysis, rehabilitation, psychiatry, spinal cord injury, learning disabilities, etc. When patients are discharged to home with further potential for recovery, identification of and referral to community based occupational therapists providing home treatment is suggested. A variety of specialists can assist in resolving problems of dysfunction.

Early identification of functional ability and disability can make the difference between recovery and decline. Patients are admitted to nursing homes with diagnoses carefully (and sometimes not so carefully) noted. Yet we all know that some stroke patients do very well, some not well at all. Some hip fracture patients walk out resuming their former life style, others assume a life of dependency and decline. Little is known of the factors which account for these differences.

Evaluation of functional performance and hindrances to that performance enables patients to be treated through instruction in methods designed to bring patients to maximal functional performance. Evaluation should include ranges of motion, strength, posture, perception in all sensory systems, functional hearing and vision, cognitive function, performance related to living skills, environmental assessment, interpersonal relations and abilities. Each of these are assessed with an eye toward intervention. It is necessary to determine which factors have been inhibiting the patient's performance in order to develop treatment plans designed to increase patients' abilities and decrease or eliminate those factors which inhibit performance. Treatment plans should be developed in conjunction with patients by identifying with patients which skills are of most critical importance to them. By utilizing patients' own goals and resolving those problems with which patients are primarily concerned, patients begin to regain feelings of self worth through decision making in their own regard. Establishing feelings of control over self and over environment are vital to speedy recovery.

REFERENCES
Chapter 9. Principles for Evaluation

1. Miller, G.A., Galanter, E. and Pribram, K.H.: *Plans and the Structure of Behavior.* New York: Holt, 1960.
2. Breines, E.: Early Intervention Through Occupational Therapy, *American Health Care Association Journal,* 5(3): 34-35; 1979.

10. Principles for Treatment

Following assessment of the patient whose capabilities and disabilities have been identified, a wide avenue of approaches is available. Many different activities may serve as therapeutic tasks. Occupational therapy is by definition a therapy which is task oriented in its approach. Therefore, all activities in which mankind engages are available for selection as avenues of treatment. Because activities and interests differ among people of various ages, time periods, sexes, cultures and educational levels, a virtually limitless range of therapeutic activities is available.

As has been previously noted, the variety of activities in which patients engage for therapeutic purpose varies significantly from clinic to clinic. Their use has been dictated because therapists have considered them valuable treatment tools for patients and frequently as well because therapists themselves have indicated special interest in those activities. Dislike for some activities on the part of therapists has assured their deletion from the list of modalities available.

Although this seeming divergence between activities available in different departments may well have contributed to occupational therapists' inability to construct a strong identity among themselves and for others, this diversity is in essence occupational therapy's greatest strength, for the use of mankind's tasks toward the achievement of its further goals is our unique skill.

Cooperative effort in tasks which appeal to both patients and therapists is a useful tool when attempting to reachieve development.

When a rationale is considered upon which to base treatment, a variety of approaches are available. Clinicians often derive their own discernible style of practice. For our own treatment theme, we look to the relational paradigm, a comprehensive construct under which occupational therapy practice can be subsumed. A gestalt approach to activity alerts us to the necessity for a comprehensive understanding of relationships inherent in activity. These relationships are in constant flux, for the world as we understand it is a mobile and transient world. Relationships which shift within a changing world are those which occur within the self, between the self and other, and between the self and others and the inanimate objects and perimeters with which and within which people are engaged in their tasks of living. Changes in relationships are particularly evident in the aging population, perhaps because those changes can be viewed as if they had been speeded up. Some things are only revealed when the whole can be viewed. For the older person the whole of life is available for analysis and the recapitulation of development occurs within a perceivable dimension.

Having made these assumptions and having selected a treatment rationale, it is then possible to apply to them the information gained in evaluation of the patient toward the development of treatment plans. Treatment should be designed to enable manipulation and control of the concrete and subjective environment in order to effect increased human performance. Context of experience must be considered in pursuit of a gestalt approach to treatment. Peripheral awareness must be incorporated into the therapeutic experience.

One description of peripheral awareness applied to treatment can be seen in terms of the following. Behavior modification is most effective when reinforcement will continue to exist as a natural course within the subject's world. If not the originally devised reinforcement, then

Principles for Treatment 199

another surrogate reinforcement must remain evident for any gains in behavior to be retained. Naturally occurring environmental conditions used as reinforcements are more effective than contrived situations such as token economies or treat reinforcements. A world which gives of its own accord can be relied upon to continue to contribute. The treatment environment is most likely to be successful if treatment takes place within the patient's natural world. The world as it exists for the patients is likely to retain its characteristics whereas artificial behavioral reinforcements are inclined to cease. Continuation of contrived reinforcement requires conscious desire on the part of some individual, a situation difficult to sustain outside of the treatment realm. Carry over is not dependably sustained. Results depend upon external forces rather than internal direction. The source and control of the reinforcement is obvious and tenuous. In an environmental approach, however, the patient is prepared to effect reinforcement from the world about him. Sources of reinforcement are everywhere and of every kind, just as they naturally exist for the developing child.

Treatment, like development, in order to be most effective, is best provided within an attuned environment. When the environment reverberates in such a way as to reinforce positive behavior, then that environment serves a developmental or therapeutic purpose. Modification of environment in such a way as to provide appropriate and graded positive experiences serves these developmental ends. Just as negative environmental experiences compound themselves, positive experience is also capable of compounding itself. A totality of experiences, in synchrony with each other, reinforces what is believed to be true. Consensus of experience can be derived by the experience of the individual or between individuals. A cognitive resolution is derived from all information and habit or reflexes available.

Utilization of a constant familiar environment in which to provide treatment is therefore suggested as a useful tool. Removing the patient with neurological dysfunction of firm or soft origin to a treatment area, although of greater convenience to the therapist, may be of questionable value to the patient. An artificial treatment environment may be conceptualized easily by the therapist while the patient receiving a new totality of experiences may be unable to benefit fully from a therapeutic learning experience without encountering inordinate distraction. That nervous system which has previously learned which of a myriad of clues are to be 'ignored' safely can concentrate on pertinent experiences and comfort. Patients who have internalized the softness of a sofa or the sounds and smells of a room can use these sure clues to better comprehend the new learning experiences now to be faced. Contextual clues are necessary to the achievement of constancy.

Repeated comparative observations of learning ability have illustrated marked differences in improvement of skills between those individuals located in their personal environment compared with the same patient treated in the traditional clinic situation. The artificiality of a treatment session away from where the patient lives and must function, must be perceived as such by the therapist. When a new environment such as a nursing home must be encountered by the patient, then a means of compensating for its unfamiliarity must be synthesized.

Movement facilitated within a new environment can serve to familiarize that environment to the patient. In order to provide effective treatment it is necessary to attend to movement which is designed to develop spatial relationships. Movement promotes recovery. Immobilization equates with disability. The mobile individual represents independence and well being. Movement is not ordinarily thought of in terms of health care other than as an adjunct to well being of the circulatory system. Movement is often considered as incidental to the care of the patient, if it is considered at all. Yet movement itself can serve as a tool for recovery if it is permitted to the patient. Since we as therapists have no magical skills with which to repair naturally failing physiology, it is our attention to the maintenance and improvement of kinesthetic functioning in integration with remaining sensory inputs which serve to keep the patient in maximum touch with his world. Reduced interaction in the environment must be avoided at all costs as this reduced interaction prevents the necessary ongoing progression of relationships vital to continuous development of perceptual functioning.

Goals for treatment are frequently numerous. If it is recalled that in aging multiple acquiring deficits are presumed, and that these deficits are experienced in association with recent or acute diagnoses, and that these multiple dysfunctions and diagnoses result in functional or performance deficits, then each of these must be attended to in order to increase functional performance. It is most desirable if they can be attended to simultaneously. Life's tasks can provide gains in strength, perceptual function and range of motion at the same time. Appropriately grading and incorporating tasks into the living day of the patient provides that patient increases in functional performance and at the same time a sense of meaningfulness, purpose and future. The occupational therapist's skilled analysis of activities for their components, in combination with skill in grading activities, will enable patients to assume more responsibility in increments which are both tolerable and therapeutic.

Early intervention is a term often used in regard to the care of infants. This concept has not been sufficiently applied to the care of the elderly ill. Yet it is of critical importance that restorative care of the elderly be instituted early in the recovery of the patient. In terms of nursing home care, immediate assessment of functional ability is vital in order to prevent the variety of problems which ensue along with serious illness. Patients can and should be seen and evaluated by the occupational therapist within twenty-four hours of admission to the facility.

Early occupational therapy intervention can eliminate undue development of an invalid personality. Being cared for, sustained over longer periods of time than necessary, creates in the patient a feeling that he has now become (and must remain) an invalid, and creates habits in patients and in staff which become difficult to alter as times goes by.

Early resumption of responsibility for self care tasks creates in the patient a feeling of self worth. Early intervention is vital following illness. If a patient views himself as an invalid he will assume the role of invalid. Roles are assumed in large part in accord with the view others have of individuals. The view one has of self influences the attitude others have of one.

Invalidism can be avoided by preventing deterioration of self worth. It is necessary at the outset of illness to establish within the patient an attitude of competency, or an expectation of the achievement of competency. The patient's assumption of an attitude of potential competency is facilitated by utilization of skills as they are acquired. Use of life skills within the daily life of the patient serves to reinforce skills and automate them so patients can resume productive and responsible lives. Although the patient usually presents a picture of weakness and dependency upon admission, one should establish for the patient an expectation that he can expect restoration to former levels of competency in areas of significant importance to himself.

Assuming more independence in an area of vital concern to the patient, reinforced by staff expectancy, will convince the patient most effectively of his potential for recovery. People tend to perform at the level at which they are expected to perform. The 'self-fulfilling prophecy' holds true. When one performs in a particular fashion, one's attitude toward the self modifies according to that performance, thus dictating the attitudes of others. An unending circle is thereby created which may revolve in either direction (Figure 10-1).

Patients who feel good about themselves and feel their needs are being met will be cooperative in their recovery. Other patients demonstrate enormous anxiety which hinders their ability to accept change. Consistent reassurance through confidence in patients' potential for recovery of skills will aid patients in accepting their own ability. But the relationship between territoriality and aggression leads us to believe that cooperation is not universally indicative of therapeutic progress. All too often the 'good' patient is considered to be the cooperative patient

Figure 10-1

```
        Performance              Self
            or                 Attitude
         Behavior

                  Attitudes
                     of
                   Others
```

Circle of Influence

Each element impacts upon each of the others.

who fits well into a treatment regimen which has been designed at base for the convenience of the staff and/or facility. Cooperation is not necessarily an asset to recovery. The good patient may indeed be the one who retains his personal integrity by expressing himself through aggressive demands in an attempt to retain or regain control over self by this means. That this therapist has encountered more cantankerous male patients than female suggests a difference which may be worthy of further investigation. As a matter of fact, the most ornery female patient ever treated by this therapist was a former corporate executive for a petroleum refinery, an unusual position for any woman, not less a woman who was employed at her trade during years that any employment of women was unusual. A study of sexuality relative to aggressive behavior would indeed be useful in helping to promote patients' assertiveness in their own behalf.

Significant persons' attitudes are critical to the patient. Among them are family, nurses, attendants, physicians and therapists. Those who are in closest direct relationship to the patient are those whose influence is enormous. If the family or nurse's aide believes that the patient is capable of self care, the patient's self-esteem increases greatly. It is not enough that the patient or therapist be aware of the patient's capabilities. Everyone must be aware of and expect to utilize the patient's skills in order that they be incorporated into a life style. The entire team, including family and patients, must be prepared to allow the patient to incorporate newly learned skills into the patient's living day in an appropriately graded fashion. A patient who can don only one shoe must be permitted to demonstrate this skill or there will be undue delay in the patient's ability to be entirely independent in the area of lower extremity dressing. A patient who can feed himself independently and has sufficient skills and endurance to traverse the distance to the dining room must be expected to arrive at that destination. Activity tolerance must be constantly reassessed and maximized. Partial skills should be used toward goals. Using learned skills increases strength and builds habits, while at the same time improving self worth. Teaching a new skill and then explicitly or implicitly denying the patient the ability to perform that skill is counterproductive to that patient's recovery.

The physician, particularly, must be made acutely aware of the patient's capabilities, as goals for medical care are often predicated upon the attitude the physician has about the patient. Too often the elderly ill are written off by their attending physcian because of their age. The determination that nursing home residency is required is often sufficient for the physician to establish an attitude of hopelessness toward that patient, thereby dictating conservatism in medical procedures. When a patient's performance abilities rise beyond originally perceived potential, a wise course of action is to review the plan of care for that individual with the physician. Often medical procedures deemed inappropriate at an earlier date may later be seen as appropriate toward effecting still further improvement. A patient for whom a prosthesis may be considered inappropriate upon first assessment, following good and effective treatment often becomes a suitable candidate at a later date. Good practice demands communication, apprising others of changes in patient capabilities in order to further advance those capabilities.

Of critical importance to the recovery of the disabled patient is the attitude of those with whom that patient is most closely associated. Attitudes about self are reflected by those with whom interactions are most closely invested. The primary caretaker often is family, nursing assistant, or professional homemaker, depending upon the environment in which the care is to be given. Notably, health care professionals are not ordinarily as significant to the patient in their role as are the non-professionals who are serving as caretakers. This may be because of the duration of time spent in the company of the patient or it may be because of the sense of reality of feedback to the patient which is afforded. It is possible that the mundane nature of job roles and tasks may be perceived by patients as closer to their own level of understanding and interest and therefore, identification with the ideas and reflections of the caretaker takes place. The health professional, on the other hand, is often seen as having different vested interests and different focus. Those issues to which people attend in their occupational association dictates attitudes and relationships in other people. Everyday tasks of living are mutually attended to by caretaker and patient. Sophisticated issues are attended to by distant professionals. Therefore, the more sophisticated the approach of the professional, the less they are perceived as having mutual interest with the patient. The professional is important, but the non-professional caretaker is perceived as vital. The dependency of the patient highlights this attitude. Therefore, attitude and performance of the caretaker is often shown to be more vital to the performance and attitude of the patient than that of the professional.

In order to effect maximum functional performance in the patient, patient competency must be demonstrated. So often, patient competency is not sufficiently demonstrated to those who are in the caretaker role. Rather than teaching others to perform our tasks, it is in demonstrated patient competency that the occupational therapist best serves as a patient advocate. Demonstrated competency indicates to the caretaker that the patient has dependable abilities. Dependable is the key word. It is not enough to demonstrate performance on single occasions. It is necessary for the patient to be repeatedly viewed as skillful in increasingly more areas of competency. Care of the patient is the responsibility of the caretaker. That responsibility can only be relinquished when the patient can be expected to be responsible for self and that responsibility is consistent and reliable. Patients must be viewed as capable of making positive change. In order to be so viewed, consistency in task performance and in role performance must be developed. The patient must expect that others have expectations for his own performance, and in order for that to occur, the caretaker must be reasonably assured of consistent patient performance.

Consistency requires repetition and appropriateness. While patients should be instructed, the therapist should not neglect alterations of the human and inert environment to assure that the patient will be permitted to practice new skills and to incorporate those skills into daily living usage. Skills taught in a splinter fashion are not easily incorporated into daily usage. This leads to the conclusion that greatest carry over occurs when treatment is provided in view of caretakers and within the environment in which the tasks are to be performed. Unskilled individuals may have difficulty translating to usage in real situations that which is performed in exclusively clinical environs. Replication of tasks learned in a contrived or simulated condition is often beyond the ability of both patient and surrogate therapist. The problem solving required for translating loci is generally not within the expertise of one who is untrained. Expertise is necessary in order to generalize treatment to all environments. The naive client and caretaker are often unable to do so easily.

Attitudes and expectations in both patients and caretakers can be successfully altered when gains can be observed as they are made. When an individual is perceived to demonstrate an increased level of competency or of potential, that perception results in a rectified self-fulfilling prophecy. Performance takes place at the level at which one is expected to perform. Expectations are based upon previously demonstrated performance.

Reassurance comes in other than verbal forms. Utilization of learned skills within the patient's life style serves to assure the patient that the 'world' expects his maximum performance and therefore regards him as having potential for recovery. Close communication between the occupational therapist and the nursing staff and families will keep everyone informed of the current level of independence the patient can assume. As a patient under treatment is expected to make gains in skills, and continued treatment is frequently dependent upon the making of gains*, it is necessary for the occupational therapist to share the patient's status as soon as the patient achieves newly gained skill or independence, for that communication facilitates further gains.

Skills and habits are demonstrations of subcorticalized behaviors. In order to perform smoothly and efficiently, it is necessary to perform without conscious attention to movement components. Incorporating learned behaviors into the daily life of the patient serves to enhance the subcorticalization of skills. Through subcorticalization of component behaviors, the patient is better able to get on with the task of living.

Treatment is based upon learning. Learning requires repetition. In order for treatment to be judged effective or ineffective, daily repetition is necessary, and not just for the duration of the treatment period. Skill being developed in the patient must be shared with those caring for that patient in order to provide immediate reinforcement. Skills are not learned in isolation from the environment. Patients must be able to perform skills within the constraints of the world in which they live. Learning of a skill that cannot actually be performed is tantamount to not having learned the skill. The patient must be provided the opportunity to perform skills he

*Insurance requirements dictate documented restoration (Medicare guidelines).

learns in order to perfect their use and habituate them. To practice an appropriate transfer to the toilet one time each day is worthless unless everyone toileting that patient utilizes the very same technique. This approach serves several ends.

1. The patient's learning is reinforced.
2. The staff and/or family feel they are contributing to the recovery of the patient.
3. Attitudes are modified from treating the patient as a recipient of total care to treating the patient as a person capable of making gains.
4. Caretakers begin to notice they are working less hard physically in the care of the patient, making them more receptive to occupational therapy, and more apt to interact with the patient more positively.
5. The patient perceives that others respond to him as having potential for gains, altering the patient's own self image.
6. The patient is more apt to set further goals.
7. The family is pleased with the gains they note. After all, they generally do not understand illness or medicine, but they are well able to assess improved function and attitude. They are more apt to provide the wherewithal to continue that treatment.

Ad infinitum. Action yields reaction. Parts relate to wholes. Naturally occurring reinforcement compounds itself.

Sounds simple. Why doesn't it happen everywhere? In order to effect change it is necessary that one have total understanding of the milieu in which one works. What are the motivators? Who holds the power? (Addicott, 1978)[1] What can be done to meet everyone's needs, including the patients? One must remember that a social system includes everyone. Interactions must be assessed as if they were occurring in group sessions. But it is not necessary that all of the group be seated in the same room. All those factors which control group behavior are at work in the treatment milieu. Being aware of that, one must come to grips with a touchy issue. Manipulation is not a dirty word. Psychotherapists do it all the time. So do mothers, teachers, and social activists. Setting up a social encounter in a task situation should not be a foreign experience for occupational therapists. It is necessary to orient toward being a psych therapist in a physical disability setting. If mind and body relate irrevocably, then our orientation is clear. Some of the most effective treatment for the patient can be to alter staff behavior. This approach requires skill and courage. The first is found in abundance in occupational therapists; the second is less abundant, but available through training and practice. Assertiveness training has been around for a while, but I venture to say it is a cop-out. Assertiveness is a polite way of avoiding acknowledgment of aggressive enterprise. Aggression is not considered a positive term for female behavior. Like it or not, occupational therapy has to this time been primarily a female profession. Aggression is not so frowned upon in male society. In fact, for men the term is often used in a complimentary fashion. "He's an aggressive businessman." This is not a derogatory remark. Aggression is admired in sports personages. Aggressiveness need not be so despised in occupational therapists. If therapists are to be role models for their patients in recapturing rights to self determination, aggression must be considered a positive trait, essentially associated with territorial behavior. Territorial excursion requires aggression. Aggression is inextricably associated with limbic function. The seat of emotion is vitally stimulated and generated by aggressive behavior. With such aggression comes increased self image and self confidence. Successful encounter cannot be achieved without confidence, a confidence which is associated with the comfort felt in appropriately demonstrated aggressive behavior.

Cooperation with the entire team is the keynote to a successful treatment program. Cooperation should be understood to derive from mutual effort rather than understood as deference. The occupational therapist does not work in a vacuum. As the patient encounters a variety of persons in his day and is dependent upon them for his needs, it is necessary to understand relationships the patient has with these persons. Family and staff must be called upon to aid the patient in achieving maximum function. Within a nursing home, maintenance, housekeeping and dietary are as vital to the life of the patient as are medicine, nursing, physical therapy and social service. All members of the team should be called upon to contribute their expertise as needed. Both therapist and patient serve to identify needs, seeking the cooperation of other team members in the solution of problems of function. When the entire team operates to provide for the patient's maximum performance, recovery can be achieved with maximum speed and cost effectiveness.

In order for the patient to be successful in the recommended environment, the cooperation of those to whom the territory 'belongs' must be effected. The patient is generally not equipped with the strength of mind, body and purpose to alter an environment over which his own rights are in question. When occupational therapists establish their own rights to alter and effect change within a territory, patients' rights are enhanced. It is the right and purpose of occupational therapists to facilitate change and plans in their clients, thereby developing for their patients their relationships with the world and the people around them.

The aggression required to establish rights in a previously unclaimed environment is not available to many occupational therapists. Training of skill in confrontation is a component seriously lacking in occupation therapy curricula and in too many of its role models, whereas it is a tool vitally important for proficient therapeutic approach. Inherent in confident assertiveness is the necessity for high personal regard both of self and of profession. Self regard on the part of the therapist is vital to the recovery of the patient. A patient will look to a confident therapist for guidance in recovery of function. Treatment demands talent from the therapist, as well as a confident awareness of that talent on the part of the treating therapist. The confident therapist who offers solutions and has been observed to have control and generate respect will be effective in generating confidence and a sense of future in clients served.

REFERENCES
Chapter 10. Principles for Treatment

1. Addicott, J.: "Occupational Therapy in Administration; Independent or Dependent Variable?" Presented at the American Occupational Therapy Association Annual Conference, San Diego, California, 1978.

11. Selected Therapeutic Techniques

The ability of the human being to interact with his environment is a developing skill. In time, vistas expand. As that expansion develops, internal recognition and awareness also develop and refine. Both egocentric and exocentric specificity refine and develop as the infant grows. Egocentric and exocentric refinement and the relationship between both are features of progressive development at later ages as well.

Egocentric and exocentric orientation depend upon constancy experiences based upon spatial coordinates. Essential to the development of reliable contexts within which to function is a clear definition of vertical and horizontal, and the ability to retain the constancy of these concepts despite functional mobility. Changes in tone and alterations in sensory integration can interfere with this facility. The establishment and reestablishment of these spatial coordinates is prior to fluid function.

Kinesthesia serves as the mechanism for the establishment of gravitational orientation. Reinforcing kinesthesia as the context for other sensory experiences provides integrated sensory performance based upon a constant gravitational field. Reverting to this basic feature of human environmental awareness through egocentric stimulation and refinement creates an improved context for further performance.

When development has been impeded by disability, that development can be recapitulated through the use of therapeutic activities. Therapeutic activities are composed of sub-skills. A number of these skills have been observed to be particularly vital to higher functional performance. Some specific techniques have been found very useful to the regeneration of skill. Descriptions of a number of these techniques follow.

Heightened Proprioceptive Awareness (egocentric)

Sometimes it is necessary to put patients in touch with the sense of how it feels to move parts of their bodies in relation to other body parts. Actions which have been 'forgotten' can be regenerated through the use of progressive resistance. These exercises should be presented to the correctly posturally aligned individual and are designed as preliminary to and facilitory to activity, not as exclusive of activity. It is vital that sitting posture be aligned vertically and horizontally (Figure 11-1). The use of pillow support is not recommended if position can be actively sustained. Rather, the patient is to develop a sense of vertical and horizontal through recognition of correct alignment. Exercises have been found most helpful when applied to trunk, neck and shoulders in order to orient the patient to space.

Trunk

Being certain the patient's buttocks are placed fully against the wheelchair seat, flex the patient forward. (Do not exceed hip fracture precautions!) Place your hands on the scapulae and encourage the patient to sit up. "Push me!" (Figure 11-1). Any movement in the correct direction is to be praised. Then place your hands on the patient's shoulders and tell the patient to "Push forward!" As the patient comprehends what is expected, increase resistance. It may take some time for the patient to break the reflex which forces him into extensor posture and thus diagonal alignment with gravity. Rudel (1979)[1] reports on the

Selected Therapeutic Techniques 215

Figure 11-1

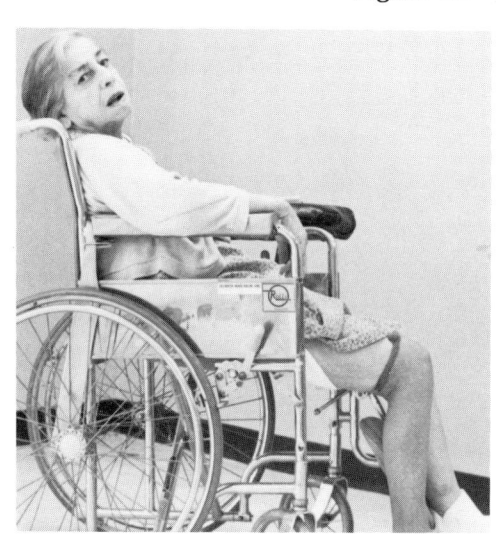

(a) Poor Posture

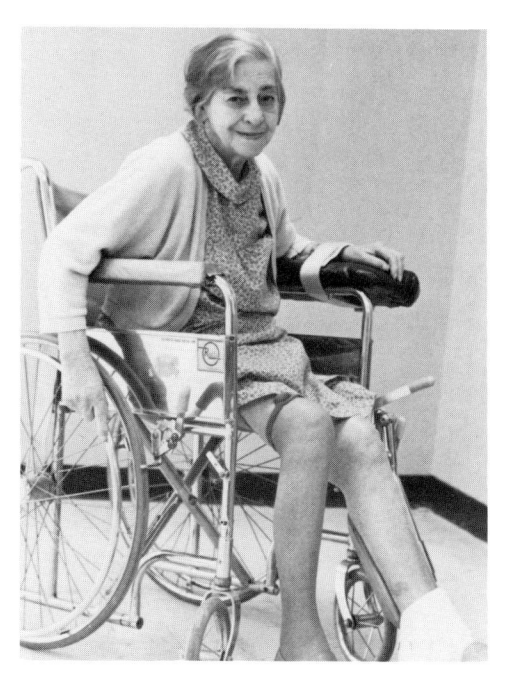

(b) Corrected Posture

Sitting Position Aligned Vertically and Horizontally

Figure 11-2

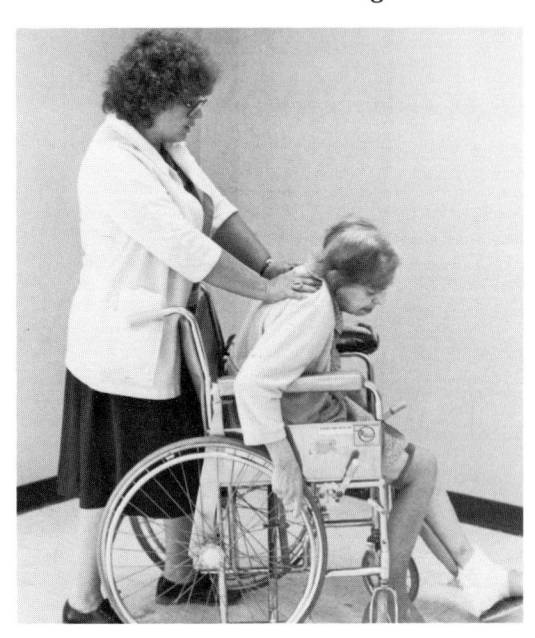

(a) Trunk Extension Exercise

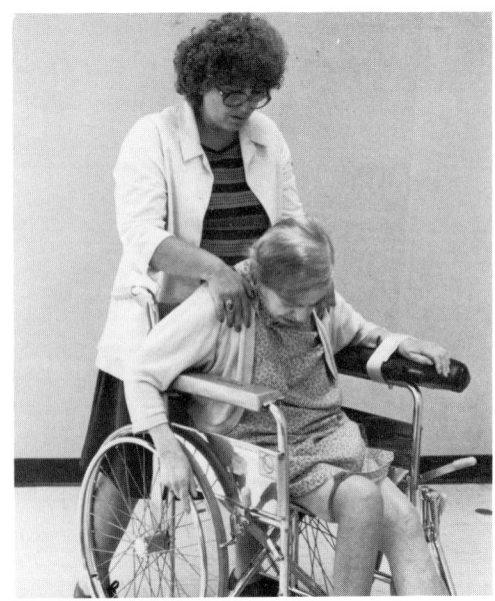

(b) Trunk Flexion Exercise

Patient is instructed to offer resistance to the therapist, first in extension, then in flexion.

Selected Therapeutic Techniques 217

Figure 11-3
Neck flexion and extension exercises

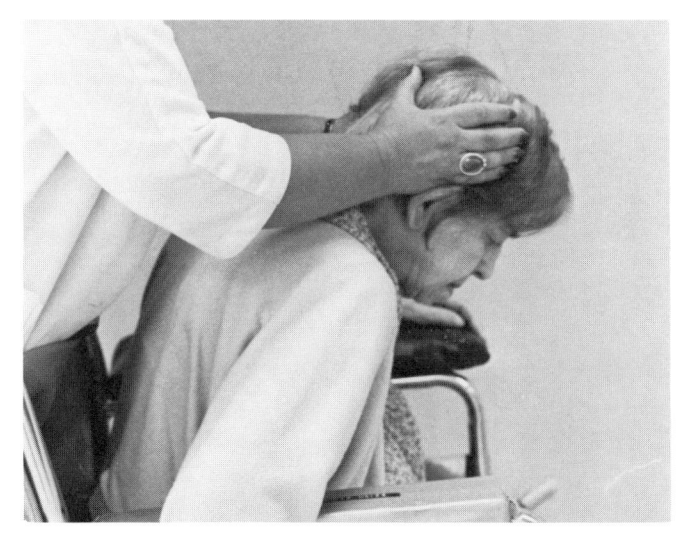

(a) Patient's head is brought to full limit of neck flexion. Patient is instructed to "Look up." Resistance is offered, but patient is permitted as much full active neck extension as can be actively performed.

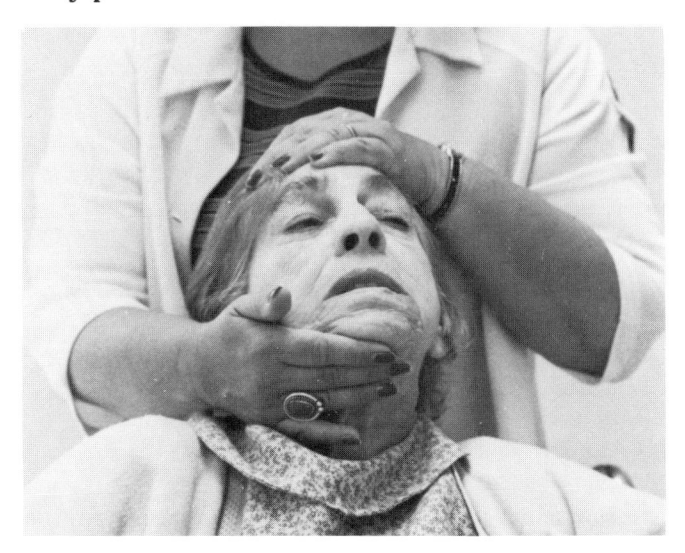

(b) Reverse procedure is followed with instructions to "Look down."

Figure 11-4
Neck rotation exercises

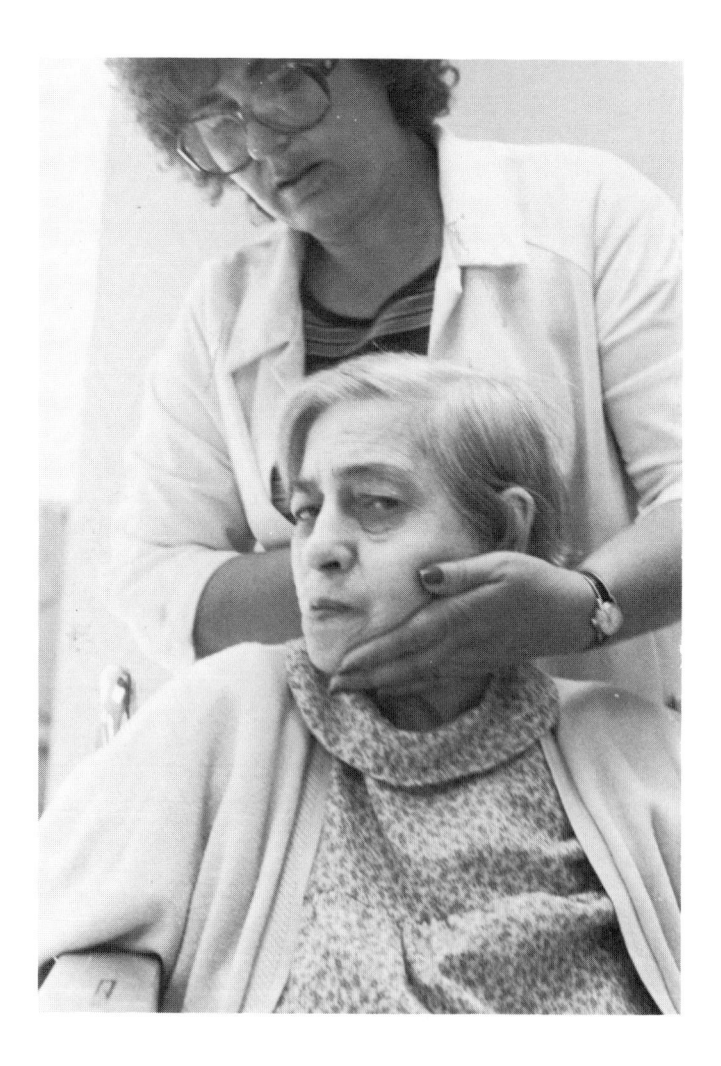

Neck rotation can be resisted with the hand placed on the lateral border of the mandible. Turn the head to full left rotation with your hand on the right jaw and say, "Turn front." Release when the head is centered. Repeat from full right rotation to center.

Selected Therapeutic Techniques **219**

Figure 11-5
Shoulder exercises

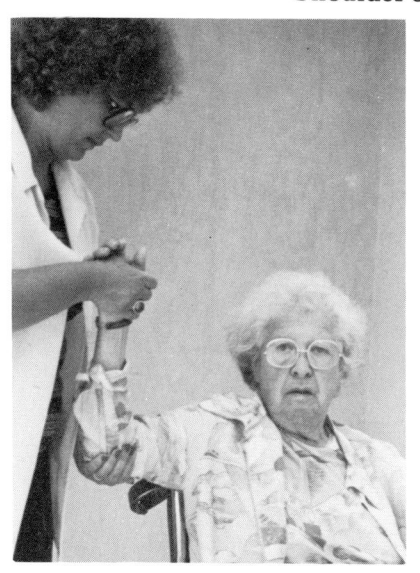

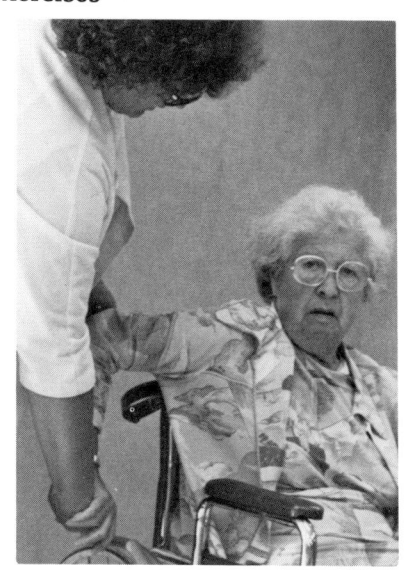

(a)

(b)

(c)

Patient is instructed:
(a) "This is up."
(b) "This is down."
(c) Detail - position of therapist's hand

difficulty persons with learning problems face when presented with tasks incorporating diagonal components. It is not necessary to belabor this exercise. It is designed to alert the patient to and reinforce conscious control of trunk mobility.

Neck

Bring the patient's head to the limit of full range of flexion and ask the patient to bring his head up. "Look up!" Apply resistance to the back of the skull (Figure 11-3). Reverse the procedure. Bring the head into full extension. Place your hand on the patient's forehead. "Put your head down." Apply only sufficient resistance so that the patient is aware of the need to exert effort, but at all times allow the patient to succeed in that effort. The object of this exercise is to heighten awareness of movement, and thus, control.

Neck rotation can be resisted with the hands placed on the lateral border of the mandible. Turn the head to full left rotation with your hands on the right jaw and say, "Turn front." (Figure 11-4) Release when the head is centered. Repeat from full right rotation to center.

Shoulder

Position the patient with arm abducted lateral to the body and flexed to 90° at the elbow (Figure 11-5). Support the elbow and hold the left hand with your left hand. Internally rotate to 0° and say, "This is down." Externally rotate to 180° and say, "This is up." "Push down." When down, state "Push up." Again, resist sufficiently to permit success.

Through these exercises the concepts of up and down, the sense of orientation to space and gravity are reinforced. It is necessary throughout the exercises that postural alignment be retained.

Patients who are experiencing difficulty in producing movement correctly can be instructed to perform these exercises with vision occluded, directing reliance upon proprioception. If proprioception and vision are unintegrated, enforcing the veridicality of proprioception may serve to transfer reliance from a misinforming visual system.

Positioning (egocentric-exocentric)

It is useful to attend to positioning to retain or enhance orientation as well as to prevent or repair physical deformity and function.

Prone lying

Many patients never have the opportunity to experience prone lying, as they are always put to bed in the supine position. The presence of decubiti may require side lying, but even this position is rarely used as other than a remediation tool. Prone lying has been found useful for several reasons. It can be used to increase range of motion to neck, hips and knees. Since prolonged supine position has been reported to be disorienting (Daffner, 1976)[2], prone lying is also recommended for its orienting capabilities.

It is not recommended that patients be left in prone position unattended unless they are capable of independent turning. Observe for redness at points of pressure.

Use prone position to teach neck rotation. Neck extensors are required to function against gravity in this exercise. It may be necessary initially to assistively rotate the head. Developmental postures can be achieved when neck tone is heightened. Gravity serves as resistance to neck, scapular musculature and trunk. The patient can be instructed to turn to the right and to the left. "Look at me." "Look at the window." Right and left are egocentric orientations. Landmarks are exocentric. Both orientations and their relationships can and should be incorporated with one another. "Look at the head board (exocentric)." "Look up (egocentric)." "Reach the call bell (exocentric)." "Turn over (egocentric)." These exercises may be performed in bed or on mats. If the therapist has no one to assist with putting the patient onto a mat, the use of the bed is often easier. There is more control available to the therapist. These exercises can

222 PERCEPTION: ITS DEVELOPMENT AND RECAPITULATION

Figure 11-6
Arm Rests

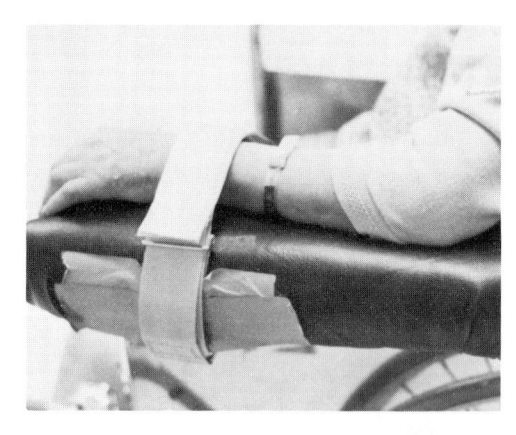

(a) Side view

(b) Front view

(c) Arm rest with tray

be incorporated into bed rolling activities. Bed rolling activities are functional and provide neck and trunk rotation and scapular resistance.

Wheelchair Positioning

Wheelchair positioning should attend to body alignment relative to verticals and horizontals. Critical attention should be paid to visual alignment of the patient. Hip flexion of 90°, with vertical trunk and horizontal shoulder position is the goal, as this position offers visual alignment with the horizon.

Arm Rests—The use of adapted arm rests for patients with hemiplegia is recommended (Figure 11-6). The arm rest provides several benefits. Subluxation is prevented, as is flexion synergy inhibited. The use of the arm rest permits the use of a weakened upper extremity as an assistive hand in a functional position. The hand is kept in view, retarding unilateral neglect. Even partial use of a paretic extremity encourages increased attention to that extremity. Spontaneous movement is permitted because the hand is not as restricted as it is when splinted. The arm rest can be contoured to provide optimal hand position.

Leg Rests—When leg extenders are used, they should fit securely so that when the leg is fully extended there is stimulation elicited should posture shift and hip extensor posture be assumed. Instruct the patient to reseat himself by pressing against the leg rests and doing 'wheelchair pushups.' Repeated reinforcement will be necessary but is justified by the success which can be achieved by attention to position.

Selective removal of leg rests should be considered. Hemiplegics can learn to maneuver their chairs when the leg rest is retained for the affected leg alone. Confused and debilitated patients often respond well to the removal of both leg rests. (Remove them entirely so that other staff do not unwittingly provide their use.) Removing leg rests provides increased motor output and increased proprioceptive input and spatial reinforcement.

Increased Shoulder Mobility (egocentric)

Older patients often have limitation in active shoulder flexion. Few activities they have been required to perform as part of their recent life tasks have necessitated shoulder flexion. When flexion is reduced, still fewer activities remain possible. Shoulder mobility can be increased by using this simple technique.

Position the patient in 90° of shoulder flexion (Figure 11-7). Hold the patient's left hand with your left hand; reverse instructions for the right side. Support the patient's elbow. Instruct the patient to push down to full shoulder extension. Instruct the patient to push up. Allow the patient to achieve the greatest degree of active shoulder flexion. Offer no resistance in flexion. Provide assistance to active motion in flexion. Instruct the patient to push down. This time, do not allow the arm to extend. Then instruct the patient to bring his hand up. Cocontraction will enable increased flexion. Repeat the procedure until the patient appears to be reaching full capability. Do not overtax the patient. Prior to the initial contraction the patient will probably be unable to flex beyond 90° without assistance; flexion will increase until a maximum is reached. Do not repeat this exercise until the next session. During each session the patient will gradually increase in muscle power and then will appear to suddenly lose all strength. Be sure to encourage the patient and say, "This is a sign that the muscles have been working. Tomorrow we'll do it again." When the patient can achieve active motion through full range, switch to an activity which incorporates this movement and grade up with increased resistance and endurance.

Finger Gnosia Training (egocentric)

It is not uncommon, following stroke, for patients to have lost the ability to discriminate between some or all of their

Selected Therapeutic Techniques 225

**Figure 11-7
Increasing Shoulder Mobility**

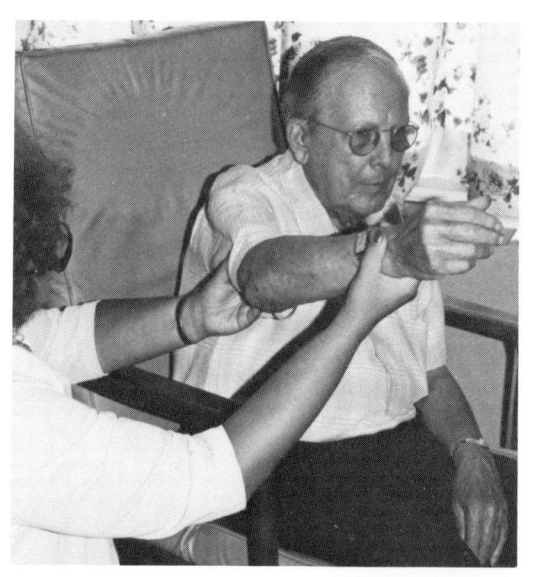

(a) 90° of Flexion

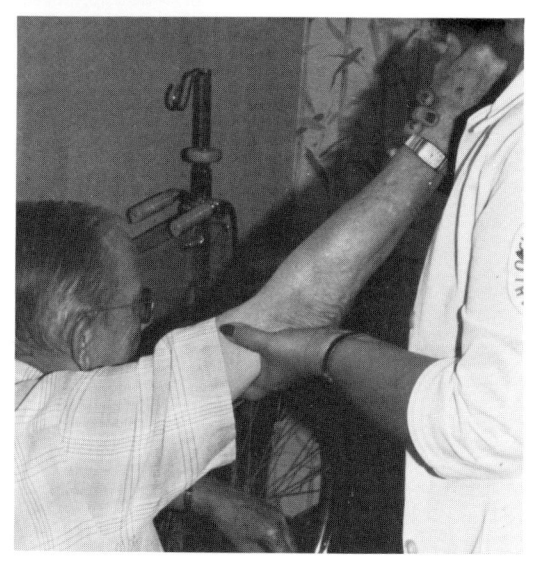

(b) Increased active range

Shoulder flexion is facilitated when cocontraction of shoulder musculature is effected. The patient is instructed to "push down" against resistance. No resistance is offered in shoulder flexion.

Figure 11-8
Finger Gnosia Training

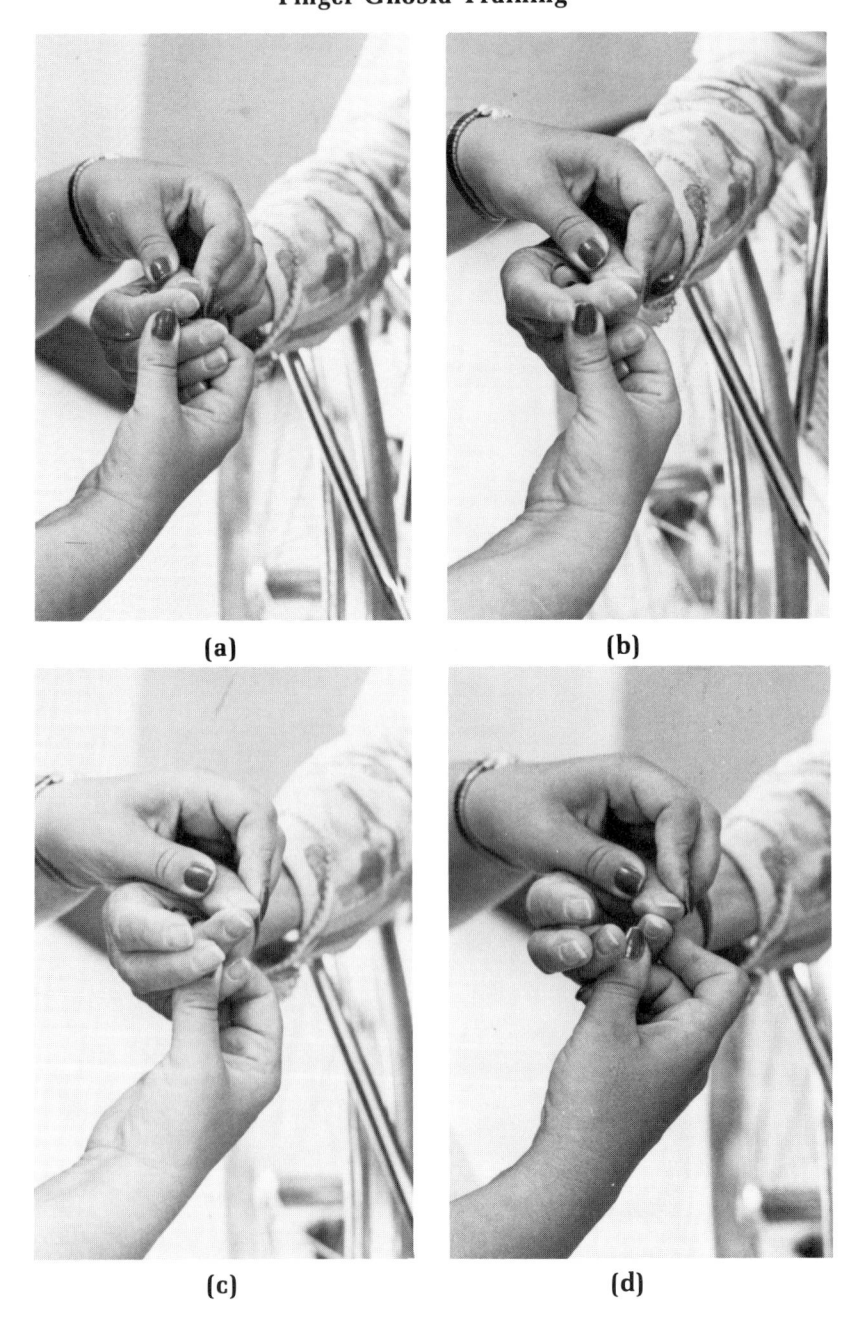

(a)

(b)

(c)

(d)

Selected Therapeutic Techniques **227**

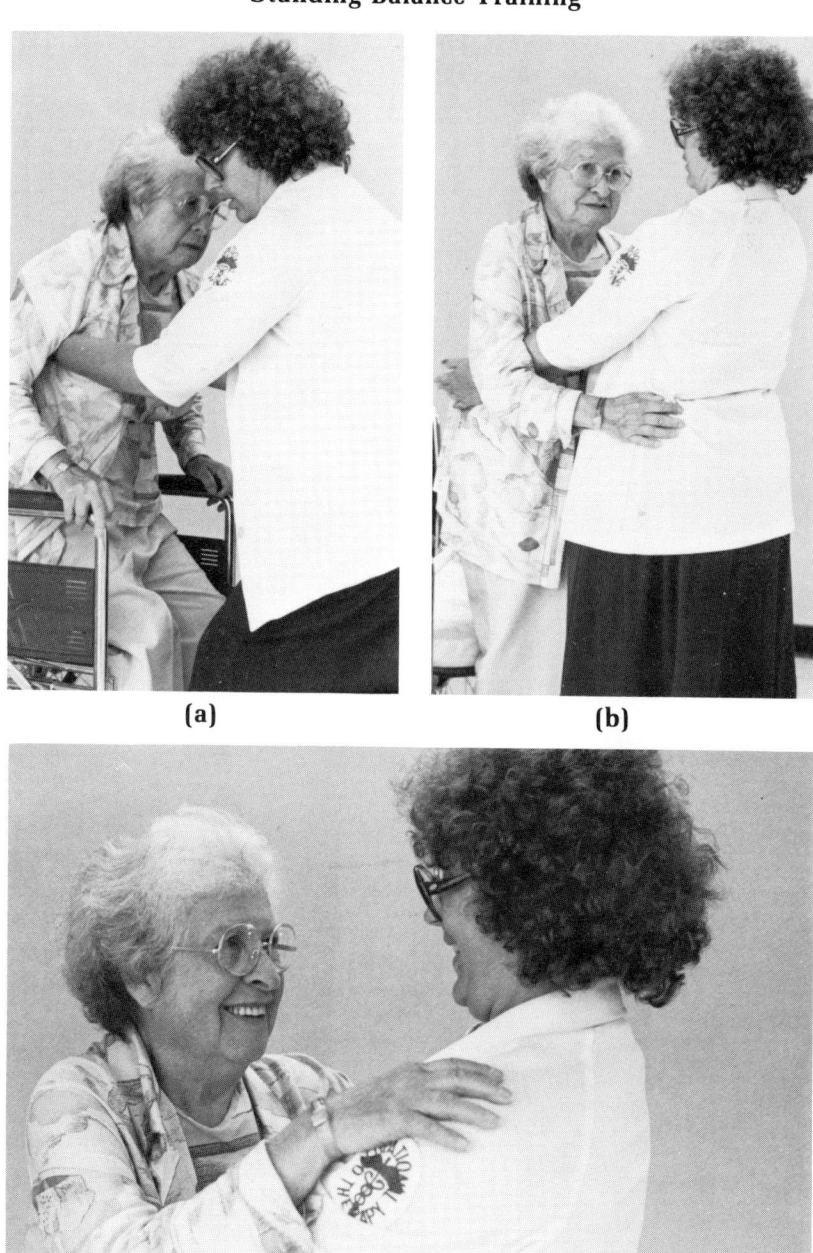

**Figure 11-9
Standing Balance Training**

(a)

(b)

(c)

**Figure 11-9 (continued)
Standing Balance Training**

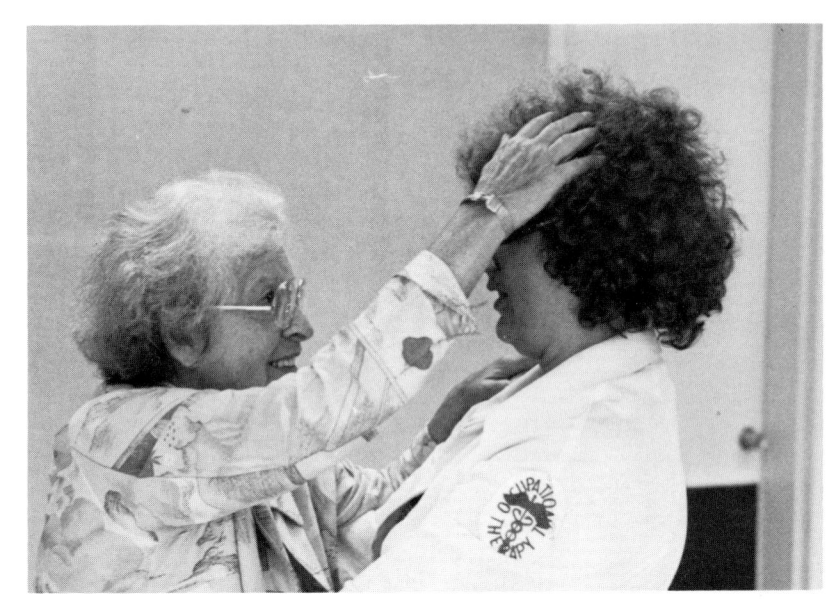

(d)

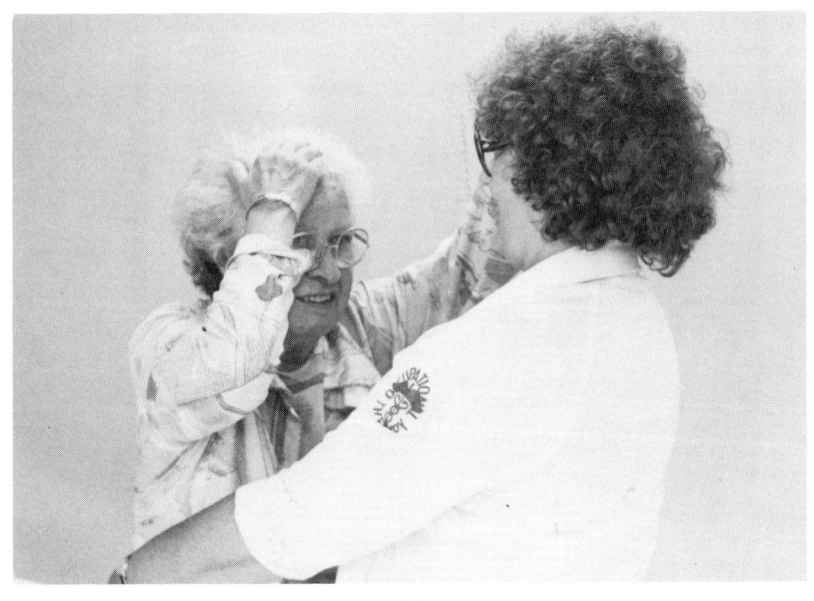

(e)

fingers on the disabled side. Absence of this ability seriously interferes with skilled hand usage. This exercise has been found useful in increasing skill in finger discrimination.

Place the patient's hand in functional position with elbow supported (Figure 11-8). Oppose the patient's thumb to the first, second, third, and fourth fingers in turn. Name each finger according to the patient's name for that finger, if the patient's name for that finger can be identified (i.e. first finger, forefinger, index finger or pointer; second finger, middle finger, tall man; third finger, ring finger; fourth finger, pinky). Be sure the hand is within foveal view. Repeat the procedure, requesting the patient to press the thumb hard against each finger in turn. Rub the thumb and each finger together in turn. Repeat touching and pressing each finger, but this time repeat the process alternately with vision and with vision occluded for each finger. Then proceed in sequence with vision occluded. Next, with vision occluded, vary the order of the fingers, requesting the patient to identify fingers when touched. If the patient continues to have difficulty, repeat the process with vision.

This disability occurs along with weakness in hand function. It is recommended that this exercise be followed by functionally directed therapeutic activity for increasing hand skill.

Wheelchair Activities (transitional)

The use of the wheelchair as a therapeutic tool should be considered. The wheelchair fulfills a variety of therapeutic needs. Positioning of the body in good postural alignment in association with ocular stimulation is enabled by the wheelchair. Self-directed propulsion through space in a wheelchair provides:

1. Bilateral shoulder movements against resistance.
2. Peripheral proprioceptive experiences.
3. Trunk shifting.

230 PERCEPTION: ITS DEVELOPMENT AND RECAPITULATION

4. Successive opportunities for progressive resistive activities for the development of upper extremity strength necessary for transfers and ambulation.
5. Change experiences to the peripheral visual field compared to foveal experiences, occurring in conjunction with proprioceptive experiences.
6. Self-induced vestibular stimulation.
7. Way finding opportunities related to the development of a cognitive map.
8. Increased patient visibility so success is apparent to staff.
9. Increased independence.
10. An activity which is measurable in terms of speed, endurance and skill.

Standing Balance (egocentric-exocentric)

Place the patient's hands on wheelchair arms with his head bent forward over his knees. Facing the patient, grasp him by his belt holding the patient on either side of the waist and while assisting the patient, instruct him to stand. Be sure to bend your knees to avoid injury to yourself. (Figure 11-9a.) The patient will be very insecure. (Figure 11-9b.) Tell him, "Grab my shoulders." (Figure 11-9c.) At this stage, patients are all too eager to grab whatever they can. They will hold very tightly. If the patient is extremely insecure, allow him to seat himself. Praise the patient and repeat the process. When the patient trusts himself and you, request that he put his right hand on top of your head and back to your shoulder. (Figure 11-9d.) Repeat with the left hand. Then seat the patient. Repeat the process. Then instruct the patient to place his right hand on his shoulder, then on your shoulder. Repeat with the left. Do not overtax the patient's tolerance for this activity, but attempt to increase the patient's capabilities each time. Progress to your waist, then to the patient's waist. His head, your head. One hand, then two. (Figure 11-9e.) The patient becomes secure that you are able to hold him and that he can sit at any time. Randomize the sequence as skill and confidence build. Begin midline crossing.

For this exercise it is necessary that the therapist be able to translate his own position relative to the patient in order not to confuse the patient with instructions. It is suggested that this skill be practiced by the therapist prior to working with a patient.

Body landmarks can be used and may include ears, nose, etc. "Put your right hand on my right ear." This exercise can evoke very funny situations. Humor is very helpful in gaining cooperation and subcorticalization of the elements of directionality associated with trunk shifting.

This activity can be adapted for use with stroke patients, hip fracture patients, and amputees. As skill increases and the therapist judges that the patient is safe, the therapist can let go of the patient's belt. Other activities can be incorporated. Reaching for objects and shifting their position will build functional skills. Items found in patients' rooms are useful. Lifting and filling suitcases, reaching into drawers and handling clothes in closets are good therapeutic activities which incorporate trunk shifting and balance.

Constancy (exocentric)

Being able to recall objects when those objects are out of sight is an ability attained within the first year of life. This ability is sometimes observed to be lost or diminished in later years. Recall is based upon recognition and is evidenced in short term and long term memory. Short term memory is more apt to be lost in later years. Retention can sometimes be enhanced through training in constancy.

Use objects the patient is apt to encounter in daily living (i.e., a spoon, a lipstick, a comb, dentures, etc.). Allow the patient to become familiar through touch with two objects. Name the objects. Have the patient name the objects. Cover the objects and request the names of the objects. Uncover them and allow the patient to reinforce accuracy or correct error. Repeat until accurate. This exercise can be varied by altering the position of the objects (right, left, front, back, under, over, in, out) or by increasing the number of objects to be remembered.

A variation of this task can be done as a game for a group of people. Prepare a tray of 10 or more objects. Allow the group thirty seconds to view the contents of the tray, and then cover the tray, concealing the objects from view. Each person is then to write down all the objects which can be remembered. Points can be awarded for correct responses.

Peripheral Stereognosis (exocentric)

Combining memory with peripheral function can be affected by this stereognosis exercise. As an adjunct to stereognostic training, use lateral space to enhance skill. Using the lateral field of upper extremity function appears to enhance stereognostic function perhaps because additional proprioceptive input is contributed by stimulation of shoulder, back and upper arm receptors.

Select a variety of familiar objects. As in the constancy exercise the objects are concealed from view, but in this instance they are placed outside of visual range, requiring the patient to reach to his side at full arm's length (Figure 11-10). The task is to identify a requested object by touch and to bring it into frontal range without looking at the object or the place where it is located. Begin with one object which has been first identified by vision. Reaching and finding the object is the initial task. Allow the patient to place the object back and forth from front to side positions until able to function skillfully. Then add another object. Start by using two objects of distinctly different dimension, texture, and **weight** (i.e. a compact and an eyeglass case). Repeat until identification of place and object becomes skilled. Then add another object. Continue to add objects until the patient becomes adept at this task. Recognition of seven objects is good skill.

Figure 11-10

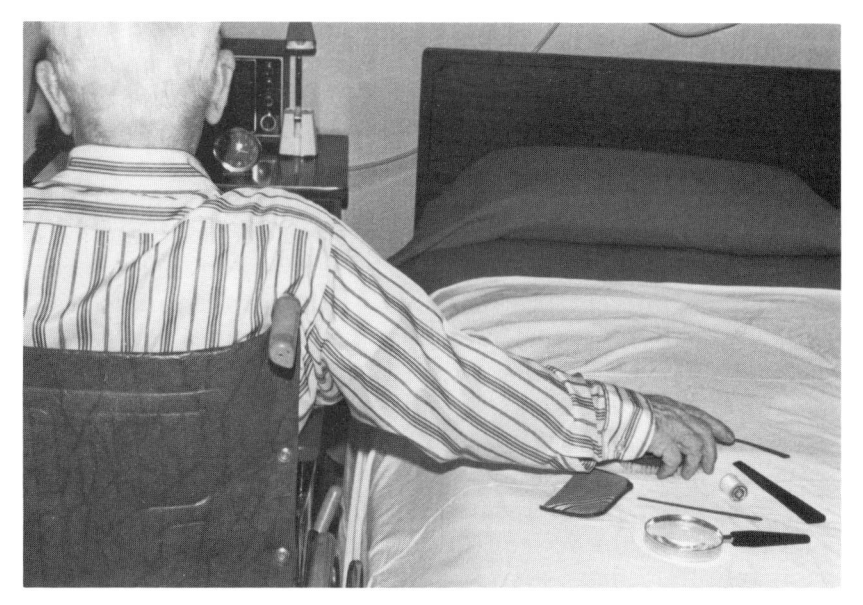

Peripheral Stereognosis Training

A variation of this exercise which incorporates lateral arm function is cone stacking. Tasks performed in the lateral areas of space appear to enhance memory and function within space. Wheelchair usage is another activity which requires skill in lateral space and enhances orientation in space.

Spatial Coordinates Applied to Perception of Environment (exocentric)

Seat the patient on a swivel chair. Restrain the patient for safety. Allow the patient to turn by instructing him to use his feet on the floor, and suggest he visually explore the environment. The corridor outside of the patient's room can be a good location to define orientation. Identify four coordinates and their relation to one another. Turn the patient quarter-turns (90°) (Figure 11-11) and state, "Here is the nurses's station, there's the door to outside, here's your room, and there's the supply closet at the other end of the hall. The nurses' station is opposite your room, the hall has a door at one end, a closet at the other." Now ask, "Where is your room? The nurses's station? Outside? The closet? Good! On your right is your room, turn to the right. On your left is the closet, turn to the left," etc. Reinforce right/left directives with place objectives. Randomly intermingle directives for right and left place. If the patient will cooperate, request the patient to close his eyes and respond. As accuracy increases, increase speed in an attempt to improve automatic responses.

This activity can be expanded to way-finding by maneuvering through space to goal directed places and events. Self-directed maneuverability through space increases skill and recall within space. Cognitive mapping is developed from familiar places out toward unknown space. Moving patients from one place to another is disorienting. Time spent in assisted way-finding, alerting patients to environmental landmarks, is useful in creating memory for space. An unfamiliar environment may be so confusing for the patient that the therapist may have to select landmarks to attend to. Be careful in your directions. What you perceive as the yellow door may be seen by the patient as white or beige. Numbers on doors may be too small to envision. Your directions may have been misheard. Give instructions in several ways. To your right, under the clock, between the windows. Repeat instructions as if you had forgotten you had given them. I understand it is not polite to ask people if they want another portion of food. Instead one should always ask, "Would you like a piece of cake?," never insinuating that someone is having seconds. Instructions can be presented in the same way. Repeat and do not stress the point. It will become clear when the patient no longer needs assistance or instruction. Interaction and independence are readily observable.

Selected Therapeutic Techniques 235

Figure 11-11

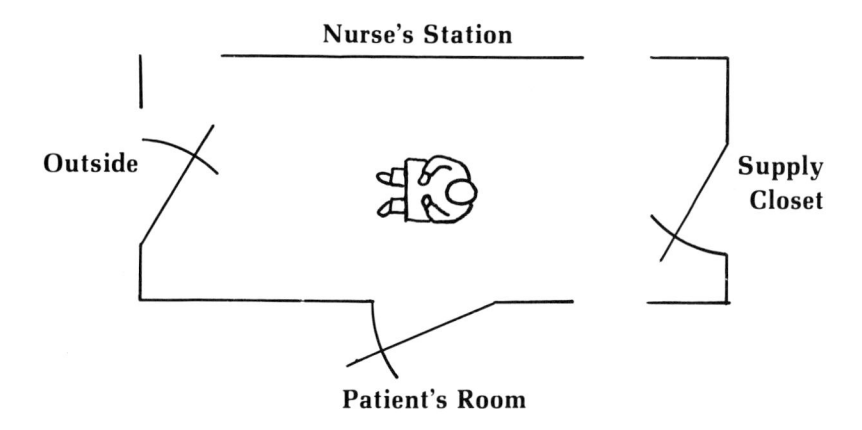

Nurse's Station

Outside

Supply Closet

Patient's Room

Overhead view of the patient in corridor for orientation training.

Weaving, Adapted (exocentric)

There are few gross craft tasks which are portable, economical, interesting and therapeutic to a variety of older persons with multiple disabilities. This is our favorite craft activity because of its universal appeal and the variety of ways it can be adapted to provide for the needs of many different patients. As adapted weaving is within the skill of all occupational therapists, merely a few adaptations will be described.

A frame with dimensions of 15 inches by 18 inches is constructed (Figure 11-12a.) Slots are routed in one-half inch increments permitting warping in either direction. For blind patients, warp threads are alternately rough, thick, and smooth, thin. For visually impaired patients, the warp is of light and dark thread. Note should be made of the ground upon which the

Figure 11-12

(a) Weaving Frame and pillow.

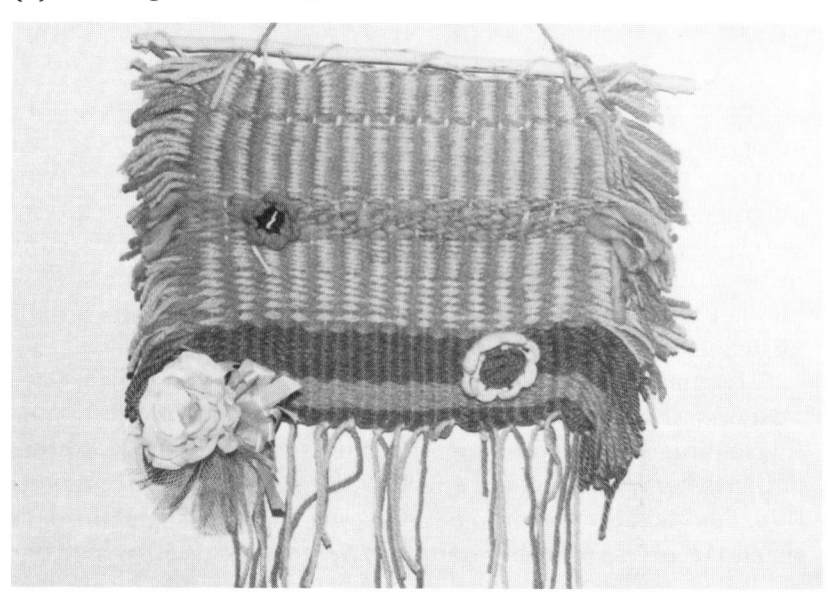

(b) Wall hanging.

work is to be done. If necessary, contrast can be provided by a colored paper which contrasts with both warp threads. Weft threads are cut to 20 inches for the 15 inch dimension. Weaving is a simple over and under, reverse pattern. Patients are instructed to alternately sequence the color of their yarn threads. "Put the blue thread under the blue thread. Put the yellow thread under the yellow thread." Yarn of any dimension can be used. Errors are easy to see and easy to correct. As skill increases, subsequent weaving projects can eliminate alternately colored warp. Sequences can be made more complex, creativity can be encouraged.

This is a project which can be left with patients for use on their own. Assignments can be given. These projects are visable and attractive and interesting to staff as well. A variety of objects can be made from the fabric. Pillows, wall hangings, walker and wheelchair bags can be designed (Figure 11-12a, b). Interest generated in this activity, although initially presented for restorative purposes, is frequently sustained, and the patient's interest can be mainstreamed into the activity or maintenance program when the patient no longer remains on restorative therapeutic program.

Ambulation

Ambulation in life spaces provides opportunities similar to those described for wheelchair activities. Sometimes patients are capable of ambulating but their life space is such that it provides confusing and disorienting stimuli which tend to interfere with balance. The following techniques have been found useful in enhancing balance while ambulating in life space.

Safe Escort

Patients who have demonstrated competency in ambulation but are not yet safe enough to be considered independent can be provided with a walker for supervised use in their life space. The therapist escorts the patient by holding the patient at the back of the waist by a belt or the trouser

Figure 11-13

Safe Escort Procedure

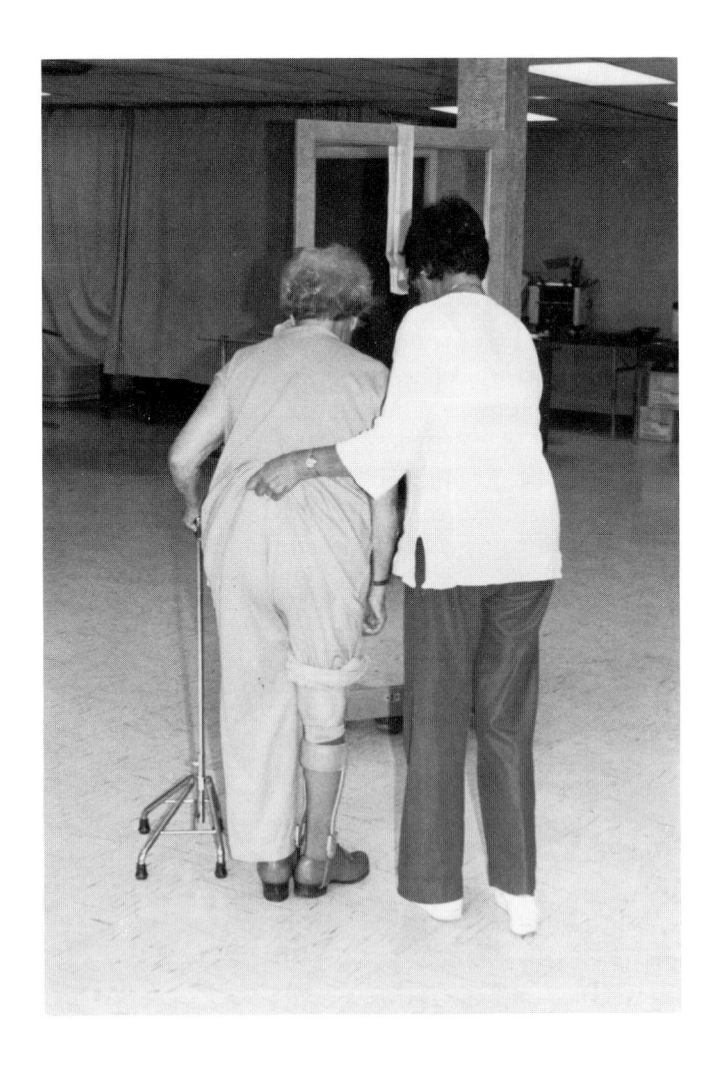

Holding patient at center back does not interfere with gravitational orientation.

waistband with one hand, (Figure 11-13) and bringing the wheelchair along so that the patient can be seated at any time. Escorting the patient by the arm alters his sense of center and encourages dependency. The therapist behind the patient and out of view of the patient provides the patient with a sense of independence while safety is assured. As balance is assured, the therapist can release the hold on the patient. Touching the patient lightly and intermittently at the center back reassures the patient of the presence of the therapist while at the same time the patient is aware that his own efforts are entirely directing his advance.

Goal Directed Ambulation

Ambulation to a goal directed event is recommended. This serves as evidence to the patient that he can resume performance in activities of meaning to him. The use of the dining room as a goal place is a good tool. The distance the patient can ambulate can be graded so that the patient can ultimately ambulate there independently. As meals are served three times per day, consistent reinforcement is provided.

Once the patient has demonstrated that he can safely traverse the distance required, it may then be necessary to wean the patient from the wheelchair. When patients show reluctance to relinquish the possession of their wheelchair, it may be possible to convince them of their ability to do without its use by folding the chair so that it remains with them, but is visibly out of service for a specified period of time (i.e. for use within the room, or to the nurse's station for medication). When patients' confidence builds, they are then usually willing to surrender their wheelchair. Spontaneous responses from other patients and staff reinforces their confidence.

REFERENCES
Chapter 11. Selected Therapeutic Techniques

1. Rudel, R.: "Oblique Mystique: Figure Perception." Presented at the Conference on Neural and Developmental Bases of Spatial Orientation, Teachers College, Columbia University, New York, November 16, 1979.
2. Daffner, C.: Personal correspondence, 1976.

12. Selected Case Studies

Recently I had occasion to give a report at one of the nursing homes we service. I was asked to present statistics regarding numbers of patients treated, numbers of treatments, and so forth. These statistics had no real meaning for me as they appeared to serve no real purpose. They were not for reimbursement purposes or to figure staffing. The intent of the administrator was for every department to inform one another of what had occurred during the past nine months as if numbers would heighten awareness. For me, the most enlightening information revealed was that we had had occasion to see better than 75 percent of those patients who were admitted to the facility during the past year. Our department had seen over 80 patients, many of whom had derived significant benefit from their evaluations and treatments. This number astounded me, for as our caseload at this facility fluctuates considerably, we usually average a case load of less than ten on any given day. It had escaped my awareness that our total census was so large and even larger when one considers those patients we have seen over the years and in multiple facilities.

During the time we have been in practice some of these patients have blurred in my memory. Some things we do are done with so many patients that their individuality escapes recollection. But some others shall never be forgotten. We have learned from every one of them.

Case Study No. 1
R.K. - Female
Left Cerebrovascular aneurysm
Right Hemiplegia

This semi-ambulatory patient entered the nursing home and was not initially referred to occupational therapy, as she offered the appearance of a functional but confused individual, needing only some ambulation training. She had been observed to be able to walk, though needing some assistance. She could move her arms and she seemed alert on initial impression. She could speak but often did not make sense. Further observation revealed that she was incapable of activities of daily living (ADL) and was incontinent. Her ensuing depression was a major problem which concerned the staff.

When her functional capacity was observed to be impaired, the referral came to occupational therapy. "See what you can find out." Initial evaluation revealed functional passive range of motion in both upper and lower extremities. Muscle power was insufficient for full active range in right shoulder flexion and abduction. Greater weakness was noted in the right upper and lower extremity than in the left where muscle power was fair. Trunk and neck musculature was generally weak. Testing revealed astereognosis in the right hand with anomia for objects in the left hand. She was able to recognize objects in the left hand by identifying their usage, indicating intact stereognostic function. She was unable to oppose her right thumb. The thenar emminence had atrophied. She was unable to raise herself from sitting to standing but was ambulatory when assisted. Her balance was impaired. She leaned to the right when seated. A mild visual field cut was noted on the right. Some difficulty was noted in following directives, possibly attributed to mild receptive aphasia, but she comprehended modeled demonstration. Mrs. K. could make herself understood, but she appeared unmotivated to make much effort on her own behalf. Praxis appeared unimpaired throughout, with the exception of right hand use. Right finger agnosia was present. The patient was dependent in all ADLs. The patient had been right hand dominant prior to her CVA. This patient was labile.

Recommendations:

1. Increase strength in both upper extremities, trunk, neck.
2. Stimulate active movement of right thumb using proprioceptive neuromuscular facilitation (PNF) techniques.
3. Increase fine motor skills in the right hand.
4. Finger gnosia training in the right hand.
5. ADL training in transfers, toileting, dressing, hygiene, grooming, feeding.
6. Improve balance.
7. Increase ambulation skills in life space.
8. Decrease depression.
9. Develop avocational pursuits within limits of patient's disability.
10. Increase activity tolerance.
11. Refer for speech evaluation.
12. Obtain wheelchair with adapted right arm rest.
13. Positioning.
14. Provide short right opponens splint.
15. Homemaking training if appropriate to discharge plans.

Training began in the patient's room by positioning the patient in a wheelchair adapted with a right arm rest in order to achieve proper body alignment as a first step toward improving balance and awareness of verticality. Trunk and neck resistance was offered to heighten proprioceptive input. The patient was instructed in transfer techniques, reinforcing "Lock your brakes." The patient became independent in transfers from wheelchair to chair and was judged safe within three days. Nursing aides were shown the technique used and were requested to use the same procedure for toilet transfers. The patient was on a bowel and bladder training program, necessitating reinforcement every three hours. Occupational therapy participated in this program, transferrng the patient to the toilet at the prescribed interval if that time occurred during occupational therapy. The patient developed bladder control and began to request toileting on her own. Up until this time the patient had been in diapers. When the patient became proficient and safe in transfers she no longer needed assistance except for resecuring the diapers and reaching toilet paper. Three courses of action were taken. Toilet paper was installed to the left side of the commode. The family was called and asked to obtain panties. Concentration was placed upon donning and doffing underpants. Since this patient's standing balance had improved this technique was quickly learned. This training was done in the toilet when the patient needed to use this skill. Nursing staff was instructed to provide continuity. Fortunately this nursing staff had long since learned that some extra time now would free them from this task later on. They were very supportive. Within three weeks this patient was totally independent in toileting, thus receiving much positive reinforcement from nursing, housekeeping (responsible for laundry), and family, not to mention occupational therapy. Her affect increased considerably. Speech evaluation had confirmed aphasia and treatment was provided. Occupational therapy and speech worked closely to coordinate treatment plans, reinforcing each others' goals. Concurrently, attention was paid to the patient's right upper extremity, particularly to the right thumb. A short opponens splint was applied to stabilize the thumb in opposition permitting grasp to be effected. This splint was removed during treatment. Antagonist cocontraction, mild stretch and tapping were used to facilitate opponens contraction. Initial treatment yielded fasciculation of the opponens. The patient was positioned in opposition to each finger in turn and was requested to "press hard." The patient was requested to do this with both vision and vision occluded in order to encourage the patient to construct a conceptualization of the motor pattern requested and in order to reinforce accurate identification of fingers through attention to sensory discrimination. When active opposition was elicited and was sufficient to sustain itself the opponens splint was discarded. Interestingly, speech appeared to return in association with thumb function. Grasp/release activities were introduced, grading those activities from gross to fine as skill developed. A series of items were used proceeding from cotton balls to gross pegs to finer graded pegs to sorting tasks of objects of various sizes and shapes and weights.

Initially, shoulder weakness had necessitated use of overhead slings which use was gradually eliminated as strength increased. As shoulder strength increased the wheelchair arm rest was removed to encourage the use of the right hand in wheelchair travel. As hand skill developed, independence in ADLs increased. As the patient gained each skill (feeding, brushing hair, dressing, etc.) the nursing aide was instructed to abstain from performing that task for the patient. The patient was not always eager to relinquish that asssistance. Reinforcement of the staff was necessary as staff changed from time to time and between shifts but overall administrative cooperation was effective in establishing our right to make these determinations regarding nursing care. All treatment was provided within view of nursing staff, making explanation easier. Feeding training was provided in a dining room where patients were fed. When the patient assumed idependence in feeding she was transferred to the Main Dining Room.

During this time the patient had been seen in physical therapy and had been instructed in the use of the walker. Techniques used in physical therapy were incorporated into ADL use. The patient was gradually encouraged to use the walker to and from chair, toilet, bed and dresser within her room. As her proficiency and safety increased, we began to ambulate the patient outside of her room toward various activities. The patient ambulated with her walker toward the dining room with us escorting her with the wheelchair at the ready. When she tired she sat and proceeded the rest of the way herself in the wheelchair. That activity was engaged in at lunch and dinner times. As her ambulation tolerance increased, the staff on all shifts was kept advised of her endurance level and a nursing aide was assigned to accompany her to meals. Once independent in one direction, she soon became independent in both. Finally, the wheelchair was removed. As the dining room was at least as far as any other location in the nursing home she was now fully independent in her ability to get around in her living environs at nine weeks post admission.

At this point the family began to believe that it would be possible for the patient to return to her home. Physical therapy began stair training. Occupational therapy began homemaker training and engaged the patient in activities requiring she ambulate on carpeting, soil, grass and concrete. She practiced getting in and out of a car. On discharge day the patient walked down the hall using a cane and carrying her own suitcase. After a brief period at home, a home she would share with an elderly sister, they both planned a trip to Las Vegas and the west coast. I understand they enjoyed the trip.

Case Study No. 2
G.H. - Male
Left below knee amputee
Urinary dysfunction

This patient had been hospitalized for three months post amputation prior to admission to the nursing home. His prolonged hospitalization was due to poor healing of the stump. During his hospital stay he was virtually bed bound. This patient was a very tall and heavy man, requiring four nurses to lift him in and out of bed. It has been reported by the family that he had not been removed from bed more than once per day and that only for short periods in which he was seated in the chair next to his bed. Other than for surgery he had never left his hospital room during his entire hospitalization. When G.H. was admitted to the nursing home he was totally dependent for all care. He was unresponsive, totally disoriented and dead weight. His urinary condition necessitated a permanent catheter with a urinary irrigant. His muscle power was poor to fair throughout his upper body. His right lower extremity measured trace to poor. His sitting tolerance was poor. He was unable to follow directions. Visual tracking was impaired. Peripheral awareness was impaired. The patient exhibited bilateral astereognosis. His head control was good even though his sitting posture was poor. All responses were diminished. Body image and directionality were impaired. He was not completely aware of the amputation and its consequences. The patient's wife was acutely ill with a cardiac condition. Two daughters shared their visits between both parents.

Recommendations:

1. Occupational therapy five times per week.
2. **PNF to right lower extremity, trunk, neck.**
3. Increase muscle power and active range of motion in both upper and right lower extremities, trunk and neck.
4. Orient patient to peripheral surround.
5. Increase visual tracking.
6. Increase movement tolerance.
7. Perceptual training - Increase body awareness, increase R/L discrimination, stereognosis training.
8. Desensitize stump. Instruct in stump care.
9. **ADL training in transfers, feeding, grooming, bathing, dressing.**
10. Adapt wheelchair with irrigant pole.
11. Wheelchair training.
12. Increase activity tolerance.
13. Increase communication skills.
14. Encourage socialization.

Treatment began with attention to the greatest problem the staff had to deal with—transfers. Policy at this nursing home required that all patients must be out of bed unless actively ill. Brief naps are permitted for certain patients for whom it has been deemed necessary for their continued health. Therefore, mobility of this patient was a critical problem. A bedside inservice was called by occupational therapy for all nursing staff who would be seeing this patient. Everyone was instructed in a technique to offer stimulation to the right lower extremity to facilitate knee extension and increase its strength. If the right leg could increase in strength sufficient to bear the weight of this large man, then he could participate in his transfers. Everyone was instructed to offer this exercise to elicit one contraction each time they had occasion to pass this patient. Remarkably, everyone participated. The staff seemed interested in being part of the rehabilitation of this patient in a concrete way. Within two weeks the patient began to be able to bear some of his own weight, reducing the staff required for transfers to two. Occupational therapy concentrated upon teaching the patient to use his arms to lift himself to standing.

As the same muscle groups are required for transfers and ambulation as are wheelchair use, wheelchair training had begun on Day 1. Wheelchair training would offer other benefits as well. Initially the patient had no awareness of the periphery, and could not tell if his hands were on the wheels or on the wheelchair arms. Movement was frightening to him. His muscle power was sufficient to propel himself a maximum of three feet. The patient appeared 'spaced out.' There was no recognition of familiar people. Wheelchair training took place around the door of the patient's room so that he would begin to develop a cognitive map encompassing territory with which he was familiar. His upper extremity strength increased. Wheelchair endurance increased. Feeding training was rapidly successful. Proper positioning in the wheelchair and patterning with a utensil in the patient's right hand was sufficient to initiate self feeding. The family was surprised and delighted to see this as this patient had been fed for the previous several months. If he could feed himself then he might have other potential. Independence in feeding also released them from their self constructed attitude that they must be there at meal times to feed him, as they had been doing during his hospitalization. Their comfort increased with the decision they had made regarding nursing home placement. When the patient was completely independent in feeding and was able to wheel his wheelchair to the Main Dining Room, the patient was transferred to eat there. Patients are more highly motivated to eat in the Main Dining Room than in the dining room near their rooms where the dependent patients are fed. The Main Dining Room offers reserved places with consistent companions. Residents eating there are more sociable and independent. Greater food choices are available. Food is served waitress style. Tables are set with cloths or placemats. It is not necessary to eat from a tray. Greater self respect is associated with the Main Dining Room so a transfer to that locale for meals is perceived by all as a successful achievement.

Being required to attend the Main Dining Room three times per day serves to further increase upper extremity strength. Propelling a wheelchair strengthens the same muscles necessary for standing and ambulation with a walker. Environmental demands help the patient make gains outside of specific attention to that exercise. Attendance at the Main Dining Room also serves to increase patient's orientation to time and space.

A technique was devised to increase peripheral awareness by developing perceptual constancy in the lateral fields of function. Familiar objects were shown to the patient. His task was to view them in the periphery, close his eyes, feel them, and then identify them with vision occluded. Objects were selected from among the patient's own possessions. Stereognosis and peripheral awareness both increased. As wheelchair travel required these skills as well, both the exercise period and life tasks supported one another.

ADL training in dressng and bathing contributed to increase perceptual functioning. Stump handling was encouraged. Dressing training was done early in the morning so the patient was gradually able to incorporate skills as they grew. Stump wrapping was included in the dressing routine. Ambulation skills in physical therapy grew. The open wound on the stump healed. A prosthesis became a possibility. Now we were dealing with a patient who was largely independent in ADLs, had good upper extremity strength, was increasingly alert, could follow directions and was sociable. His memory for short term and long term events had increased. His sitting balance was improved permitting removal of a previously required chest restraint.

At this point the physician determined that surgery could be attempted to correct his urinary disorder. He was discharged to the hospital, had uneventful and successful surgery. Toilet training was instituted. Transfers to the toilet were included in his regimen. The patient soon became independent in toileting and became fully independent in dressing and mobility. He had received his prosthesis and was learning to put it on and take it off. The family, at this point, began to plan to take the patient home. A decline in affect and skills resulted. This patient did not want to go home. He did not want to live with his daughters. His wife, with whom he had apparently not had a good relationship, had died early in his nursing home residency. He enjoyed the attention he received from the young women caring for him in the nursing home. He was emotionally tied to those who had helped him to recover. But he refused to tell his daughters how he felt. A family conference was suggested by the patient review committee. Social Service, Nursing and Occupational Therapy, the family and the patient attended the conference. The family decided to take the patient home. The MSW requested that reconsideration be made subsequently if things did not work out at home. She kept in touch with the family. The patient came back to visit several times. When the family went on vacation, G.H. came back to the nursing home for his vacation. Ultimately, he returned and remains a permanent resident, contented and involved, caring for himself, and good humored in his relationships with staff and residents alike.

Case Study No. 3
E.B. - Female
Arteriosclerotic cardiovascular disease (ACVD)
Arthritis
Decubitus
Chronic organic brain syndrome (COBS)

Mrs. B. was admitted to the nursing home amongst much grief and fanfare on the part of her family. She had been living at home with the family and they had come to a difficult decision - nursing home placement. Upon admission an occupational therapy evaluation was performed which indicated that there was full range of motion in the right upper extremity. The left upper extremity was limited in active range to 100° shoulder flexion, and 145° passive range. The patient was avoiding use of the left hand, was less accurate in stereognostic testing on the left, but not entirely dysfunctional. No diagnosis accounted for these losses other than arthritis. If a stroke had occurred, no medical confirmation existed. Peripheral vision was intact on both the right and the left sides. Manipulative skills were good. She was able to feed herself but handled her food excessively. She discriminated right from left accurately, and identified her body parts accurately. Some apraxia was noted. She was unable to stand and transfer. She was somewhat confused, but her statements were not worse than could be misinterpreted from a confusing set of circumstances. Some paranoid ideation was noted. Recommended were the following:

1. Occupational therapy five times per week.
2. ADL training.
3. Increase range of motion in the left upper extremity.
4. Increase bilateral upper extremity function.
5. W/C training.
6. Reality orientation.
7. A physical therapy consultation was recommended.

The family refused all restorative treatment. Funds were not available, and it was feared by the family that we would be demanding too much effort from the patient. Even a wheelchair was denied. Mother was too weak; she needed support for her head in order that she be 'comfortable.' It was requested that we not see the patient as we would make too many demands upon her. Mother needed to be cared for, which included feeding her. A well padded semi-reclining, geri-chair was obtained and there she remained for 15 months, a total care patient, disoriented, belligerent at times, developing contractures of both knees and ultimately a decubitus in the sacral area. When the decubitus did not respond to treatment, she was sent to the hospital for surgical debridement. Upon her readmission to the nursing home she became eligible for Medicare benefits and thus for occupational therapy services. The family offered no objection to our intervention at this time. An evaluation was ordered and performed. At this time the patient was found to have poor to fair muscle power of both upper extremities, trunk and neck. Active and passive range of motion were limited in both shoulders and hips. Both knees were contracted to 90°. Stereognosis was impaired in both upper extremities. The patient was unable to follow directions, directionality was impaired, tracking was diminished, peripheral awareness was absent. Frontal vision and hearing were functional. She was unable to perform any purposeful acts, but many of her verbal responses did not appear to be as disoriented as initial impression suggested. Treatment recommended was as follows:

1. Occupational therapy 5 times per week.
2. Increase ROM in both upper and both lower extremities, trunk and neck.
3. Increase muscle power throughout.
4. Increase endurance.
5. Perceptual training.
6. ADL training.
7. W/C training.
8. Provide wheelchair with leg extenders.

Early attention was to positioning, in both bed and wheelchair. A complicated schedule was adopted early on as it soon became evident that occupational therapy and nursing could not both meet the patient's needs without careful attention to time. Care of the decubitus required treatment every two hours. Occupational therapy was anxious to get this patient up and about as soon as possible before her benefits ran out. Occupational therapy treatment began with attention to those features of treatment which would facilitate nursing care and at the same time be concerned with positioning and mobility. Bed rolling activities led to solving the problem of positioning this patient in abdominal lying which was designed to allow treatment of the decubitus as well as reduce hip flexion and stimulate neck extension. In return, nursing assisted in getting the patient up in her wheelchair as frequently as her treatment permitted. Occupational therapy took over the responsibility for this patient's feeding for two meals per day, formerly a nursing task.

Trunk strengthening exercises were offered when the patient was seated in the wheelchair, exercises which enhanced weight shifting, again concerned with reducing sacral pressure. Wheelchair training was begun. Wheelchair activities would strengthen both upper extremities, particularly in those muscles which would be required for ambulation and transfer, as well as stimulate perceptual orientation through movement, and permit socialization and independence. Cooperation was initially difficult to obtain from the patient. The patient was tactile defensive. She was disturbed by forward propulsion through space. Geri-chairs are pulled from behind when they are moved. This patient had not been moved forward in a head erect position for at least one year and possibly for many years before that. The therapist stood behind the patient placing the patient's hands upon the wheels, moving the wheels with the patient's hands, repeating, "Push, push!" Brief but frequent treatment was provided (five minutes, several times per day). Within two days the patient was able to comprehend and execute forward movement dependently, although her endurance and strength were poor. Active range of motion and perceptual exercises were provided with a variety of activities such as cone stacking, hair brushing, ball throwing and some contrived grasp/ release activities using familiar objects. Self stimulation using lotion was encouraged to reduce tactile sensitivity. The use of scented cosmetics also was designed to increase the patient's self image and heighten sensory stimulation. Bilateral activities were encouraged to provide trunk stabilization and lateral orientation.

Feeding training began. This patient's asocial behavior interfered with treatment. She was not averse to spitting her food. This behavior was dealt with by the therapist with such statements as, "That's rude!" or "Grown women do not spit their food and you are a grown woman." "It's not pleasant for me to visit with you when you spit. If you continue, I'll have to leave. I'll be back when you stop."

This patient had difficulty discriminating figure from ground of the visual array of her tray and seemed confused by the variety of items presented to her, so food items were initially presented sequentially rather than all at once. Nursing aides were instructed to follow this procedure on all shifts permitting the patient to become increasingly independent in feeding. A colored placemat was placed under her food to assist in discrimination. A white cup holding milk on a white placemat was invisible to her. As this patient's skill increased, additional items were added until she was able to feed herself independently with good speed and considerably improved manners.

As this patient's skills in dyadic interaction improved and as tolerance for activities increased, treatment was provided in a group situation so that social awareness and skill could increase. She became more involved with other patients and began to interact with them more appropriately and spontaneously. As her skill grew in feeding and wheelchair mobility, a campaign was begun to encourage this patient to be perceived by others as a more competent individual, toward encouraging her transfer to the Main Dining Room.

In terms of time, the patient's recovery was as follows: By two and one half weeks, her tolerance for activity and handling had increased. At the end of the third week, the patient wheeled herself to the activity room, and became involved in a game of ball with other patients. She was reluctant at first, but did become involved with encouragement.

At this point a physical therapy consult was requested. The patient's gains had been considerable to this point and would be enhanced further if her knee contractures could be reduced so that she could ambulate and transfer. Physical therapy had not been considered earlier as ambulation had not initially been considered as potentially possible for her. Occupational therapy had not been aware that physical therapy had not been ordered to that point, and so, recommended physical therapy toward the end of reducing both knee contractures when this need became evident. At five weeks, sequencing activities showed increased accuracy. Bilateral skills were markedly improved. In the sixth week, she was increasingly alert, more involved in group activities, anticipating and comprehending directions, had increased memory for names, exhibited increased attention span, followed numbers called at Bingo, and was singing in German, her native tongue. At seven weeks, the patient propelled her wheelchair twenty-five feet using her feet to assist in propulsion. Activities to increase midline crossing were incorporated into treatment. At eight weeks, the patient was very cooperative, and spoke very sensibly. This was a marked difference from her previous performance, and she stated, "I didn't know I could do it." At nine weeks she was transferred to the Main Dining Room which she was then able to get to independently, with reminders necessary only regarding time.

This patient's strength, mobility, affect, behavior and perceptual skill increased as did her decubitus heal. Time confusion remained, but did not seriously hamper her function nor her contentment. Difficulty was encountered in the reduction of this patient's knee contractures, preventing success in ambulation, transfer training, lower extremity dressing and independence in toileting. Both occupational and physical therapists determined that success in these areas could not be achieved and further attempts in these directions were discontinued. This patient was now feeding herself, was mobile and sociable, and required nursing care only for toileting and for A.M. and P.M. care. She spent her day busily engaged, requiring far less care than formerly. It was decided that restorative treatment be discontinued.

This patient was on an active restorative program for sixty-three days. Following discontinuation of formal treatment, the patient has been noted to have become increasingly more alert and sociable; trunk and upper extremity mobility have continued to increase. Her sense of time is now intact. The family still needs occasional reminders that they stop feeding Mother when they visit bringing treats with them, but they are more comfortable with her increased gains in independence, awareness and sociability. One must wonder what this patient's functional level would be to date had treatment been provided upon her initial admission to the nursing home, prior to the time that contractures developed.

Case Study No. 4
M.S. - Female
Chronic obstructive pulmonary disease (COPD)

Upon admission to the nursing home, this patient's activity level was extremely diminished. Sitting in a chair was exhausting. Dyspnea was evident. This patient required constant oxygen for survival and would always continue to do so. Testing revealed that the patient was intact in all perceptual systems. She was alert, intelligent and having difficulty coping with the inordinate restrictions upon her life.

Inquiry was made regarding oxygen equipment. A portable oxygen tank called a Linde tank was identified. This tank, fully charged, weighed 11 pounds and was portable. Carrying this tank was beyond the capabilities of our patient. Treatment recommendations were:

1. Occupational therapy five times per week.
2. Increase independence in ADLs.
3. Decrease stress.
4. Increase activity tolerance.
5. Increase muscle power and endurance to enable the patient to carry 11 pounds a distance of fifty feet.
6. Homemaking training — energy conservation techniques.

Goals were set in consultation with the patient. It was explained to the patient that we would gradually increase demands upon her, but we would only increase demands based upon her ability to tolerate activity. We began by adapting the nasal catheter by increasing its length so that the patient could reach the bathroom, closet and dresser drawers so that her restrictions would not be further enhanced by her distance from the oxygen tank. Mild upper extremity exercises were provided through table activities, setting up a timed regimen, requesting increased involvement as stamina increased. When sitting tolerance increased and her pulse stabilized training began in activities of daily living. Ambulation to and independence in toileting was of primary concern to this patient. For the first week she was accompanied to the toilet, then she gained sufficient strength and confidence to reassume her independence in toileting. Dressing independence was encouraged by grading difficulty of garments, leaving the patient's clothes within her reach. As the patient became independent within her room and could obtain her own clothes, dress and toilet herself, we began to consider her discharge. It was felt that this patient would have greater freedom at home because the recreational areas and the dining room within the nursing home permitted smoking and this precluded her presence as with this patient came her oxygen supply.

When the decision to opt for discharge was made, we began to train the patient in the use of the Linde tank. The use of the Linde tank would enable her to travel in an automobile to the doctor and for any other necessary visit. She could even visit a neighbor. We began to build her ambulation endurance. As no further than twenty-five feet was anticipated, it was decided to enable her to ambulate twenty-five feet to and fro. This patient's pulse was monitored daily before and after activity and after five minutes of rest. No increase in demand was instituted unless there had been demonstrated a reduction in pulse following activity from that recorded the previous day, and a decrease in the time for her pulse to return to the resting rate. The patient was instructed in transferring her dependence from the oxygen tank to the

Linde tank. She learned to operate the equipment which heightened her tolerance of it and reduced her anxiety. The family was requested to obtain a light knapsack for the patient to carry. In stages, as the patient was able to tolerate, weight was added. We used objects as weights which would be found in the patient's home. A one pound jar of applesauce was placed into the knapsack for the patient to carry. Not only was this amusing, but it also converted the concept of one pound to a readily translated object, leading the patient to understand her capabilities in terms of potential for homemaking tasks. The weights were concretely measurable, increasing in time. The patient was thrilled with herself when she became able to trade in four one-pound objects for one five-pound object, a bag of sugar. When ten pounds was able to be tolerated, the patient next carried her own tank. Needless to say, her sense of accomplishment was extraordinary. Once she became independent in ambulating fifty feet carrying the eleven pound Linde tank, homemaking training enabled her to prepare a simple breakfast, sandwiches, and beverages. She would have most other chores performed for her at home by a homemaker. This patient was now able to live at home, capable of meeting her own needs. She was discharged to home and lived there for several months until her death later that year.

Case Study No. 5
Fr. F. - Male
Colostomy
Dehydration
Reactive psychosis

This patient had been found on the floor at home covered with feces, weak, incoherent, making little sense in a Slavic tongue, even when translated. He was admitted to the nursing home by parishioners for whom he had served as priest emeritus. Apparently he had been discharged to home by the hospital post-surgery, to the charge of friends who understood little English. They delivered their charge to his home where he lived alone, whereupon the patient apparently suffered a psychotic episode, reliving a former concentration camp experience, and suffering denial of what had recently occurred to his body. There he remained, unattended, for two or three days.

Upon admission to the nursing home he was weak, unable to comprehend directions, frightened and disoriented. The occupational therapy evaluation was necessarily very subjective. A seminarian who was fluent in the patient's native tongue was requested to participate in the evaluation as translator. The patient exhibited paranoid ideation, accusing people of having stolen money from him. He was very agitated. It was determined that occupational therapy would attend to the following:

1. Decrease anxiety.
2. ADL training in dressing, colostomy care.
3. Increase activity tolerance.
4. Vocational retraining.
5. Homemaking retraining.

In order to reduce the patient's perception of himself as a prisoner, and to increase his strength, we provided him with a wheelchair and instructed him in its use, orienting him to the nursing home environs. He was instructed in colostomy care, using sign language and critical words derived from translators whom we were able to identify and reach by phone. Lots of touching of equipment and of self were encouraged. The patient gradually was encouraged to become more and more involved in the procedure until he became fully independent. This required close communication between the nursing staff and occupational therapy so that the patient would always be performing up to maximum capabilities. Occupational therapy scheduled time for participating in the change of the colostomy bag one time per day. Nursing attended to any other colostomy care required at other times. As the patient's strength increased through ambulation endurance training, wheelchair use was reduced until the wheelchair was removed.

As suspicion was still a feature of this patient's interactions, it was felt that the reality of his potential could be assessed and cooperation effected if we could arrange for him to attend his church. In order not to jeopardize the patient's Medicare benefits we received medical orders indicating that his attendance at church was necessary for his rehabilitation. Parishioners picked up the patient on Sunday and returned him to the nursing home after services. He tolerated the trip well. The patient's ability to communicate with us increased. We planned for the next week, with the cooperation of congregants, that the patient would participate in the service. This, again, was tolerated well.

Inquiry with parishioners revealed that this man had followed the practice of walking many miles daily attending to his vocation. Endurance training in ambulation was encouraged in and outside of the nursing home to a greater degree. Homemaking training prepared Fr. F. for discharge. His judgment, clarity and affect improved. His tolerance for activity was such that he could safely return to home and be independent in his care. We occasionally hear from those who know Fr. They report that he has fully resumed his former vocation, is responsible for himself, and is providing meaningful attention to a variety of parishioners to whom his visits are essential.

Case Study No. 6
B.F. - Female
Pathological Fracture Left Hip

Mrs. F. entered the nursing home subsequent to a fall at home which caused her to fracture her hip. Cooperation was not her strong point. Her life had been full and she was angry and frightened that she could no longer retain her former life style. She was unable to accept the fact that if she would modify some of her demands, her independence would increase. Rather, she resorted to increased dependence out of her anger about her present condition. Evaluation revealed weakness impairing function in both upper and both lower extremities. She was intact in all perceptual areas. Her vision and hearing were functional. She was highly intelligent and had been engaged in the translation of a book prior to her injury. Recommendations were:

1. Occupational therapy five times per week.
2. Increase muscle power in both upper and both lower extremities, trunk.
3. Observe partial weight bearing status per M.D.
4. Increase sitting tolerance.
5. ADL training in transfers, toileting, dressing.
6. W/c training.
7. Increase ambulation tolerance within living environs.
8. Decrease anxiety.
9. Adapt environment to enable patient to resume former occupational pursuits.
10. Homemaking training.
11. Decrease w/c dependency when patient's condition warrants.

Initially, it was difficult to gain cooperation from this patient. She was terrified of moving. This was the second hip fracture she had sustained. The doctor had told her that she must be VERY careful. She interpreted this to mean that she was forbidden to move. She dwelled upon the delay in her goal, the completion of a translation of a book written by an ancestor who had been an early settler of this country. Being a creature of habit, she felt she could only work at home, and looked upon her nursing home sojourn as a necessary evil she would have to endure before resuming work. She saw no alternative solution. Although it was not impossible for her to continue her work in the nursing home, the patient was unwilling to make compromises in the method she had been using at home. This method required her own typewriter and a space to work in privately and comfortably, as well as the cooperation of her niece who had been engaged with the patient in this effort cooperatively.

During each treatment session we attended to the various functional treatments as adjuncts to plans to work on the book. Each restriction that Mrs. F. presented was approached as a problem to be solved. Each functional skill was dealt with in terms of its usefulness toward the accomplishment of her goal. Sitting tolerance would enable her to sustain her activity. Transfers would enable her to resume independence so she could control the time she would be engaged in work, not necessitating her dependence upon aides, and thus not being subject to their time constraints. We arranged for her typewriter to be brought in. To alleviate the patient's fears, a place was found to keep her machine safe. A schedule was set up with her niece so that they could work together. The physical therapy room was selected since it was not in use during the evening. An office area was set up for their use. Mrs. F. was involved in all arrangements. She was accompanied in her visits to each department head to make these arrangements. These visits were set up by the therapist in order to provide goal directed wheelchair use in order to offer the patient a sense of control over her life, and at the same time offer exercise in upper extremity function. Her niece was urged to refrain from assisting Mrs. F. in wheeling her chair when she visited.

Weaning the patient from her wheelchair proved as difficult as accustoming her to its use had been. Careful positive weaning took place, substituting ambulation with the walker in graded tolerance, per consultation with physical therapy. As Mrs. F. became increasingly able to ambulate she began to ambulate to the dining room, to her work, and to other activities in turn. When able to demonstrate her capability to ambulate wherever her needs required, we discussed the removal of her wheelchair. The patient reluctantly agreed to relinquish its use but was afraid to relinquish its possession. We agreed to leave the wheelchair within her room until she was assured that she no longer needed it. As a sign to her that she would be giving up this support, we folded the wheelchair. It remained there folded for two days before its removal. This way she retained the security that it would be there if she proved to need it.

Mrs. F. never completely lost her arrogance and

belligerence, but she resumed her purpose and completed her book within several months of her discharge, immediately prior to her death. We always felt that the time she used in the nursing home enabled her to complete that task she felt compelled toward finishing.

Case Study No. 7
B.P. - Male
Chronic Heart Failure (CHF)
Arteriosclerotic Heart Disease (ASHD)
Hypertension
Organic Brain Syndrome

When B. entered the nursing home he was confused, disoriented and expressed feelings of emasculation. Not listed among his admitting diagnoses was a urinary disorder requiring a permanent catheter. He was totally dependent in all ADLs. He was weakened throughout. He was slow to respond to direction. His motor planning was impaired. His stereognosis was intact. Time and space concepts were impaired. Short term and long term memory were impaired. He fixated in his conversation upon his desire to repair automobiles as the only reason for his existence. If he could not do so there was no reason for continuing to live. He was clearly devastated by his perception of himself as a weak, incompetent, dependent person. He was considered to be a permanent resident in the nursing home. Recommendations were:

1. Occupational therapy five times per week.
2. Increase muscle power throughout.
3. Increase activity tolerance.
4. ADL training in dressing, transfers, toileting, grooming.
5. Wheelchair training.
6. Increase ambulation endurance within living environs.
7. Alleviate depression.
8. Improve masculine identification.
9. Instruct patient in catheter care.
10. Orient to nursing home.

Clothes were obtained for the patient from home. A wheelchair was obtained from which the leg rests were removed to encourage active movement of both lower extremities as well as to increase sensory input to both feet in coordination with the resistance offered to both upper extremities by the wheelchair. We began by instructing the patient in wheelchair techniques leading to transfer training. He had difficulty remembering his room number so the wheelchair was labeled with the number. He needed repeated reminders to lock his wheelchair. Concentration was placed upon improving his memory for safe procedures. Then the patient was taught to shave himself once again. He objected to the use of an electric shaver so his safety razor was obtained and he was supervised in its use until he was observed to be safe in its use. As wheelchair endurance increased the patient was transferred to the Main Dining Room for meals. His orientation and way finding improved through the repetition offered by this activity. In order to reduce the visibility of his catheter and to facilitate independent ambulation, a leg bag was provided. The patient was pleased when the bag was no longer visible. Dressing training was successful and the patient became safe in dressing and needed assistance only with the catheter. As his balance improved, the patient expressed the desire to resume his habit of standing while shaving. This need was met by using the walker. As his skill in ambulation had increased in physical therapy, a walker was obtained for his use in his room. The patient began to perform his ADLs by maneuvering about his room using the walker. As proficiency increased, we began to supervise the use of the walker outside of his room, increasing his distance and destinations daily. The leg bag required adaptation as it had been restricting full knee extension. By trying all skills where the patient was going to use these skills, any problem he would experience was resolved under supervision, and that supervision was provided until he demonstrated sufficient skill for that supervision to be discontinued. Endurance increased in ambulation using first the walker, then a cane, then independent ambulation. As physical therapy taught the newer skill, the patient was able to continue to use the former skill to participate in living skills until his proficiency increased sufficiently to enable the use of the newer ambulation techniques and ultimate independence.

The patient's affect, memory, and appropriateness considerably improved. Dependence upon the nurses for his catheter care remained a problem to this patient. In cooperation with nursing the patient was instructed in techniques to measure urine output accurately. He quickly acquired skill in this area. To this point, B. had been a patient for four weeks.

When the patient demonstrated improved affect, heightened sociability and independence, he then presented a picture of a patient with increased potential. A consult with a urologist was recommended to the patient's physician by the team. A transurethral resection was recommended, and successfully performed. Upon readmission to the nursing home, the patient was again weakened but still was stronger than upon his first admission. He showed none of his former cognitive or affective disorders. We reinstituted strengthening activities, and endurance increasing activities, first in the wheelchair and then in ambulation. He quickly recovered his full capacities, becoming totally independent in all ADLs. He visited and socialized with everyone. His nursing home residency was then questioned, as a sheltered environment no longer seemed appropriate for him. The family and social service arranged for his discharge.

Every so often, B. would drop by for a visit, delighting everyone, staff and patients alike, with his good humor and with the success he exemplified. He lived at home and travelled, reporting on his adventures each time he visited.

Ultimately he became ill again, his kidneys functioning precariously. Upon readmission, the patient was determined by his physician to be terminally ill and the physician ordered no restorative services, feeling the patient had no potential, and that independence would be too exhausting. The patient reassumed his depressed affect and became totally dependent although he never again became confused or disoriented. He remained a patient, receiving neither treatment nor hope, and fulfilled his physician's prophecy eight months after his final readmission.

Case Study No. 8
B.L. - Female
Terminal Metastic Cancer

When B.L. was admitted to the nursing home the picture presented was of a disoriented bed patient, too weak to turn in bed. She covered her face with her blanket and offered no communication. It was as if her contract with life had ended when her admission to the nursing home took place. Evaluation revealed weakness throughout, but strength was sufficient to perform basic ADLs with assistance. She was not in undue pain. Her perceptual systems appeared to be intact. She was paralyzed by fear. Treatment recommendations were:

1. Occupational therapy five times per week to be reduced to necessary level to sustain maximum level of function.
2. Increase muscle power in both upper and, both lower extremities, neck, trunk.
3. Increase tolerance to out of bed activities and sustain at maximum activity level.
4. Decrease anxiety through orientation to nursing home environs.
5. Provide adaptive equipment such as long bath brush, long shoe horn, reacher tongs.
6. Counselling and assistance in resolving terminal plans.

Although the patient did not initially desire to leave her bed, she responded to her desire to use the toilet. An attitude expecting her capability and cooperation was sufficient to gain that cooperation. Once she was aware that she was able to become independent in toileting, she accepted this self responsibility. Meals were served in the dining room, requiring that she be up in her wheelchair going to and from meals three times per day, and that further, she be dressed for the occasion since she would be in the company of others. Sensitivity to her level of endurance was considered at all times. Her independence in wheeling her own chair increased until she could go back and forth for all meals.

Because the staff obviously expected that this patient was capable of living according to the mode of the nursing home, requiring no special apprehension due to her diagnosis, the patient began to communicate to a greater extent. She saw we were more concerned with her life than her death. This patient began to explore her feelings about her ensuing death. She was assured that we would be of assistance in resolving any problems as they arose. As she became more ill, her body became edematous. When her underpants no longer fit her, the aides put diapers on her, reducing her ability to care for herself. When we became aware of this, her own underpants were adapted so that she could continue to wear them, sustaining her dignity. Table activities were provided, graded toward reduced muscle power while attempting to sustain maximum range of motion.

This patient became a good listener and welcomed visits from other residents. Her affect altered into a serene resolve. She eagerly petted the fluffy dog I brought in to visit her one Friday. She died quietly in her sleep that weekend.

Case Study No. 9
E.L. - Female
Rheumatoid Arthritis

This patient had been transferred to this nursing home after having been a resident at another nursing home for several years. Her funds had been exhausted and she had been unable to stay. This patient was totally dependent in all ADLs, was depressed, emotionally labile, angry at her circumstances, and in constant pain.

Occupational therapy evaluation revealed limitation in all joints. Finger deformities were severe and no corrective surgery was anticipated. Vision was poor due to cataracts and unsuccessful surgery. Her hearing was excellent. Her memory and intelligence were also excellent. The patient was compulsive in her habits. Treatment was recommended as follows:

1. Occupational therapy five times per week.
2. Increase range of motion in both shoulders and elbows, and neck.
3. Increase dexterity.
4. Increase strength in both upper extremities.
5. Increase ADL skills in feeding, grooming.
6. Develop avocational skills within severe joint and mobility limitations.
7. Obtain electric wheelchair with removable arms and desk arms to reduce pain experienced during transfers.
8. Develop and provide adaptive equipment as necessary.
9. Splints to both upper extremities to stabilize wrists in neutral position and decrease ulnar deviation.

The patient cooperated in passive and active range of motion despite the pain she experienced. Her ability to bring her hand to her mouth and sustain those movements for sufficient time to endure self feeding increased. Adapted utensils were provided but the patient preferred to use standard utensils and indeed did as well with them as shoulder and elbow range increased. Her range of reach increased so she could reach all tray items she chose. In an attempt to provide an activity in which she could engage, straw weaving was attempted, but the patient found it too unstable and not satisfying. We then warped a simple loom with alternately colored yarns. Threads were used which were 5 inches wider than the width of the warp so that it would not be necessary to manipulate a shuttle. Splints were worn during this activity. An orthoplast hook was appended to the right splint. The patient used the hook to retrieve the weft thread using supination and elbow flexion to draw the thread up from between the warp threads. She was instructed to go under the dark and over the light threads when going left to right, and to reverse when going right to left. The patient was able to weave only one half of a row per day at first. It soon became apparent that this activity was well suited to this patient's compulsivity. Although slow, her work was extremely neat. She was unsatisfied with less than quality work. She derived a great deal of attention and many compliments from everyone. She was very pleased with the attention and with her own success. Ultimately this patient increased her speed so that she could finish a pillow per week. She began to take orders and has continued to be in production varying her designs with each new pillow. She no longer wears her splints. Her dexterity has increased so that she can use her fingers to continue her work.

She remains dependent in all ADLs other than feeding. She is easier to transfer with the removed arm rest, using either a transfer board or being lifted. Although still depressed much of the time, her humor often comes through. She is totally aware of all nursing home events and is the best source of gossip if she deems you trustworthy. Although she still gets upset when any changes in her routine are made, she has made a reasonably good adjustment to her disability and to her life space.

The request for an electric wheelchair for this patient was denied by her funding agency on the grounds that she could get anywhere in the nursing home if someone pushed her. She remains totally dependent for mobility.

Case Study No. 10
D.P. - Female
First Admission: S/P Right Cerebral Vascular Accident
Diabetes
Second Admission: Gangrene Right Lower Extremity
Third Admission:
Right Above Knee Amputtee

This patient has been known to this therapist for a period of four years. Over time she received treatment from occupational therapy for repeated circumstances.

Her initial admission to the nursing home was as a patient

who had deteriorated in function at home. Evaluation revealed impaired right opposition. Right hand sensory loss was noted. She had astereognosis on the right and appeared to have right hemianopsia and right sided neglect. She had full range of motion in both upper extremities and good muscle power in both upper extremities. Shape discrimination was intact. Color identification was good, but she appeared to have difficulty naming colors. She was totally dependent in all ADLs. The patient was cooperative, but labile. The evaluation suggested that a recent stroke had taken place contralateral to the previous CVA, despite the absence of motor losses, compounding her dysfunction. Treatment recommended:

1. Occupational therapy three times per week (Occupational therapy was only available three times per week at this time.)
2. Stereognosis training.
3. ADL training.
4. Training in compensation for visual field cut.
5. Recommend speech evaluation.

An attempt to initiate stereognosis training revealed that the patient was unable to tolerate this activity. It was decided to concentrate on transfers and dressing. These revealed further perceptual dysfunction. The patient had difficulty in identification of right and left, crossing the midline, and finding body parts. The patient was distracted by and unable to cope with a wide array of objects presented at once, as on a food tray. Wheelchair training was begun. It was necessary to reinforce position of hands on the wheelchair. Bilateral activities were instituted to reinforce coordinated movements. Ball playing elicited good automatic movements and the patient enjoyed this activity. Within three weeks there was good carryover in ADL. The patient was more alert, interested in other patients, could maneuver her wheelchair to the Main Dining Room and feed herself. Difficulty remained in sequencing, requiring direction in dressing. The patient remained labile and began to complain of pain in her right foot. As no further gains were noted, occupational therapy was discontinued. One month later the patient's medical and emotional status improved and nursing requested that we reinstitute treatment. ADL training was resumed. Toilet transfers improved. The patient began to use panties rather than diapers and was reliabily continent. It was noted that the patient continually crossed her right leg over her left knee. The patient was reminded to desist from this action. An attempt was made by maintenance, at our request, to adjust the wheelchair leg extenders to better fit the patient. The patient became independent in toilet transfers but difficulty in sequencing remained, requiring continued assistance in dressing. The patient's independence had increased to the point that she was transferred to a reduced care wing where she lived and socialized. She remained there for approximately a year.

We reencountered D.P. as a patient when she returned to the nursing home from a brief hospital stay necessitated by a flareup of a preexisting diabetic condition. Although we had seen D. frequently during the year she had been in the nursing home, she had not been an occupational therapy patient following her initial treatment program. During her hospitalization D. suddenly developed gangrene of the right foot. Upon her readmission to the nursing home an occupational therapy evaluation was requested.

Evaluation revealed that she was tired and cold to the touch. She had retained full range of motion in both upper extremities. Some weakness was noted in her right hand. She was verbally unresponsive. She did not recognize me. She was dependent in all ADLs. Her right lower extremity was held in fetal position. She was in a great deal of pain. Surgery had not been recommended due to the severity of her medical condition. We recommended an attempt at increasing her activity level, ADL training, and attempting to position both lower extremities to prevent contractures. Treatment was now available five times per week.

We attempted dressing and transfer training and attempted to build wheelchair tolerance. The patient was encouraged to feed herself. It soon became evident that treatment would not be successful as the patient was in constant pain and could concentrate on nothing else. She became confused and was often unaware of her circumstances. At this point occupational therapy was discontinued.

Although we were not actively treating this patient our interest in her remained. We felt that if her pain were not present, her potential for resumption of independence was still good.

Two months later we were again asked to see the patient. At this time her right knee was contracted. Her sitting posture was poor. She was unable to be pulled up to the dining room table. It was primarily to resolve the positioning problem that we were consulted. We provided the patient with a lap board. Despite the pain and weakness she had been experiencing, the patient's medical condition had stabilized. We requested that the patient be reviewed by the staff and it was suggested that surgery be reconsidered. Neither physician nor family was eager to make this decision. Nursing consulted with the surgeon and it was agreed that the risk was worthwhile at this time. The son had a great deal of difficulty dealing with this problem. It was determined through his tears that he wanted his mother to make this choice herself. At this point it was necessary to determine the competency of the patient. When her competency was assured, it remained to pose the question of amputation to her. The RN and OTR offered to assist in this task. The son was unable to bear the independent burden of this responsibility. He was unable to speak. In his presence we spoke for him, while he nodded in agreement. Our patient agreed to surgery. The moment she agreed, her son was then able to speak with his mother and they made plans together.

D.P. returned to the nursing home with a right above knee amputation. But her experience had taken its toll. She was totally hypotonic. She was unable to actively hold her head erect. She could not speak. She was dependent upon others for everything. She did not even cry any longer. She was totally without affect. Occupational therapy was again reinstituted.

It was first necessary to increase tone in neck and trunk to assure stabilization. PNF was instituted. The staff was trained in positioning techniques as reinforcement would be provided at all times. Abdominal lying was introduced into the patient's regimen to increase extensor tone in the neck musculature and to decrease the hip contracture which had developed during the period prior to surgery. Progessive resistive exercises were offered to her left lower extremity. The patient was not allowed to permit her head to droop while in occupational therapy treatment. She became so angry that she began to scream and thrash out at this therapist. She was told in very angry tones that I cared about her even if she did not care about herself. The anger displayed heightened her tone. The sight of me from then on was sufficient to reawaken her anger. As tone increased, progressive resistive exercises and activities were introduced to increase muscle power. Exercises were adapted to wheelchair activities and the nursing staff was instructed in performance of these exercises to develop voluntary and automatic control in the sitting position.

The patient had reverted to the perceptual dysfunctions she demonstrated the previous year so perceptual training was reinstituted. These tasks were incorporated into ADL tasks in feeding and bathing. Standing balance exercises were begun as soon as strength was sufficient in the left lower extremity to support her weight. A "Simon Says" type of game was used. When the patient was first stood facing the therapist, she was encouraged to hold onto the therapist's shoulders. As tolerated, she was then asked to "Look up. Look at me." "Put your right hand on my head, back on my shoulder. Left hand on my head, back on my shoulder." Then to her own shoulders, to her head, to my waist, to her waist, etc. Each movement required subtle trunk shifting. Gradually, from day to day, new instructions were added and speed was increased. Balance steadily improved.

D. practiced these skills daily. As her skills improved new tasks were incorporated into her treatment regimen and her ADL performance, each time working with nursing toward including independence in those skills in her daily tasks. The nursing staff was instructed in the type of support they could, and should not, offer. This positive attitude of the nursing staff enhanced her feelings of self worth. Eventually, Mrs. P. learned to get into and out of bed safely by herself, how to use the toilet, dress herself, and care for her own needs. She began to resume her interest in life and the world about her. For some reason unknown to us, she spontaniously resumed her ability to speak sentences, and although she would initially speak only with the Certified Occupational Therapy Assistant who was now treating her, with that therapist's support she became more willing to share her new found skill. She began to participate in a graded variety of craft activities designed to remediate her perceptual disorders. She lost her dysfunction in sequencing.

As her independence increased she was again transferred to the reduced care wing of the nursing home, returning to the friends she had made when she had previously lived there. Her affect is better. She takes the bus trip weekly and participates in many acitivites.

Occupational therapy remained in touch with this patient once a week for the next six months, primarily reinforcing staff so that the gains made through treatment would not deteriorate before habits were firmly established.

Mrs. P. remains a patient at the nursing home, functioning at a much higher level than had been expected at the time of her initial admission, despite the multiple crises she had endured.

Summation

A variety of cases have been selected and presented to demonstrate how occupational therapy can be provided within a milieu approach. Those cases selected, although each unique, are by no means unusual. All patients admitted to nursing homes are unique, not only in the diagnoses and dysfunctions they present, but in their heritages and experiences.

It may be noted that no ages were associated with any of the case studies presented. This reflects my own prejudice regarding the patients with whom I work. I have long since ceased inquiring about patients' ages. If it is someone's birthday, the subject comes up, but other than that I have noticed over the years that age is not a significant factor in the recovery of the patients I have treated, so I refrain from asking. In general, the cases included patients from approximately 65 to 90 years of age, although we frequently see patients who exceed these limits.

The cases selected have varied in their characteristics, but there are some universal points to be noted regarding the treatment provided. Mobility is the feature most central to all treatment; mobility of self or of self through space. Mobility is designed to facilitate the reintegration of all sensation as a base for the establishment of constancy and, thus, confident behavior. Choice, decision making, the making of plans, is a further element of all treatment, either using patient motivation as a starting point, or when that motivation is not available, enabling the patient to develop sufficient skill using component behaviors and skills to bring the patient to the point to which choice becomes possible. Striving and goal setting are significant elements which can be integrated into all treatment regardless of diagnosis, age or environment. Occupational therapists' skill in functional analysis, activity analysis, and activity grading makes them ideally suited to style their treatments in this manner. This scheme provides a developmental approach affording recapitulation of ontogenetic development Recapitulation of development following disability in the elderly through occupational therapy has here been termed gerontogeny.

There is no way to predict who will benefit from treatment prior to the administration of that treatment. Further, there is no reliable way to predict longevity to determine the worth of providing treatment. Patients who one would least expect to survive may live for years, and others not. The length of human life is beyond human prediction. We can only presume that as long as life persists it is worth attention so that striving can be facilitated.

From birth to death we are engaged in a developmental

process. The stages are delineated, but each person follows his own course. The joy of working with the aged is based upon the vicarious experiences of lifetimes. When it is considered that each aged person brings to the therapeutic encounter a life history rich in world experience, the value to the therapist cannot be measured. Hundreds of years of history and learning are there for the taking. With maturity there seems to come a surety of knowledge of self and personal philosophy willingly shared if one is but willing to receive. Listen very carefully to the needs you hear expressed and you will also hear your needs fulfilled.

Birth is a beginning
And Death a destination.
And life is a journey:
From childhood to maturity
And youth to age;
From innocence to awareness
And ignorance to knowing;
From foolishness to discretion
And then, perhaps, to wisdom;
From weakness to strength
Or strength to weakness-
And, often, back again;
From health to sickness
And back, we pray, to health again;
From offense to forgiveness,
From loneliness to love,
From joy to gratitude,
From pain to compassion,
And grief to understanding-
From fear to faith;
From defeat to defeat to defeat-
Until, looking backward or ahead,
We see that victory lies
Not at some high place along the way,
But in having made the journey, stage by stage,
A sacred pilgrimage.
Birth is a beginning
And Death a destination.
And life is a journey,
A sacred pilgrimage-
To life everlasting.

Gates of Repentence
Central Conference of American Rabbis
and Union of Liberal and Progressive
Synagogues
5738 New York 1978

BIBLIOGRAPHY

Addicott, J.: "Occupational Therapy in Administration; Independent or Dependent Variable?" Presented at the American Occupational Therapy Association Annual Conference, San Diego, California, 1978.

Altman, I.: *The Environment and Social Behavior.* Belmont, California: Wadsworth, 1975.

Ardrey, R.: *The Territorial Imperative.* New York: Dell, 1966.

Asch, S.: *Social Psychology.* Englewood Cliffs, New Jersey: Prentice Hall, 1952.

Asch, S.: Opinions and Social Pressure. *Scientific American,* 193(5): 31-35; 1955.

Austin, W.T. and Bates, F.L.: Ethological Indicators of Dominance and Territoriality in a Captive Human Population. *Social Forces,* 52: 447-455; 1974.

Ayres, A.J.: *Sensory Integration and the Treatment of Learning Disabilities.* Los Angeles: Western Psychological Services, 1972a.

Ayres, A.J.: *Southern California Sensory Integration Tests.* Los Angeles: Western Psychological Services, 1972b.

Bartley, S.: *Principles of Perception.* New York: Harper and Row, 1969.

Bender, M.: The Incidence and Type of Perceptual Deficiencies in the Aged. In *Neurological and Sensory Disorder in the Elderly,* edited by W.S. Fidlds. New York: Stratton Intercontinental Medical Book, 1975.

Berkeley, G.: *Toward A New Theory of Vision.* New York: Dutton, 1954. First published 1709.

Botwinick, J. and Storandt, M.: Speed Functions, Vocabulary, Ability and Age. *Perception and Motor Skills,* 36(3), Part 2; June 1973.

Breines, E.: *The Effects of Familiarity of Environment on Perception in an Aged Population.* Bound Brook, New Jersey: New Jersey Occupational Therapy Association, 1977.

Breines, E.: Early Intervention Through Occupational Therapy. *American Health Care Association Journal,* 5(3): 34-35; 1979.

Breines, E.: *Proprioceptive Memory; The Recall of Frontal and Lateral Space in Upper Extremity Function.* Previously unpublished, 1979.

Breines, E.: *Perceptual Changes in Aging.* Lebanon, New Jersey: Geri-Rehab, 1980.

Bremner, V.G.: Spatial Errors Made By Infants: Inadequate Spatial Cues of Evidence of Egocentrism? *British Journal of Psychology,* 69: 77-84; 1978.

Bronowski, J.: *The Origins of Knowledge and Imagination.* New Haven, Connecticut: Yale University Press, 1978.

Brown, H.: *Brain and Behavior.* New York: Oxford University Press, 1976.

Browning, R.: *Andrea del Sarto (The Faultless Painter),* poem, line 97.

Buell, S.J. and Coleman, P.D.: Dendritic Growth in the Aged Human Brain and Failure of Growth in Senile Dementia. *Science,* 206: 854-856; November 1979.

Cantor, B.: "Age," poem. In *The Outlook.* Green Brook, New Jersey: Greenbrook Manor Nursing Home, October 1979.

Castenada, C.: *Journey to Ixtlan; The Lessons of Don Juan.* New York: Pocket Books, 1972.

Corso, J.: Sensory Processes and Age Effects in Normal Adults. *Journal of Gerontology,* 26: 9-105, 1971.

Daffner, C.: Personal correspondence, 1976.

Daffner, C.: An Occupational Therapy Model for Treatment of Learning Disabilities. *Journal of New Jersey Speech and Hearing Association,* 15(1): 14, 1977.

Darwin, C.: *The Origin of Species.* New York: MacMIllan, 1962.

DeLong, A.J.: Territorial Stability and Hierarchical Formation. *Small Group Behavior:* 55-63; February 1973.

Denny, N.: Classification Abilities in the Elderly. *Journal of Gerontology,* 29: 309-314; 1974.

Dinnerstein, D.: Previous and Concurrent Visual Experience as Determinants of Phenomenal Shape. *American Journal of Psychology,* 78: 235-242; 1965.

Dinnerstein, D., Cursio, F. and Chinsky, J.: Contextual Determination of Apparent Weight as Demonstrated by the Method of Constant Stimuli. *Psychological Science,* 5: 251-252; 1966.

Downs, R.J. and Stea, D. (Editors): *Image and Environment: Cognitive Mapping and Spatial Behaviro.* Chicago: Aldine, 1973.

Eccles, J.C.: *The Understanding of the Brain.* New York: McGraw Hill, 1972.

Edney, J.J.: Property, Possession and Permanence; A Field Study in Human Territoriality. *Journal of Applied Social Psychology,* 275-282; July 1972a.

Edney, J.J.: Place and Space: The Effects of Experience With a Physical Locale. *Journal of Experimental Social Psychology,* 8: 124-135; 1972b.

Edwards, B.: *Drawing on the Right Side of the Brain.* Los Angeles: J.P. Tarcher, 1979.

Esser, A.: *Behavior and Environment: The Use of Space by Animals and Men.* New York: Plenum Press, 1971.

Feffer, M.: Private manuscript, 1979.

Festinger, L.: *A Theory of Cognitive Dissonance.* Evanston, Illinois: Row, Peterson, 1957.

Fidler, G.: Professional or Nonprofessional? In *Occupational Therapy 2001 A.D.* Rockville, Maryland: American Occupational Therapy Association, 1979.

Fiorentino, M.: *Normal and Abnormal Development.* Springfield, Illinois: Charles C. Thomas, 1972.

Fiske, D.W. and Maddi, S.R.: *Functions of Varied Experience.* Homewood, Illinois: Dorsey Press, 1961.

Foley, J.M.: "Sensations and Behavior." In *Neurological and Sensory Disorders in the Elderly,* edited by W.S. Fields. New York: Stratton Intercontinental Medical Book, 1975.

Fraiberg, S.: Parallel and Divergent Patterns in Blind and Sighted Infants. *Psychological Study of the Child,* 23: 264-300; 1968.

Gaylord, S.A. and Marsh, G.R.: Age Differences in the Speed of a Cognitive Process. *Journal of Gerontology,* 30: 674-678; 1975.

Gibson, E.: The Development of Perception as an Adaptive Process. *American Scientist,* 58: 98-107; 1970.

Gibson, J.J.: *The Senses Considered As Perceptual Systems.* Boston: Houghton Mifflin, 1966.

Gilfoyle, E. and Grady, A.: A Developmental Theory of Somatosensory Perception. In *Body Senses and Perceptual Deficit,* edited by Henderson and Coryell. Boston: Boston University Press, 1973.

Ginsburg, H. and Opper, S.: *Piaget's Theory of Intellectual Development.* Englewood Cliffs, New Jersey: Prentice Hall, 1969.

Goldberg, M.: "Parietal Neuron Activity in Moving and Attending." Presented at the Conference of Neural and Developmental Bases of Spatial Orientation, Teachers College, Columbia University, New York, November 18, 1979.

Goldstein, A. et. al.: Structured Learning Therapy: Development and Evaluation. *American Journal of Occupational Therapy,* 33: 635-639; 1979.

Goodall, J. VL.: (see Van Lawick-Goodall, J.)

Griffin, D.: Topographical Orientation. In *Image and Environment,* edited by R.H. Downs and D. Stea. Chicago: Aldine, 1973.

Grundy, D. and Wilson, S.F.: Diagnosis and Planning of a Community Residence; A Sociometric Study. *Small Group Behavior,* 4: 206-226; 1973.

Haley, A.: *Roots.* Garden City, New York: Doubleday, 1976.

Hart, R.: "Facilitating Children's Orientation Abilities." Presented at the Conference on Neural and Developmental Bases of Spatial Orientation, Teachers College, Columbia University, New York, November 16, 1979.

Held, R.: Plasticity in Sensorimotor Coordination. In *Neuropsychology of Spatially Oriented Behavior,* edited by S.J. Freedman. Homewood, Illinois: Dorsey Press, 1968.

Hermelin, B.: "Seeing and Hearing and Space and Time." Presented at the Conference on Neural and Developmental Bases of Spatial Orientation, Teachers College, Columbia University, New York, November 17, 1979.

Hock, H., Gordon, G.P. and Whitehurst, R.: Contextual Relations: The Influence of Familiarity, Physical Plausibility and Belongingness. *Perception & Psychophysics,* 16: 4-8; 1974.

James, W.: *Principles of Psychology.* New York: Holt, 1890.

Johannsen, G.: Colloquium Lecture at the Institute for Cognitive Studies, Rutgers University, Newark, New Jersey, Winter 1978-79.

Johnson, J.: Occupational Therapy: A Model for the Future. *American Journal of Occupational Therapy,* 27: 1-7; 1973.

Johnson, R.N.: *Aggression in Man and Animals.* Philadelphia: W.B. Saunders, 1972.

Kaplan, S.: Cognitive Maps in Perception and Thought. In *Image and Environment,* edited by R.H. Downs and D. Stea. Chicago: Aldine, 1973.

Kephart, N.C.: *The Slow Learner in the Classroom.* Columbus, Ohio: Charles E. Merrill, 1960.

Kielhofner, G.: General Systems Theory: Implications for Theory and Action in Occupational Therapy. *American Journal of Occupational Therapy*, 32: 637-645; 1978.
King, L.J.: A Sensory-Integrative Approach to Schizophrenia. *American Journal of Occupational Therapy*, 28: 529-536; 1974.
King, L.J.: Toward A Science of Adaptive Responses. *American Journal of Occupational Therapy*, 32: 429-437; 1978.
Klopfer, W.G.: The Rorschach and Old Age. *Journal of Personality Assessment*, 38: 420-422; 1974.
Knickerbocker, B.: Lecture to New Jersey Occupational Therapy Association, Princeton, New Jersey, March 1976.
Knickerbocker, B.: *A Holistic Approach to the Treatment of Learning Disorders*. Thorofare, New Jersey: Charles B. Slack, 1980. (See Figure 40, page 215).
Knickerbocker, B.: Personal correspondence, 1976.
Krocher, T.: *Ishi, the Last of his Tribe*. Oakland, California: Parnassus, 1964.
Kubler-Ross, E.: *The Final Stages of Growth*. Englewood Cliffs, New Jersey: Prentice Hall, 1975.
Lee, T.: Psychology and Living Space. In *Image and Environment*, edited by R.H. Downs and D. Stea. Chicago: Aldine, 1973.
Levy, J., Trevarthen, C. and Sperry, R.W.: Perception of Bilateral Chimeric Figures Following Hemispheric Deconnexion. *Brain*, 95: 61-78; 1972.
Levy, J.: Psychobiological Implications of Bilateral Asymmetry. In *Hemisphere Function in the Human Brain*, edited by S.J. Dimond and J.G. Beaumont. New York: John Wiley & Sons, 1974.
Levy, J.: Manifestations and Implications of Shifting Hemispheric Attention in Commisurotomy Patients. In *Advances in Neurology*, edited by E.A. Weinstein and R.P. Freidland, Volume 18. New York: Raven Press, 1977.
Lewis, S.: *The Mature Years: A Geriatric Occupational Therapy Text*. Thorofare, New Jersey: Charles B. Slack, 1979.
Lieberman, M.: Relocation Search and Social Policy. *Gerontologist*, 14: 494-501; 1974.
Llorens, L.: *The Occupational Therapy Sequential Care Record, Revision II*. Gainesville, Florida: University of Florida, 1976.
Lorenz, K.: *On Aggression*. New York: Harcourt, Brace, 1974.
Luckiesh, M.: *Visual Illusions, Their Causes, Characteristics and Applications*. New York: Dover, 1922, 1965.
Luria, A.: *The Mind of A Mnemonist: A Little Book About A Vast Memory*. Chicago: Contemporary Books, 1976.

Lynch, K.: Some References to Orientation. In *Image and Environment*, edited by R.H. Downs and D. Stea. Chicago: Aldine, 1973.

Milgram, S.: Behavioral Study of Obedience. *Journal of Abnormal & Social Psychology*, 67: 371-378; 1963.

Miller, G.A., Galanter, E. and Pribram, K.H.: *Plans and the Structure of Behavior.* New York: Holt, 1960.

Miller, N.E. and Dollard, J.: *Social Learning and Imitation.* New Haven, Connecticut: Yale University Press, 1941.

Montegu, A.: *Man and Agression.* London: Oxford University Press, 1973.

Moore, J.: Behavior, Bias and the Limbic System. *American Journal of Occupational Therapy*, 30: 11-19; 1976.

Moore, J.: "Neuroanatomical Aspects of the Vestibular System." Presented at the Conference on the Vestibular System, Washington University, St. Louis, Missouri, June 1978.

Mosey, A.: The Concept and Use of Developmental Groups. *American Journal of Occupational Therapy*, 24: 272-275; 1970.

O'Neill, P.M. and Calhoun, K.S.: Sensory Deficits and Behavioral Deterioration in Senescence. *Journal of Abnormal Psychology*, 84: 579-582; 1975.

Olton, D.: Spatial Memory. *Scientific American*, 236: 82-98; 1977.

Orne, M.T.: On the social psychology of the psychological experience: with particular reference to demand characteristics and their implications. *American Psychologist*, 17(11): 776-783; 1962.

Paillard, J. and Brouchon, M.: Active and Passive Movements in the Calibration of Position Sense. In *Neuropsychology of Spatially Oriented Behavior*, edited by S.J. Freedman. Homewood, Illinois: Dorsey Press, 1968.

Papulia, D.E. and Reily, D.D.: Cognitive Function in Middle and Old Age Adults; A Review of Research Based on Piaget's Theory. *Human Development*, 17: 424-443; 1974.

Pastalan, L.: The Stimulation of Age-Related Losses: A New Approach to the Study of Environmental Barriers. *New Outlook for the Blind*, 68: 356-362; 1974.

Piaget, J.: Intellectual Evaluation From Adolescence to Adulthood. *Human Development*, 151: 1-12; 1972.

Piaget, J. and Inhelder, B.: *The Child's Conception of Space.* London: Routledge and Kegan, 1973.

Pick, H.: "Children's Cognitive Maps." Presented at the Conference on Neural and Developmental Bases of Spatial Orientation,

Teachers College, Columbia University, New York, November 16, 1979.
Polanyi, M.: *Personal Knowledge: Towards a Post-Critical Philosophy.* Chicago: University of Chicago Press, 1958.
Pribram, K.H. and Goleman, D.: Holographic Memory. *Psychology Today,* 79-84; February 1979.
Price, A.: "Laterality Revisited." Presented at the American Occupational Therapy Association Annual Conference, Detroit, Michigan, 1979.
Ravens, J.C.: *Coloured Progressive Matrices (Sets A, Ab and B).* London: Lewis, 1956, 1962.
Reilly, M.: Occupational Therapy Can Be One Of The Great Ideas Of Twentieth Century Medicine. *American Journal of Occupational Therapy,* 31: 1-9; 1962.
Rennick, H.L.P. and Cantor, J.M.: Suicide and Aging. In *Readings in Gerontology,* edited by H. Brown. St. Louis, Missouri: C.V. Masky, 1978.
Riegal, K.: Dialectic Operation, The Final Period of Cognitive Development. *Human Development,* 16: 346-370; 1973.
Rist, R.C.: On the Means of Knowing; Qualitative Research in Education. *New York University Education Quarterly,* New York, Summer 1979.
Rock, I.: *An Introduction to Perception.* New York: MacMillan, 1975.
Rossi, A.M.: General Methodological Considerations. In *Sensory Deprivation: Fifteen Years of Research,* edited by J.P. Zubek, New York: Appleton-Century Crofts, 1969.
Rudel, R.: "Oblique Mystique: Figure Perception." Presented at the Conference on Neural and Developmental Bases of Spatial Orientation, Teachers College, Columbia University, New York, November 16, 1979.
Schactel, E.G.: *Metemorphosis; On the Development of Affect, Perception, Attention and Memory.* New York: Basic Books, 1959.
Schreiber, F.R.: *Sybil.* New York: Warner, 1974.
Schultz, N.R. and Mayer, W.J.: Feedback Effects on Spatial Egocentrism in Old Age. *Journal of Gerontology,* 31(1): 72-75; 1976.
Selye, H.: *Stress and Distress.* New York: Lippincott, 1974.
Sheehy, G.: *Passages: Predictable Crises of Adult Life.* New York: Dutton, 1976.
Smith, A.D.: Response Interference with Organized Recall in the Aged. *Developmental Psychology,* 10: 867-870; 1974.

Smith, C.U. and Smith, W.M.: *Perception and Motion.* Philadelphia: W.B. Saunders, 1962.

Sommer, R.: *Personal Space.* Englewood Cliffs, New Jersey: Prentice Hall, 1969.

Stratton, G.: Some Preliminary Experiments on Vision Without Inversion of the Retina. *Psychological Review,* 3: 611-617; 1896.

Stratton, G.: Upright Vision and the Retinal Image. *Psychological Review,* 4: 182-187; 1897.

Stratton, G.: VIsion Without Inversion of the Retinal Image. *Psychological Review,* 4: 341-360; 1897.

Suedfeld, P.: Changes in Intellectual Performance and in Susceptibility to Influence. In *Sensory Deprevation: Fifteen Years of Research,* edited by J.P. Zubek. New York: Appleton-Century Crofts, 1969.

Sundstrom, E. and Altman, I.: Field Study of Territorial Behavior and Dominance. *Journal of Personality and Social Psychology,* 1: 115-124; 1974.

Taub, E.: Prism Compensation as a Learning Phenomenon. In *Neuropsychology of Spatially Oriented Behavior,* edited by S.J. Freedman. Homewood, Illinois: Dorsey Press, 1968.

Thatcher, R.W. and John, E.R.: *Functional Neuroscience, Volume I: Foundations of Cognitive Processes.* Hillsdale, New York: Lawrence Erlbaum, 1977.

Thomas, L.: *The Medusa and the Snail.* New York: Viking, 1979.

Trevarthen, C.: Vision in Fish: The Origins of the Visual Frame for Action in Vertebrates. In *The Central Nervous System,* edited by D. Ingle. Chicago: University of Chicago Press, 1968.

Van Lawick-Goodall, J.: *In the Shadow of Man.* Boston: Houghton Mifflin, 1971.

Wallach, H.: *On Perception.* New York: Quadrangle, New York Times Book, 1976.

Washburn, S.L.: Tools and Human Evolution. *Scientific American.* 203(3); 1960.

Waugh, N.C., Fozard, J.L., Tolland, G.A. and Erwin, E.D.: Effects of Age and Stimulus Repetition on a Two Choice Reaction Time. *Journal of Gerontology,* 28: 466-470; 1973.

White, R.: Ego and Reality in Psychoanalytic Theory. *Psychological Issues,* 3(3). New York: International Universities Press, 1963.

Wigginton, E. (Editor): *The Foxfire Book.* Garden City, New York: Anchor, 1972.

Wilbarger, P.: "Clinical Aspects of Vestibular Stimulation." Presented at the Conference on the Vestibular System, Washington University, St. Louis, Missouri, June 1978.

Zubek, J.P. (Editor): *Sensory Deprivation: Fifteen Years of Research.* New York: Appleton-Century Crofts, 1969.

Zuckerman, M.: Hallucinations; Reported Sensations and Image. In *Sensory Deprivation: Fifteen Years of Research,* edited by J.P. Zubek. New York: Appleton-Century Crofts, 1969.

Index

A

activities of (daily) living, 40, 98, 193, 243, 245, 247, 249, 251, 252, 259, 261, 263, 265, 271, 273
activity analysis, 201
activity grading, 201
adapt (ive) (ation), 35, 48, 51, 55, 59, 68, 69, 75, 76, 79, 87, 90, 97, 98, 110, 137, 139, 153, 155, 156, 178, 190, 191, 235
Addicott, J., 208
advocates for human performance, 10
affect, deficiency in skill for measuring, 8
affective domain, 7
aggression, 79, 80, 83, 103, 151, 202, 209, 210
agnosia, 243
alerting, 35
Allport, 50
Altman, I., 89
analytic (al), 29
ambiguity, 25, 60, 63, 69, 71
anomia, 242, 261
anonymity of the experiment, 6
antigravity responses, 63
Apollo, 86
appropriateness of behavior, 6
Ardrey, R., 79
artifacts, 6
Asch, S., 41, 103
astereognosis, 169, 193, 242, 247
asymetrical tonic neck reflex, 63
attend (tion), 35, 36
attitude, shifts in, 7
Austin, W.T., 88
autokinetic, 69
automatic performance, 3, 5, 6, 21, 103
Automatic Pilot Principle, 181
awareness, shifting, 13, 15
awareness, subjectivity of, 10
Ayres, A.J., 22, 27, 48, 52, 64, 151
axes, 52

B

Bartley, S.H., 50, 65, 156
behavior modification, 198
behavior of religious converts, 7
behavior, standards for, 5, 6
behavioral objectives, 7
behavioral plans, 15, 16
Behlen, F., 1
beliefs, 5
Bender, M., 127
Berkeley, J., 65
bias, 7
bicameral (ity), 29, 51, 79
bilateral (ity), 34, 41
Botwinick, J., 135
Breines, E., 154, 160, 167, 183
    Automotive Principles, 181
Bremner, V.G., 66

Bronowski, J., 60
Brouchon, M., 84
Brown, H., 48
Browning, R., 16
Bruner, 87
Buck, P., 111
Buell, S.J., 138

C

Calhoun, K.S., 131
Cantor, B., 100
Cantor, J.M., 120
caring, 7, 8
Castenada, C., 95
centration, 39, 41, 42, 91, 106
circle of inclusion, 24, 202
clarification of the role of OTs, 11
cognition, 6, 7, 23, 24
cognitive dissonance, 7
cognitive map(ping), 85
cognitive psychology, 10
Coleman, 138
collagen(ous), 118, 126
communal, 97, 102
concept(ual), 6, 7, 9, 11, 14, 16, 42
conflict, 64, 71, 103, 136
conscious attention, 3
conscious awareness, 5
conserver (ation), 60
consensus (t) (tual), 5, 7, 9, 23, 41, 98, 102, 104
consolidation 60, 64, 70
constancy, 62, 91, 133, 135, 136, 249
constant stimuli, 62
context, 13, 15, 23, 61-63, 91, 104, 198, 213
context/constancy relationship, 23, 33, 39, 47, 59, 62, 91
converts, 7
Corso, J., 127, 128, 135, 136, 160
cost effectiveness, 13, 99, 103, 104
creativity, 10, 35, 54, 56
curricula, 8
custom, 6, 11

D

Daffner, C., 63, 130, 221
Darwin, C., 80
death, 120
decision making, 5
deficiency in skill for measuring affect, 2
definition of OT, 11, 15
delayed independence, 99
De Long, A., 89
demonstration of success, 12
Denny, N., 132
dentrites (tic), 138
dependency, 99, 105
detail, 13
development (al), 14, 15, 23, 98
development of OT, 9, 15
Dinnerstein, D., 47, 62
disability areas, 12
disregard, 35
dissonance, cognitive, 7
display behavior, 80
distance sensors, 56, 66
distortion, 50
Dollard, J., 103
Downs, R.H., 85, 87
dreaming, 57

E

early intervention, 201
Eccles, J.C., 138
Edney, J.J., 50, 87, 88, 90, 149
Edwards, B., 29
education, 9
educators, OT, 8
efficacy, 41
egocentric (ity), 66, 67, 213, 214, 221, 224, 230
Einstein, A., 27
empirical observations, 10
enzyme production, 127
equilibration, 21
Esser, A., 77, 87
ethology (ist)(ical), 76, 77, 82, 88, 89

evolution, 97
experimental design, 6, 7
expertise of OTs, 12-15
exocentric, 66, 213, 221, 230-233, 235

F

facilitation, 12, 14, 64, 71, 132, 200
faith, 12
familiar (ity), 47, 55, 84, 89, 90, 147, 148, 150, 154, 156, 160, 161, 174, 199, 249
feedback, 41, 48, 51, 126, 136, 156, 183
Feffer, M., 60
Festinger, L., 7
Fidler, G., 9, 14
Fiorentino, M., 80
finger gnosia, 228, 243
Fiske, D.W., 75
fixed-action pattern, 80, 83
flight, 82, 147
fluctuating, 46
Foley, J.M., 131, 137
formal research, 9, 10
foveal, 38, 150
Fraiberg, S., 67
Freud, S., 7, 10, 22, 56, 81, 82
future, 15, 16

G

Galanter, E., 48, 64, 183
ganzvelt, 128
Gaylord, S.A., 134
gender behavior, 83
generalists, 14
genetic potential, 117
gerontogeny, 139, 275
gerontology, 11, 13, 14, 111
gerontological specialists, 123
Gestalt, 10, 21, 29, 40
Gibson, E., 36, 37
Gibson, J.J., 29, 37
Gilfoyle, E., 14
gnosia, 224, 243

goals, 5, 10, 16, 185, 196, 239
Goldberg, M. 361
Goldstein, A., 40
Goodall, J., 27, 78, 79, 81
Goodenough, 53
Grady, A., 14
graphesthesia, 138
grasp reflex, 99
gravity, 63, 84, 130, 213
Grey Panther, 121
Griffin, D., 86
griot, 106
Grundy, D., 89

H

habit (uated), 40, 70, 71, 90, 178, 179, 208
Haley, A., 101
hallucination, 130
hand rehabilitation, 11
handedness, 79
Hart, R., 85, 90
Heisenberg uncertainty principle, 6
Held, R., 77
Hermelin, B., 27, 28, 137
hippocampus, 34
history, 9, 97
Hock, H., 90
Holland Tunnel Principle, 90, 181
holographic memory, 55
horizontal positioning, 130
Hot Wire Principle, 181
Hugo, V., 113
humans, as subject, 6
Hunterdon County Office on Aging, 161
hypothesis, 160, 170
  formulation of, 6, 7
  the OT, 8

I

illusions, 7, 50, 63
independence, 64, 99
individuality, 10

induced movement of the self, 39, 69
inferiority, 133, 149
Inhelder, B., 85
insecurity, 12
integrated neural (sensory) functioning, 9, 178
internuncial neuron, 51
invalidism, 201
investigator, 7
isolation, 118, 132

J

James, W., 27
Johanssen, G., 39
John, E.R., 126, 138
Johnson, J., 15
Johnson, R.N., 79
judgment, 21

K

Kaplan, S., 86
Kean College, 2, 114
Kephart, N.C., 40
Kielhofner, G., 41
kinesthesia (tic) 66, 68, 130, 152, 213
King, L.J., 14, 22, 151
Klopfer, W.G., 133, 149
Knickerbocker, B., 52, 64
knowledge base, 8
Kubler-Ross, E., 120

L

laboratory experiments, 6
laterality, 9, 39, 63
learning, 10, 58
Lee, T., 83, 86
Leeper, 57
legislative, 112, 114
Levy, J., 29
Lewis, S.C., 127
Lieberman, M., 119

life's tasks, 7
limbic function, 82, 209
  system, 151
Llorens, L., 3, 9
longevity, 117
Lorenz, K., 79, 151
Luria, A. 15
Luckiesch, M., 50
Lynch, K., 87

M

Maddi, S.R., 75
Mandler, 87
map making, 90
Marsh, G.R., 134
Master of Behavioral Planning, 16
measurement of human behavior, 6, 7
Medicare, 207
Mehta, Y., 104
memory, 10, 53, 56, 58, 135, 188, 249, 255, 264, 265
midbrain, 36
midline, 38
mind/body impairment, 10
mind/body paradox, 22
Milgram, S., 103
Miller, G.A., 48, 64, 183
Miller, N.E., 103
Mitchell, 85
mobility (motility, motion, movement), 29, 33, 39, 48, 51, 52, 53, 89, 126, 127, 131, 151, 153, 154, 156, 159, 174, 181, 200, 253, 255, 268
modalities, 12
modeling, 4, 242
Montegu, A., 79
Moore, J., 82, 152, 153
morality, 103
Mosey, A., 65
motivation, 16, 185, 275
motoric performance, 16
muscle, origin and insertion, 23, 24

N

Nazism, 103
neck righting, 63
Necker cube, 47
need for OT, 8
negative self image, 13
neural end plates, 126
neurogenic bias, 4
neurotransmission capability, 126
New Car, Old Car Principle, 182
New York University, 1
non-segmental rolling, 63
non-parametric statistics, 171

O

object world, 23
observation of human behavior in natural settings, 7
occupational therapy educators, 8
occupational therapy hypothesis, 8
occupational therapists, as advocates for human performance, 10
occupational therapists, recognition of own skills, 13, 14
O'Keefe, 34
Olton, D., 34
O'Neill, P.M., 131
ontogeny (ic)(isis), 81, 84, 139, 275
optic chiasma, 37
orientation, 25
origin, 23
Orne, M., 6

P

Paillard, J., 84
Papulia, D.E., 133
paradigm, relational, 10
Pastalan, L., 154
pediatric practice, 11, 13

periphery (al), 13, 36-39, 41, 91, 150, 159, 169, 172, 189, 190, 198, 229, 232, 247-249, 251, 252
personally constructed concept, 22
personal space, 83
perspective, 7, 23, 25
Pettigrew, 50
phylogenetic (ally)(phylogeny), 38, 51, 76, 80, 84
physical disabilities, 11, 13
physics, study of, 6
Piaget, J., 7, 10, 16, 54, 59, 62, 64, 66, 85, 133, 139
Picasso, P., 104
Pick, H., 34, 66, 85
plans, 15, 16
plasticity, 51
Plato, 31
Polanyi, M., 10, 21
power of consentual agreement, 6
practice of OT, 1, 3, 9-14, 22
presbycusis, 128
presbyopia, 121
Pribram, K.H., 48, 55, 64, 183
Price, A., 9
primitive, 36, 63, 81
Principles of Perception, 72
prism adaptation, 50, 68
problem solving, 21, 150
profession, 11-15
progressive resistive activities, 71, 230
projective techniques (tests), 25, 53, 130
proofs of formal derivation, 6
property possession, 87
proprioception (ive), 38, 49, 50, 53, 83, 152, 159, 169, 172, 180, 214, 243
proprioceptive neuromuscular facilitation techniques, 64, 71, 243
pseudochromatic plates, 57
psychiatric practice, 11, 13
psychology, cognitive, 10, 23

psychology, social, 10
psychosomatic medicine, 22

Q

qualitative research, 7
quantification, 6, 7, 9
questionable data, 6

R

Ravens Coloured Progressive Matrices, 50, 161, 163, 166
reaction (response) latencies, 134, 135
reality, 23, 24
recall, 55, 56, 70
recognition, 47, 55, 70
Reffler, R., 3
reduction of cognitive dissonance, 7
reflexive performance, 16
reference, 24
Reigel, K., 133
Reily, D.D., 133
Reilly, M., 8, 41
reincarnation, 111
reinforcement, 3, 15
relational concepts, 24, 33, 35, 46, 47
relational paradigm, 10, 42
relativity, 15, 27
religion, 111, 120
relocation, 70, 119, 146, 156
Rennick, H.L.P., 120
Renshaw, 65
repetition, 47
research, 6, 9, 10
responsibility, 96, 105, 206
  for elderly, 112
  of OT, 11
restructuring of behavior, 5
reticular formation, 152
reticular activating system, 50
retirement, 113-117
reversible figures, 24
risk, 148

Rist, M., 7
Rock, I., 39, 50, 51, 57, 62, 65
roles, 5, 10, 95, 96, 98, 102, 104, 205
roles of women, 112
roles of patients, 202
role of OT, 10, 11, 155
Rorschach, 25
Rossi, A.M., 129
Rutgers Institute for Cognitive Studies, 4

S

Sammons, F., 13
Schactel, E.G., 147
scientific studies, 6, 7
Schreiber, F.R., 71
Schultz, N.R., 149
self constructed plans, 15
Selye, H., 71
senile (ity), 193
sensory deprivation, 128-132, 136, 152, 153, 155
sensory dominance, 65
sensory integration, 13, 14, 64, 71, 213
sequential (ly), 15, 27, 28, 40, 58, 64, 177, 255
sexual outlets, 120
sharing, 7, 8, 13
Sheehy, G., 71
Shepard, 85
shifting awareness, 13
sign learning, 21
simultaneous, 28
skill, 11-16, 39, 40, 48, 49, 54, 76, 105, 110, 138, 173, 202, 207
sub-skill, 214
sleeping, 57
small groups,
Smith, A.D., 135
Smith, C.U., 50-52
Smith, W.M., 50-52
social psychology, 10
Sommer, R., 83
Southern California Sensory Integration Tests, 39

Spatial Illusion Test for Midpoint Identification, 160, 162, 163
specialists, 195
specialization, 13-15
speech, 79, 147
speed, 24
Sperry, R.W., 29
splinter skill, 40, 59, 60
standards of behavior, 6
statistical procedures, 7
status, 7
Stea, D., 85, 87
stereognosis, 191, 232, 242, 249, 251
Storandt, M., 135
Stratton, G., 50
stress diseases, 22
striving, 16
style of interaction with patients, 3
subcortical, 3, 90, 182, 207
subjective (ity), 8, 10
subjects, human, 6
success, 8, 11, 12, 98
Suedfeld, P., 130
suicide, 120
Sundstrom, E., 89
supine posturing, 130
synapse, 126
systems theory, 41

T

task, 10, 11, 40, 41, 98, 99, 110, 173, 174, 186, 197, 198, 201, 205
task groups, 71
Taub, E., 81
territorial (ity), 2, 76-80, 82, 87-89, 151, 209, 210
testing, 13
thalamic, 152
Thatcher, R.W., 126, 138
Thematic Apperception Test, 25
theory (etical), 9, 10
therapeutic (treatment) techniques, 8-11
Thomas, L., 60
thumb, 39, 78

time (temporal), 15, 26-29, 37, 46, 69, 104, 136, 255
tolerance of shifts in attitude, 7
Tolman, 85
tonic labrynthine supine, prone, 63
Trevarthen, C., 36
triangulation 34
trust, 104
truth, 6, 7, 23

U

unilateral dominance, 9
Union County Technical Institute, 1
uniqueness, 9, 10, 12, 13
unity, 6, 14
unresolved conflicts, 71

V

Van Lawick-Goodall, 77, 79, 81
vestibular, 151, 230
vested interests, 7
vibratory sensitivity, 127
vision's capture of touch, 65
visual overlay color cube projections, 127

W

Wallach, H., 24
Washburn, S.L., 78, 79, 97
Waugh, N.C., 134
way-finding, 87, 234
Werner, 85
White, R., 41, 81
white noise, 128
Wigginton, E., 101
Wilbarger, P., 151
Wilson, S.F., 89
worth 9, 41, 196

Z

Zubek, J.P., 166
Zuckerman, M., 130, 152